SOURCEBOOK

OF

CONTEMPORARY

NORTH

AMERICAN

ARCHITECTURE

SOURCEBOOK

OF

CONTEMPORARY

NORTH

AMERICAN

ARCHITECTURE

From Postwar to Postmodern

Sylvia Hart Wright

VNR VAN NOSTRAND REINHOLD
New York

This Book Is Dedicated to Rustin Wright
and to
Paul Fletcher, Blithe Spirit

Printed in the United States of America

Designed by Keano Design Studio

Van Nostrand Reinhold
115 Fifth Avenue
New York, New York, 10003

Van Nostrand Reinhold International Company Limited
11 New Fetter Lane
London EC4P 4EE, England

Van Nostrand Reinhold
480 La Trobe Street
Melbourne, Victoria 3000, Australia

Macmillan of Canada
Division of Canada Publishing Corporation
164 Commander Boulevard
Agincourt, Ontario M1S 3C7, Canada

16 15 14 13 12 11 10 9 8 7 6 5 4 3 2 1

Library of Congress Cataloging in Publication Data

Wright, Sylvia Hart.
    Sourcebook of contemporary North American Architecture from postwar to post-modern/Sylvia Hart Wright.
        p. cm.
    Includes indexes.
    ISBN 0-442-29190-6
    1. Architecture—North America. 2. Architecture, Modern—20th century—North America. I. Title.
NA703.W75 1989
720'.973—dc 19

CONTENTS

PREFACE

For more than 500 of the most widely discussed buildings and complexes completed in North America, 1947–1987, this book supplies basic information: architect, building name or names, location, completion date,[1] a short description, major awards won, and so on. Photos illustrate almost half these projects. The entry for each project also contains a selective bibliography of two to six sources—typically journal articles and parts of books—where the reader can find more comprehensive descriptions. These usually include numerous photos, plans, elevations, and sections of the project as it was actually built. (Reviews of proposed versions that subsequently were redesigned generally are not listed.) Architects, whatever their nationality, are included if they have designed especially noted projects erected in the United States, Canada, or Puerto Rico.

Almost all major building types are represented: aquariums and office buildings, churches and jails, rapid transit stations, concert halls, and factories, among others. Some outstanding examples of adaptive reuse, such as Ghirardelli Square in San Francisco, Faneuil Hall in Boston, the Seagram Museum in Waterloo, Ontario, and St. Louis's Union Station, have been included. However no attempt has been made to cover either individual residences (which alone could fill several volumes this size) or open space developments such as plazas and malls unless they incorporate buildings as well. The few primarily landscape projects that have been included, such as the Vietnam Veterans Memorial in Washington and the Piazza d'Italia in New Orleans, are here because they have attracted a great deal of interest within the architectural community.

In selecting projects for this book, as for its more modest predecessor, *Highlights of Recent American Architecture,* the author has striven to avoid subjective judgments. She has relied on a system of objective criteria that was devised with advice and assistance from experts in the fields of architecture, architectural history, and librarianship.

---

[1] No attempt has been made to supply starting dates. Dates of completion have been taken, whenever possible, from the most reliable contemporary sources or from information supplied by the architectural firms involved. If inconsistencies in the literature could not be resolved, alternate dates may be shown with a slash between them, for example, 1968/1970. Because the "completion" of a building may be dated from the completion of its final drawings, the issuance of its occupancy certificate, or the occasion of its dedication, and since inevitably some buildings are refined after their official opening, more than one completion date may be arguable.

First, an exhaustive inventory was made of all contemporary architects whose works had won significant awards, had been featured on the covers of leading architectural journals, or had been given substantial mention in major books. Then their leading projects in North America were identified. Points were awarded for each honor any such project might have won, each weighty reference to it in a book, and each article about it in an architectural magazine. Those that scored the most points were included. Although this system could not guarantee that all the best architectural works would be included (unfortunately, many a fine project is built to bloom unheralded), it did tend to ensure the inclusion of the best known—the most controversial as well as the most celebrated.

Several unusual features of this book provide shortcuts to frequently sought information that's often hard to find. For instance, most magazine indexes and catalogs of books assume that the researcher already knows the name of the architect whose building is to be studied. Yet, in reality, students and architecture buffs frequently plunge into a search knowing little more than the names and locations of the buildings that interest them—and they may not be sure of those. Unless they wish to embark on a costly and intricate computer search or have entree to an extensive architectural library and the patience and/or skilled help to explore it at length, they may be stymied in their efforts to find the data they want.

Similarly, the young architect or architectural student with a project to design may be interested in studying examples of a particular building type, but may have no idea *which* examples to study. An up-to-date book on the appropriate building type may be impossible to locate. Indexes to journal articles are tedious to use; besides, they don't distinguish between *major* projects and those that have attracted just one critic's attention.

Here, however, readers can choose among five different routes to the information they are seeking. They can search by architect, by building type, by the name of the building or complex, by geographical location, and by the name of a given design or construction professional. The main body of this sourcebook, "Guide to Contemporary Architects and Their Leading Works," is arranged alphabetically by architect's last name. Detailed indexes provide the four alternate routes.

The Building Type Index[2] should prove particularly helpful to architects and architecture students. With it, they can quickly identify the best known recent examples of the kind of building they've been called on to design. Then, moving on to individual entries, they can decide which ones particularly interest them and can easily locate the best articles and books from which to learn more about these projects.

This book has grown out of the author's experience since 1976, as librarian-in-charge at the architecture school of the City College of the City University of New York. It aims to answer the kinds of questions that have recurred in her library over the years. Her earlier book, *Highlights of Recent American Architecture,* originally devised primarily for use by librarians, was a first step in this direction. Published in 1982 to highly favorable reviews, *Highlights* covered 378 projects completed 1945–1978 and contained 49 photos. The author—and many of her colleagues in other libraries—have been using it successfully ever since to serve architecture students and faculty members.

Sourcebook of Contemporary North American Architecture comprises virtually all the information previously contained in *Highlights,* plus an additional 135 entries—most of them dating from the mid-1970s on—and *five times* as many photographs. Many of the older entries have been updated to reflect changes in the name, use, or structure of projects. Bibliographies also have been expanded: more sources are listed for individual works and, whenever

---

[2] Each project is listed under all building types that apply. For instance, Benjamin Thompson's Harborplace, Baltimore, appears under "Piers and Waterfront Complexes," "Recreational Buildings and Complexes," and "Stores, Markets, Shopping Centers, and Showrooms"; while Arthur Erickson's Robson Square and the Law Courts Complex, Vancouver, appears under both "Courthouses," and "State Capitols, City Halls, and Civic Centers." Numerous cross-references guide the reader to the appropriate subject headings.

possible, retrospective evaluative articles have been included in the lists of readings on older buildings. Similarly, information about awards won by individual architects and architectural firms has been expanded and updated.

Nonetheless, however comprehensive and evenhanded the author has sought to be, gaps and inequities doubtless remain. Some very promising and widely reviewed young architects are not represented here—generally because the bulk of their *oeuvres* is individual residences, a topic not covered in this book. Other distinguished architects, still creating outstanding projects, are represented here only by older buildings. Unfortunately, just such vagaries follow from the system of objective criteria that has dictated choices for inclusion in this book. Only those "superstar" nonresidential projects that have gained wide attention in the journals for which indexing was available and in the books that already were in print to be surveyed have scored enough points for inclusion here.

The author is painfully aware that, despite her best efforts, some worthy subjects may have been overlooked while others less worthy have been included. For any such shortcomings, she offers her apologies. It is hoped that at some future date such oversights may be corrected in a revised and enlarged edition.

ACKNOWLEDGMENTS

It is a pleasure for me to acknowledge the many individuals and institutions whose help and cooperation have enabled me to create this book and my earlier work, *Highlights of Recent American Architecture,* from which this *Sourcebook* draws a great deal of data.

I am deeply grateful to The City College, City University of New York, for granting me a year's fellowship leave, 1979–80, and a second leave, 1987–88, and to the City University's Research Foundation for giving me two PSC-CUNY Research Awards that helped fund my efforts during those periods. Special thanks also are due to two men who, in different ways, served as my mentors when I first set out to write an architectural reference book.

Bernard P. Spring, my then dean at the School of Architecture and Environmental Studies, gave me much valuable encouragement and advice, and put me in touch with experts elsewhere such as Richard Freeman at the American Institute of Architects, Jeanne Butler Hodges at the AIA Foundation, and Leslie H. Gillette at the American Institute of Steel Construction. The distinguished architectural historian and, now, Avery Librarian Emeritus, Adolf K. Placzek was a never failing source of clarification and reassurance as I labored at Columbia University's magnificent Avery Library. I shall always be grateful for his guidance in planning *Highlights* and bringing it to completion.

Conversations with a number of other people early on helped me formulate my research strategies and criteria. These included the architectural writer and author John Fondersmith, Catha Grace Rambusch, then of the Committee for the Preservation of Architectural Records, William O'Malley at the Avery Library, many of my colleagues in the Association of Architecture School Librarians, and several of my fellow faculty members at The City College of New York. The informed advice of Profs. Norval White, Robert Alan Cordingley and Paul David Pearson of the Architecture School and Profs. Elizabeth Rajec and Robert Kuhner of the Library Department were especially useful. Among those who supplied me with hard to find information for *Highlights* were Prof. Carol Krinsky of New York University and Imre Meszaros of Washington University, St. Louis.

Once *Highlights of Recent American Architecture* was in print, it was a delight—and an education—for me to use it in serving the students and faculty at the City College Architecture School. Their questions and comments gave me insight into the book's most crucial functions for architectural research and heartened me to take on the job of updating and expanding it to create this book. I am most grateful to the good people at my former publisher, Scarecrow Press, for their cooperation.

By the time I returned to Avery Library to pursue my research for *Sourcebook,* Angela Giral had replaced Mr. Placzek as Avery Librarian. I'm deeply indebted to Ms. Giral and her staff for their unfailingly knowledgeable and gracious assistance. On my own campus, I owe a special debt to Guy Westmoreland for his extensive computer searching on my behalf, and to my chief librarian, Dr. Ann K. Randall, for her good offices in obtaining my leave of absence for the 1987–88 academic year.

The Royal Architectural Institute of Canada gave me invaluable assistance in identifying their nation's prize winning architectural projects and locating their top architectural firms. My very obliging contacts there were Mary-Dale Farrell and Alexandra Fitzgerald.

For word processing and related technical assistance, thanks are due to Jerome McCoy and to the computer mavens at DataScan, in Manhattan. For guiding me through the paperwork entailed by my two research awards, thanks are due also to the staff of the Research Foundation of the City University of New York, in particular to Miriam Korman and Brenda Newman.

Two research assistants helped me to put this book together. I cannot praise Genevieve Dejean and Susan Bogaty too highly for their patience, their determined accuracy, and their unfailing goodwill. Similarly praiseworthy were my assistants on *Highlights,* Marie-Alice Souffrant and Susan Kaplan.

Here at Van Nostrand Reinhold it has been my good fortune to be associated with a succession of capable and agreeable professionals. My sincere thanks go especially to Wendy Lochner, who first accepted this book for publication, to Everett W. Smethurst, genial and accommodating, who took it on after she left, to Cynthia Zigmund, who steered it deftly through the early stages of its editing, and to Jim Woods, who probably merits the title of fastest editorial supervisor in the East.

Finally, it is a pleasure to affirm here my abiding gratitude for the wealth of photographs that inform this book while they lend it flair and excitement that my words alone never could express. Our limited budget did not allow us to give those who supplied them the compensation they truly deserved. For the most part, we were dependent on the generosity of the architectural firms that had designed the outstanding buildings described here, and on the generosity of corporations and cultural institutions—museums, universities and the like —associated with the projects shown. Often the architectural photographers themselves—masters of a métier which demands complex technical skills along with an artist's eye—accepted far less than their due. This book, in large measure, is a tribute to them and their work.

USER'S GUIDE

Entries in the main body of this book are arranged alphabetically by last name of architect, or by firm name if—like Arquitectonica or Centerbrook—that appellation does not comprise any personal names. In alphabetical headings, the given names of architects appear in lower case. Under each heading by architect or firm name, individual projects are listed alphabetically.

The first sentence of each entry supplies basic information in the following order: Building Name; Location; Date of Completion.

In accordance with the scheme recommended by the United States Postal Service, the fifty states, the District of Columbia, and Puerto Rico are abbreviated as follows:

AK	Alaska	LA	Louisiana	OH	Ohio
AL	Alabama	MA	Massachusetts	OK	Oklahoma
AR	Arkansas	MD	Maryland	OR	Oregon
AZ	Arizona	ME	Maine	PA	Pennsylvania
CA	California	MI	Michigan	PR	Puerto Rico
CO	Colorado	MN	Minnesota	RI	Rhode Island
CT	Connecticut	MO	Missouri	SC	South Carolina
DC	District of Columbia	MS	Mississippi	SD	South Dakota
DE	Delaware	MT	Montana	TN	Tennessee
FL	Florida	NC	North Carolina	TX	Texas
GA	Georgia	ND	North Dakota	UT	Utah
HI	Hawaii	NE	Nebraska	VA	Virginia
IA	Iowa	NH	New Hampshire	VT	Vermont
ID	Idaho	NJ	New Jersey	WA	Washington
IL	Illinois	NM	New Mexico	WI	Wisconsin
IN	Indiana	NV	Nevada	WV	West Virginia
KS	Kansas	NY	New York	WY	Wyoming
KY	Kentucky				

NOTES ON ABBREVIATIONS AND HONORS

AIA   The American Institute of Architects

AIA ARCHITECTURAL FIRM AWARD   Initiated in 1962, since 1967 this award has been given annually by the American Institute of Architects to "a firm which has consistently produced distinguished architecture for a period of at least ten years."

AIA BICENTENNIAL LIST   The July 1976 issue of the *AIA Journal* contained a section entitled "Highlights of American Architecture, 1776–1976." It summarized the responses of 46 architectural "practitioners, historians and critics" who had been asked "to nominate up to 29 of what they considered the proudest achievements of American architecture over the past 200 years."

AIA HONOR AND MERIT AWARDS   In 1949, the American Institute of Architects initiated the practice of annually conferring both Honor Awards and Awards of Merit on outstanding architectural achievements, many but not all of which had been completed within the previous year. In 1967, the Awards of Merit category was discontinued.

AIA TWENTY-FIVE YEAR AWARD   Each year since 1969, with the exception of 1970, the American Institute of Architects has selected one project, at least twenty-five years old, to receive this award "given in recognition of architectural design of enduring significance."

AISC ARCHITECTURAL AWARDS OF EXCELLENCE   Since 1960, the American Institute of Steel Construction has conferred Architectural Awards of Excellence on buildings in which steel has been used with particular distinction. At first several awards were granted each year but since 1981 this competition has been held biennially.

BARD AWARD   From 1964–1979, the City Club of New York annually conferred the Albert S. Bard Award for Excellence in Architecture and Urban Design on outstanding examples of architectural achievement in New York. In recent years, the award has been conferred less frequently, at irregular intervals.

BARTLETT AWARD   Named for the late Senator E. L. Bartlett of Alaska, author of Public Law 90-480 on barrier-free design, this award is bestowed annually by the American Institute of Architects on those AIA Honor Award winners that are judged to be most accessible to the handicapped and the elderly. It has been granted since 1969.

CRSI DESIGN AWARDS   Since 1974, these awards have been conferred by the Concrete Reinforcing Steel Institute. At first their awards program was annual but since 1977 it has been biennial.

GOVERNOR GENERAL'S MEDAL FOR ARCHITECTURE   In 1982 and 1986, the Governor General of Canada awarded a number of medals to recognize outstanding achievement in the field of Canadian architecture. As of 1988, it was anticipated that the Governor General's Competition would be held every three to four years thereafter.

KEMPER AWARD   The Edward C. Kemper Award is given each year by the American Institute of Architects to "one AIA member who has contributed significantly to the Institute and to the profession."

MASSEY MEDAL FOR ARCHITECTURE   At two or three year intervals between 1950 and 1970, Massey Medals for Architecture, sponsored by the Massey Foundation and The Royal Architectural Institute of Canada, were conferred to recognize outstanding examples of Canadian achievement in the field of architecture.

PA AWARD CITATIONS, DESIGN AWARDS, AND DESIGN CITATIONS   Since 1954 *Progressive Architecture,* one of the leading architecture magazines in the United States, has conferred awards on distinguished architectural projects, announcing winners regularly in its January issue. Unlike other honors listed here, PA's awards are conferred for designs that at the time have not yet been built.

PRITZKER ARCHITECTURE PRIZE   Created in 1979 by the Hyatt Foundation, this annual international award is modeled loosely after the Nobel Prize. Given in recognition of an architect's entire career, not a specific building, it consists of a $100,000 grant and a sculpture.

R. S. REYNOLDS MEMORIAL AWARD   This award, sponsored by the Reynolds Metal Company, is administered by the American Institute of Architects. Each year it honors one "permanent, significant work of architecture, in the creation of which aluminum has been an important contributing factor."

RIBA   Royal Institute of British Architects

ROYAL GOLD MEDAL   Since 1848, the British sovereign each year has conferred one Royal Gold Medal for the Promotion of Architecture "on some distinguished architect, or group of architects for work of high merit, or on some distinguished person or group whose work has promoted . . . the advancement of Architecture."

NOTES ON JOURNALS CITED

Architecture   Citations to *Architecture,* for issues dating from July 1983 or later, refer to *Architecture: The AIA Journal.* Citations to *Architecture* for 1976 and 1977 refer to a journal that was published briefly in Paris and written primarily in French. It evolved from *Architecture Française.*

L'Architettura   The full name of this Italian journal is *L'Architettura; Cronache e Storia.*

RIBA Journal   For many years this was the full name of a publication of the Royal Institute of British Architects. Its present name is *The Royal Institute of British Architects Journal.*

GUIDE TO CONTEMPORARY ARCHITECTS
AND THEIR LEADING WORKS

Alvar AALTO

Winner of Royal Gold Medal, 1957, and AIA Gold Medal, 1963.

■ 1

Baker House, Massachusetts Institute of Technology; Cambridge, MA; 1948 (see Illus. 1).
Built as a senior dorm and including a large dining hall, it winds, serpentine fashion, along the banks of the Charles River and is accented by a huge **V** of outdoor staircases hung dramatically against one long side.
Associated architects: Perry, Shaw & Hepburn. Contractor: Aberthaw Co.

See: Architectural Forum 91 (August 1949): 61–69. Henry-Russell Hitchcock and Arthur Drexler, eds., *Built in USA: Post-War Architecture* (New York: Museum of Modern Art, 1952), 38–39.

■ 2

Mount Angel Abbey Library; St. Benedict, OR; 1970.
This library for a Benedictine monastery fans out over its site on a wooded knoll. Inside, it features a 3-story-high reading and stack area enhanced by a curving skylight overhead.
Designer in charge for Alvar Aalto: Erik T. Variainen; executive architects: DeMars & Wells. Structural engineer: S. J. Medwadowski. Acoustical consultant: Walter Soroka. Contractor: Reimers & Jolivette.

See: Architectural Record 149 (May 1971): 111–16. *Architectural Review* 151 (June 1972): 344–48. *Alvar Aalto,* Architectural Monographs, no. 4 (New York: Rizzoli, 1979).

Max ABRAMOVITZ

■ 3

Avery Fisher Hall, Lincoln Center; New York, NY; 1962—interior frequently reconstructed thereafter.
Originally designed to seat 2,644 and to be the permanent home of the Philharmonic orchestra, this concert hall —originally known as Philharmonic Hall —proved to have such disappointing acoustics that its interior, housed within a

travertine and glass facade, was repeatedly modified. In 1976 it was completely gutted and rebuilt, with what appeared to be satisfactory results.
For original structure: Engineers: Ammann & Whitney (structural); Syska & Hennessy (mechanical/electrical). Acoustical consultants: Bolt, Beranek & Newman. *For interior reconstruction,* 1976. Architects: Philip Johnson and John Burgee. Consultants: Cyril Harris (acoustical); Ammann & Whitney (structural); Syska & Hennessy (mechanical).

See: Architectural Record 132 (September 1962): 136–39. *Progressive Architecture* 58 (March 1977): 64–69. *L'Architecture d'Aujourd'hui,* no. 106 (February–March 1963): 34–37.

AFFLECK, DESBARATS, DIMAKOPOULOS, LEBENSOLD, MICHAUD, and SISE

■ 4

Grande Salle, Place des Arts; Montreal, Quebec; 1963.
Operas, ballets, symphonic concerts, and musical comedies all can be staged in this 3,000-seat hall, centerpiece of Montreal's performing arts center. Like a Continental opera house, it has an orchestra with no center aisle, three shallow balconies, and three horseshoe-shaped tiers of boxes; no seat is more than 135 feet from the stage.
Partner in charge of design: Fred Lebensold. Structural engineers: Brouillet & Carmel. Mechanical and electrical engineers: McDougall & Friedman. Acoustical consultants: Bolt,

Beranek and Newman. General contractor: Quemont-Duranceau Entreprise Conjointe.

See: Architectural Record 136 (December 1964): 136–39. *RAIC Journal* 40 (November 1963): 32–50. *Canadian Architect* 8 (November 1963): 47–65.

AFFLECK, DESBARATS, DIMAKOPOULOS, LEBENSOLD, SISE

■ 5

National Arts Centre; Ottawa, Ontario; 1969.
Three handsome theaters, ranging in size from a 2,300-seat opera house to a 300-seat "studio," are located within a complex replete with plazas and terraces, cafés and shops. The center, sited on the edge of a canal and built primarily of concrete, has for its base a huge underground parking garage.
Canadian Department of Public Works (J. A. Langford, chief architect). Consulting architects: Affleck, Desbarats, Dimakopoulos, Lebensold, Sise. Partner in charge: D. F. Lebensold. Project architect: A. B. Nichol. Engineers: Adjeleian & Associates (structural); Granek, Chisvin, Crossey (mechanical and electrical). Consultants: Bolt, Beranek & Newman and N. J. Pappas & Assoc. (acoustical); Sasaki, Strong & Assoc. (landscaping).

Honors: Massey Medal for Architecture, 1970.

See: Architectural Forum 131 (October 1969): 46–53. *Architecture Canada: The RAIC Journal* 46 (May 1969): 29–52. *Canadian Architect* 14 (July 1969): whole issue.

1 Baker House, Massachusetts Institute of Technology; Cambridge, MA; 1948. *See* Entry 1. (Courtesy Massachusetts Institute of Technology; Cambridge, MA.)

■ 6

Place Bonaventure; Montreal, Quebec; 1967.
A multiuse complex that has been called "an underground city," it comprises such varied facilities as shopping arcades, office space, a large hotel, and an exhibition hall —all served by a 1,000-car garage and a weather-protected pedestrian network. Partner in charge: R. T. Affleck. Structural consultants: R. R. Nicolet & Associates; Lalonde, Valois, Lamarre, Valois & Associates. Mechanical and electrical consultants: James P. Keith & Associates. Contractor: Concordia Estates Ltd.

Honors: Massey Medal, 1970.

See: Architecture Canada/RAIC Journal 44 (July 1967): 31–39. *Modulus,* no. 5 (1969) 62–70. Leon Whiteson, *Modern Canadian Architecture* (Edmonton: Hurtig, 1983), 214–17.

■ 7

St. Gérard Majella Church and Presbytery; St. Jean, Quebec; 1963 (see Illus. 2).
Gracefully undulating lines dominate the roofline of this church and the unusual ceiling of its sanctuary underneath; several of its outer walls, like those of old Quebec churches, are curved as well. Brick-faced but built of reinforced and precast concrete, it has a raised basement necessitated by a high water table, and an attached presbytery. Partner in charge: Guy Desbarats; design developer: Eva Vecsei. Engineering consultants: Bourgeois & Martineau (structural); Laflamme, Lefrancois & Gauthier (mechanical and electrical). General contractor: Désourdy Frères.

2 St. Gérard Majella Church; St. Jean, Quebec; 1963. *See* Entry 7. (Courtesy Guy Desbarats, Architect; Ottawa, Ontario. Photographer: Hans Samulewitz.)

Honors: Massey Medal, 1964.

See: Architectural Record 138 (November 1965): 133–42. *L'Architecture d'Aujourd'hui* 36 (April–May 1966): 40–41. *Canadian Architect* 8 (September 1963): 57–61.

AFFLECK, DESBARATS, DIMAKOPOULOS, LEBENSOLD, SISE with Norbert SCHOENAUER, town planner

---

■ 8

Fathers of Confederation Memorial Buildings; Charlottetown, Prince Edward Island; 1964.
This complex, built on a 6.3-acre site bounded on three sides by shopping streets, pays homage to the place where the nation of Canada was founded, the 3-story neo-Palladian Provincial Building, constructed of reddish brown sandstone in 1847. Monumental in style, yet no taller than the building it cradles, the complex —faced in matching sandstone— comprises a theater, art gallery, museum, memorial hall, and library, and a sequence of plazas at different levels. Partner in charge: Dimitri Dimakopoulos. Structural consultants: Adjeleian & Associates. Theater design consultant: George C. Izenour. Contractors: Pigott Construction.

Honors: Massey Medal, 1967.

See: RAIC Journal 41 (December 1964): 19–

49. *Canadian Architect* 9 (November 1964): 39–59. Leon Whiteson, *Modern Canadian Architecture* (Edmonton: Hurtig, 1983), 254–57.

Lawrence B. ANDERSON, supervising architect

■ 9

Suburban campus, Rochester Institute of Technology; near Rochester, NY; 1968.
When this privately supported technical school decided to move to a 1-mile-square suburban site, design responsibilities were shared by landscape architect Dan Kiley and five architects— Edward Larrabee Barnes, Kevin Roche and John Dinkeloo, Hugh Stubbins, and Harry M. Weese—cooperating under the supervision of Lawrence B. Anderson of Anderson, Beckwith and Haible. Exteriors throughout were faced with identical pinkish brown brick.

Honors: New York State/AIA Award for Community Design.

See: AIA Journal 57 (April 1972): 46–50. *Architectural Record* 143 (May 1968): 164–65; 144 (November 1968): 123–34.

John ANDREWS

■ 10

George Gund Hall, Harvard University; Cambridge, MA; 1972 (see Illus. 3).
This building houses all programs and facilities of the Graduate School of Design and features a grandly spacious central studio shared by architects, planners, urban designers, and others. Designers: John Andrews, Edward R. Baldwin, and John Simpson; partner in charge: Edward R. Baldwin. Engineers: LeMessurier Assoc. (structural); G. Granek & Associates (mechanical). Landscape architects: Richard Strong Associates.

Honors: AIA Honor Award, 1973; Bartlett Award, 1973.

See: AIA Journal 68 (January 1979): 52–61. *Architectural Forum* 137 (December 1972): 50–

55. *Architectural Record* 152 (November 1972): 95–104. *Progressive Architecture* 54 (February 1973): 62–63.

■ 11

Scarborough College, University of Toronto; Scarborough, Ontario; 1966.

This blocky, angular megastructure, 5 to 6 stories high and shaped in plan rather like a question mark, comprises science and humanities wings, an administrative area, and a refectory. Skylighted or glass-walled pedestrian streets tie these spaces together, making the campus weatherproof.
Associated architects: Page & Steele; planner: Michael Hugo-Brunt; landscape architect: Michael Hough & Associates. Engineering consultants: Ewbank Pillar & Associates.

See: *Architectural Forum* 124 (May 1966): 30–41, 52–55. *Architectural Record* 140 (September 1966): 161–64. *Architectural Review* 140 (October 1966): 245–52. Leon Whiteson, *Modern Canadian Architecture* (Edmonton: Hurtig, 1983), 124–27.

ANSHEN & ALLEN

■ 12

Chapel of the Holy Cross; Sedona, AZ; 1956.

A Roman Catholic chapel in a rugged mountain setting, it is designed to seat 50 to 150 worshipers. The great cross centered in its southwest wall soars upward 90 feet from its base, framed between massive boulders.
Engineers: Robert D. Dewell (civil/structural);

Earl & Gropp (electrical/mechanical). Sculptor of Corpus over altar: Keith Monroe.

Honors: PA Award Citation, 1954; AIA Honor Award, 1957.

See: *Architectural Forum* 105 (December 1956): 97–99. *Architectural Record* 120 (October 1956): 173–82. *Architettura* 3 (May 1957): 42–43; *Architect and Building News* 219 (March 1961): 346–49.

The ARCHITECTS COLLABORATIVE (TAC)

Winner of the AIA's Architectural Firm Award, 1964. This firm's senior and probably most famous member, Walter Gropius (1883–1969), won Great Britain's Royal Gold Medal in 1956 and the AIA Gold Medal in 1959.

■ 13

American Institute of Architects National Headquarters Building; Washington, DC; 1973.

In 1963, Mitchell/Giurgola Associates won a competition to design AIA headquarters; however, they met with a series of adverse rulings from the city's Fine Arts Commission. Ultimately, TAC's design was adopted instead. A low, modern office building, it curves gracefully around its historic neighbor, the Octagon, built in 1800 and occupied briefly by President Madison.
Principal in charge: Norman C. Fletcher. Landscape designers: Knox C. Johnson, Hugh T. Kirkley. Engineers: LeMessurier Associates (structural); Cosentini Associates (mechanical).

See: *AIA Journal* 59 (June 1973): 19–56; 66 (July 1977): 32–39. *Architectural Record* 153 (May 1973): 131–40.

■ 14

C. Thurston Chase Learning Center, Eaglebrook School; Deerfield, MA; 1966.

A cluster of three low-slung, understated buildings houses classrooms, a language lab, a science wing, a meeting hall, and an inviting, airy library.
Associated architects: Campbell, Aldrich & Nulty. Structural engineers: Souza & True.

Honors: AIA Honor Award, 1967; AISC Architectural Award of Excellence, 1968.

See: *AIA Journal* 47 (June 1967): 62. *Architectural Record* 139 (February 1966): 163–82.

■ 15

CIGNA South Office Building; Bloomfield, CT; 1983.

Despite its huge size—890 by 260 feet, encompassing over 500,000 square feet of space—this dignified megastructure is elegantly detailed. Four stories high, its two facing wings enclose a large atrium that provides light and a view of greenery to offices and balcony corridors. Sophisticated lighting strategies, which include a motorized shading system in the atrium roof, reflective "light shelves" on the south facade, and venetian blinds adjusted semiannually to accommodate sun angles, conserve energy while they optimize comfort.
Principal in charge: John C. Harkness. Co-principal and project manager: Richard A. Sabin. Engineers: LeMessurier Associates/SCI (structural); Syska & Hennessy (mechanical/electrical). Construction manager: Turner Construction.

Honors: AISC Architectural Award of Excellence; Landscape Architecture Merit Award, 1985; also, the CIGNA Corporation was designated Owner of the Year, 1985, by *Building Design and Construction* for "Best Balance of Cost Effectiveness and Design Sensitivity."

See: *Architectural Record* 173 (March 1985): 136–43. *Architecture* 73 (October 1984): 60–63. *Corporate Design and Realty* 4 (July–August 1985): 62–69. *Building Design and Construction* 26 (August 1985): 60–63.

3 George Gund Hall, Harvard University; Cambridge, MA; 1972. *See* Entry 10. (Courtesy Harvard News Office; Cambridge, MA. Photographer: Laura Wulf.)

■ 16

Children's Hospital Medical Center; Boston, MA; 1970.
To accommodate a growing medical center, TAC created a tall residential tower to house hospital staff, flanked by a low, street-oriented "Children's Inn" for ambulatory patients accompanied by parents.
Principals in charge: John C. Harkness, Roland Kluver, Jean Fletcher. Engineers: Souza & True (structural); Metcalf & Eddy and Francis Associates (mechanical). Landscape architect: Laurence Zuelke. General contractor: Turner Construction Co.

Honors: AIA Honor Award, 1971.

See: AIA Journal 55 (June 1971): 45–55. *Architectural Record* 140 (October 1966): 204–5. *Baumeister* 67 (September 1970): 1018–21.

■ 17

Harvard University Graduate Center; Cambridge, MA; 1950 (see Illus. 4).
Aiming for "the illusion of motion," the center's eight buildings—most of them linked by covered walks—enclose a series of quadrangles. Seven of the eight are dormitories; the eighth, the Commons, provides dining rooms, lounges, and space for large meetings.
Job captain: Walter Gropius. For Commons building: Norman Fletcher; for dormitories: Robert McMillan; site improvements: Louis McMillen. Technical associates: Brown, Lawford & Forbes. Engineers: Maurice A. Reidy (structural); Charles T. Main (mechanical). Contractor: George A. Fuller & Co.

Honors: AIA Bicentennial List, one nomination.

See: Architectural Forum 93 (December 1950): 62–71. *L'Architecture d'Aujourd'hui,* no. 28 (February 1950): 30–33. Henry-Russell Hitchcock and Arthur Drexler, eds., *Built in USA: Post-War Architecture* (New York: Museum of Modern Art, 1952), 62–63.

■ 18

Johns-Manville World Headquarters; near Denver, CO; 1976.
Deftly engineered and sleekly sheathed in aluminum, this corporate headquarters spans a wide reach of foothills and looks out over a desert valley.
Principals in charge: William Geddis, Joseph D. Hoskins; project architects for design: John P. Sheehy and Michael Gebhart. Landscape: Robert DeWolfe and David Mittelstadt. Consultants: LeMessurier Associates, SCI (structural); Golder, Fass Assoc. (foundations); Cosentini Associates (mechanical/electrical/acoustical). Construction manager: Turner Construction Co.

Honors: AIA Bicentennial List, one nomination; AIA Honor Award, 1979.

See: AIA Journal 67 (mid-May 1978): 106–11. *Architectural Record* 162 (September 1977): 89–100 and cover. Paul Goldberger, *On the Rise* (New York: Times Books, 1983), 96–99.

■ 19

Social Science Center (1961) and Academic Quadrangle (1962), Brandeis University; Waltham, MA.
Both of these campus clusters are built of reinforced concrete enlivened by meticulous attention to detail. Edges and corners are rounded, a carefully selected range of colors in the aggregate is brought out by bushhammering, and rosy brick walls lend contrast inside and out.
Partner in charge: Benjamin Thompson. Engineers: Simpson, Gumpertz and Heger (structural, for Social Science Center), Goldberg LeMessurier & Associates (structural, for Academic Quadrangle); Reardon & Turner (mechanical). Contractor: G. B. H. Macomber Co.

Honors: AIA Merit Award, 1963, for Academic Quadrangle.

See: Architectural Record 116 (January 1962): 121–26. *Architectural Design* 32 (April 1962): 194–97. *L'Architecture d'Aujourd'hui,* no. 100 (February–March 1962): 36–39.

ARCHITECTURAL ASSOCIATES COLORADO

■ 20

Engineering Science Center, University of Colorado; Boulder, CO; 1965 (see Illus. 5).
Stone, precast concrete, and concrete block combine to shape "a campus within a campus," varied environments for labs, classes, offices—and, in an unexpected courtyard, quiet reflection.
Architectural Associates Colorado: William C. Muchow Assoc.; Hobart D. Wagener & Associates; Fisher & Davis. Partner in charge: William C. Muchow. Design consultants: Pietro Belluschi, and Sasaki, Dawson, DeMay Associates (site planners and landscape architects). Structural engineers: Ketchum & Konkel.

Honors: PA Design Citation, 1963.

4 Harvard University Graduate Center; Cambridge, MA; 1950. *See* Entry 17. (Courtesy The Architects Collaborative: Cambridge, MA. Photographer: The Architects Collaborative.)

5 Engineering Science Center, University of Colorado; Boulder, CO; 1965. *See* Entry 20. (Courtesy Office of Public Relations, The University of Colorado; Boulder, CO. Photographer: Ken Abbott.)

5

See: Progressive Architecture 47 (July 1966): 47; 47 (November 1966): 118–31. *Baumeister* 64 (April 1967): 409–15.

ARQUITECTONICA

■ 21

The Atlantis on Brickell; Miami, FL; 1982 (see Illus. 6).
This 20-story beachfront condominium asserts its presence brashly. Faced with reflective glass, it is ornamented in crayon colors: red columns at its entry and a red pyramid at one end of its roof; a huge blue grid laid across one side; four giant, triangular, yellow balconies in a cluster; and a 37-foot-square hole "punched" through the building to create a "sky patio" with a red staircase spiraling within it. This last appears regularly in the opening footage of "Miami Vice."

Consultants: O'Leary-Schafer-Cosio, landscape; John Ross Assoc., structural/mechanical/civil engineering. General contractor: Cohen-Ager.

Honors: PA Citation for Architectural Design, 1980.

See: Progressive Architecture 64 (February 1983): 99–107 and cover. *Process: Architecture,* no. 65 (February 1986): 40–44. *GA Document,* no. 7 (August 1983): 22–27. *Architettura* 31 (March 1985): 206–7.

Warren H. ASHLEY

■ 22

Edgemont Junior-Senior High School; Greenburgh, NY; 1956.
Inexpensively built and energy efficient, this clean-lined, suburban educational complex makes canny use of its 70-acre site.
Site planners: C. A. Currier & Associates. Engineers: Marchant & Minges.

Honors: AIA Honor Award, 1957.

See: Architectural Record 116 (November 1954): 185–86; 120 (September 1956): 205–9.

ASHLEY, Myer see Hugh STUBBINS; ASHLEY, Myer

Edward Larrabee BARNES

Winner, AIA Architectural Firm Award, 1980.

■ 23

Crown Center; Kansas City, MO; 1968– . (see Illus. 7).
This privately financed urban renewal development—an 85-acre "city-within-a-city"—is sponsored by Hallmark Cards, Inc. By 1988 it comprised two large office complexes; two hotels, the Westin Crown Center and the Hyatt Regency Crown Center; a 400,000-square-foot shopping center with extensive dining and cultural facilities; 245 residential units; parking for 6,000 cars; a 10-acre central square with a skating rink; and other amenities.
Coordinating architect and master planner: Edward Larrabee Barnes. *For Westin Crown Center Hotel,* architect: Harry Weese & Associates. *For Crown Center Office Complex,* architect: Edward Larrabee Barnes. Associated architects: Marshall & Brown. Landscape consultant: Peter C. Rolland & Associates.

6

6 The Atlantis on Brickell; Miami, FL; 1982. *See* Entry 21. (Courtesy Arquitectonica; Coral Gables, FL Photographer: Norman McGrath.)

See: *Architectural Record* 154 (October 1973): 113–25. *Buildings* 69 (January 1975): 40–46. *Process: Architecture,* no. 11 (1979): 82–87.

■ 24

IBM Building (590 Madison Avenue); New York, NY; 1983 (see Illus. 8).
Located across the street from Johnson/Burgee's AT&T Building (see entry no. 194), this sleekly simple, 43-story office slab, faced in gray-green granite and blue-green glass, shares its site with a spectacular 68-foot-high greenhouse whose informal seating amid clusters of tall bamboo invites use by neighborhood people as a public square. At street level, the office tower's corners are clipped off, leaving its upper floors to cantilever overhead dramatically.
Associates in charge: John M. Y. Lee and Armand P. Avakian; project architect: Richard Keibschon. Engineers: The Office of James Ruderman (structural); LeMessurier Associates/SCI (structural consultant); Joseph R. Loring & Assoc. (mechanical/electrical). Landscape architects: Zion and Breen. General contractor: Turner Construction.

See: *Architectural Record* 169 (March 1981): 130–33; 172 (May 1984): 146–55. *Space Design,* no. 250 (July 1985): 61–65.

■ 25

Walker Art Center; Minneapolis, MN; 1971.
A mannerly backdrop for the art it houses and a harmonious neighbor for Ralph Rapson's Guthrie Theater (see entry no. 339), with which it shares a glass-walled entrance, it has been called "a minimal sculpture inside and out."
Associate in charge: Alistair M. Bevington. Engineers: Paul Weidlinger, and Meyer, Borgman & Johnson (structural); Gausman & Moore (mechanical/electrical).

Honors: AIA Honor Award, 1972.

See: *AIA Journal* 57 (May 1972): 38. *Architectural Record* 150 (July 1971): 34. *Design Quarterly,* no. 81 (1971): whole issue.

S. B. BARNES see KISTNER, WRIGHT & WRIGHT; Edward H. FICKETT; S. B. BARNES

Donald BARTHELME

■ 26

West Columbia Elementary School; West Columbia, TX; 1952.
"Neighborhoods" of classrooms oriented around courtyards, airy patterns of exposed steel joists, and ingenious use of colorful and varied materials characterize this cheerful and unusual school.
Structural engineer: Walter B. Moore.
Contractor: Fisher Construction Co.

See. *Architectural Forum* 97 (October 1952): 102–9. *Werk* 41 (March 1954): 76–79. Henry-Russell Hitchcock and Arthur Drexler, eds., *Built in USA: Post-War Architecture* (New York: Museum of Modern Art, 1952), 46–47.

Fred BASSETTI (subsequent name of firm: BASSETTI NORTON METLER)

■ 27

Ridgeway Men's Dormitories, Phase 3, Western Washington State College; Bellingham, WA; 1966.
Twenty-six suite-towers progressing down a steep and heavily wooded hillside provide housing and lounge facilities for 450 students. Each room has its own private outdoor entrance via a stairway or bridge.
Engineers: Norman Jacobson & Associates (structural); Richard M. Stern (mechanical). Landscape architects: Richard Haag Associates.

Honors: PA Design Citation, 1965; AIA Honor Award, 1967.

See: *AIA Journal* 47 (June 1967): 51. *Architectural Record* 141 (June 1967): 50–55. *Progressive Architecture* 46 (January 1965): 144–45.

Welton BECKET

■ 28

Hyatt Regency Hotel and Reunion Tower; Dallas, TX; 1978 (see Illus. 9).
This dazzler stars in the opening footage of the TV soap "Dallas." Seven towers of different heights, all faced with reflective glass, meld into one skyscraper hotel with 1,000 guest rooms arranged around a 200-foot-high atrium. The towers, structurally innovative, resist wind forces with steel-plate shear walls rather than concrete walls or steel trusses, thus saving money and interior space. Alongside, Reunion Tower (nicknamed "the electric dandelion") is topped by a brightly lit geodesic dome, which contains a restaurant and observation deck.
Director: Alan Rosen; director of design: Louis Naisdorf; project designer: Victor Chu. Engineers: Welton Becket Assoc. (structural); Herman Blum Consulting Engineers (mechanical/electrical). Landscape architects:

9 Hyatt Regency Hotel and Reunion Tower; Dallas, TX; 1978. *See* Entry 28. (Courtesy Welton Becket Associates: Santa Monica, CA.)

Myrick-Newman-Dahlberg. General contractor: Henry C. Beck Co.

Honors: CRSI Design Award, 1979, for Reunion Tower.

See: *Architectural Record* 164 (mid-August 1978): 116–17; 164 (October 1978): 107–12. *Contract Interiors* 138 (August 1978): 72–77. *Abitare,* no. 205 (June 1982): 62–65. Charles Jencks, *Architecture Today* (New York: Abrams, 1982), 68–69. F. Hart et al., *Multi-Storey Buildings in Steel,* 2d ed. (New York: Nichols Publishing Co., 1985), 72–73.

■ 29

Kaiser Center: Oakland, CA; 1960 (see Illus. 10).
This landmark on the shores of Lake Merritt is actually a complex of buildings dominated by a gleaming, 28-story office

10 Kaiser Center; Oakland, CA; 1960. *See* Entry 29. (Courtesy Welton Becket Associates: Santa Monica, CA. Photographer: Kaiser Graphic Arts.)

tower whose faces curve in a dramatic arc. Featuring materials manufactured by Kaiser companies, its curtain wall combines natural-finish aluminum frame, gray glass, and gold anodized aluminum panels.

Engineers: Murray Erick Associates (structural); Dames & Moore (soil mechanics). Landscape architect: Osmundson & Staley. Contractor: Robert E. McKee General Contractor, Inc.

See: *Architectural Record* 128 (December 1960): 117–22. *Interiors* 121 (April 1962): 109–13. *Arts + Architecture* 77 (December 1960): 10–13.

■ 30

North Carolina Mutual Life Insurance Company; Durham, NC; 1965 (see Illus. 11).

Headquarters for the largest black-owned insurance company in the United States, this imposing office building gains symbolic strength from an interplay of massive vertical columns and broad horizontal Vierendeel trusses. Structurally innovative, it was the first to use segmental post-tensioned construction in a tall building.

Associated architect: M. A. Ham Associates. Structural/mechanical electrical engineers: Seelye, Stevenson, Value & Knecht. Landscape architect: Richard C. Bell Associates.

See: *Progressive Architecture* 46 (September 1965): 166–71; 47 (April 1966): 222–26. *Concrete* 3 (September 1969): 356–59.

■ 31

Southland Center; Dallas, TX; 1959 (see Illus. 12).

The 42-story Southland Life office tower and the 28-story, 600-room Sheraton-Dallas Hotel soar above a terrazzo-paved and attractively planted plaza. Through connections under and above the plaza, they offer "bulk space" on their lower floors for convention use.

Consulting architect: Mark Lemmon. Structural engineers: Murray Erick Associates. Consulting mechanical engineers: Zumwalt & Vinther. General contractor: J. W. Bateson Co.

Honors: AISC Award of Excellence, 1960.

See: *Architectural Forum* 111 (August 1959): 94–101. *Architectural Record* 126 (August 1959): 141–46. *Arts + Architecture* 77 (August 1960): 10–11.

11 North Carolina Mutual Life Insurance Company; Durham, NC; 1965. *See* Entry 30. (Courtesy Welton Becket Associates; Santa Monica, CA. Photographer: Balthazar Korab.)

12 Southland Center; Dallas, TX; 1959. *See* Entry 31. (Courtesy Welton Becket Associates; Santa Monica, CA.)

11

12

Welton BECKET and J. E. STANTON

■ 32

Police Facilities Building, Civic Center; Los Angeles, CA; 1955.
Occupying a full city block, this building comprises an information center, offices, a laboratory, an auditorium, and a jail. The richly finished main lobby features a 36-foot-long glass mosaic mural designed and executed by Joe Young.
Director of design: Maynard Woodard. Engineers: Murray Erick and Paul E. Jeffers (structural); Ralph E. Phillips, Inc. (mechanical/electrical). Associated general contractors: Ford J. Twaits Co. and Morrison-Knudsen.

Honors: AIA Merit Award, 1956.

See: Progressive Architecture 37 (March 1956): 108–15, 145. *Arts + Architecture* 73 (July 1956): 12–13. *Architect & Engineer* 205 (May 1956): 8–13.

William S. BECKETT

■ 33

William Beckett's office; Los Angeles, CA; 1951?
When this young architect gutted a former boys' club and, at modest cost,

transformed it into a simple yet elegant space for his offices, the results caught the fancy of architects around the world.

Honors: AIA Honor Award, 1952.

See: Architectural Forum 94 (June 1951): 138–40. *Domus* 278 (January 1953): 12–15. *L'Architecture d'Aujourd'hui,* nos. 50–51 (August 1953): 94–96.

Herbert BECKHARD see Marcel BREUER and Herbert BECKHARD

Pietro BELLUSCHI

Winner, AIA Gold Medal, 1972.

■ 34

Equitable Savings and Loan Building; Portland, OR; 1948.
This trim, compact office building, originally 12 stories high and later 13, set styles for hundreds that came after. It was the first to be sheathed in aluminum, the first to employ double-glazed window panels, and the first to be completely sealed and fully air-conditioned.
Mechanical engineer: J. Donald Kroeker. General contractor: Ross B. Hammond.

Honors: AIA Twenty-Five Year Award, 1982.

See: AIA Journal 71 (July 1982): 84–89. *Architectural Forum* 89 (September 1948): 98–106; 128 (June 1968): 40–45. *Architectural Record* 138 (December 1965): 144–45.

■ 35

Juilliard School of Music, Lincoln Center; New York, NY; 1969 (see Illus. 13).
A complex building, it contains four theaters as well as classrooms, studios, and other school facilities. The 960-to-1,026-seat Juilliard Theater has a movable ceiling that adjusts to three positions within a 7-foot range. Its neighbors are Alice Tully Hall (1,096 seats), Paul Recital Hall (277 seats), and a small Drama Workshop.
Associated architects: Eduardo Catalano and Helge Westermann. Engineers: Paul Weidlinger (structural); Jaros, Baum & Bolles (mechanical/electrical). Stage design consultant: Jean Rosenthal Associates, Inc. Acoustical consultant: Heinrich Keilholz. Contractor: Walsh Construction Company.

Honors: Bard Award, 1970.

See: Architectural Forum 131 (December 1969): 78. *Architectural Record* 147 (January 1970): 121–30. *Progressive Architecture* 51 (December 1970): 55, 65–72.

13 Juilliard School of Music, Lincoln Center; New York, NY; 1969. *See* Entry 35. (Photographer: Ashod Kassabian: New York, NY).

13

BELT, LEMMON & LO; John Carl WARNECKE

■ 36

State Capitol; Honolulu, HI; 1969.
Openness is the theme of this gracious and dignified statehouse; it is built, with rings of verandas, around a great courtyard that itself has no walls at street level on two sides. Local natural features —ancient banyan trees and volcanic mountains—are said to have suggested other design elements: stately columns and a curved, fluted roof.
Architect in charge of design: John Carl Warnecke. Engineers: Donald T. Lo (structural); Soderholm, Sorensen & Associates (mechanical). Landscape architect: Richard Tongg. General contractor: Reed & Martin, Inc.

Honors: PA Design Citation, 1962.

See: Architectural Record 145 (May 1969): 117–28. *Progressive Architecture* 42 (June 1961): 67–68; 43 (January 1962): 126–31.

Gunnar BIRKERTS

■ 37

Federal Reserve Bank of Minneapolis; Minneapolis, MN; 1973 (see Illus. 14).
Here is an engineering tour de force, an office building built like a bridge, with a column-free span of 275 feet. Framed by its two titanic concrete towers, a sleekly paved plaza lies underneath; protected facilities for security operation are housed beneath the plaza.
Project director: Charles Fleckenstein. Engineers: Skilling, Helle, Christiansen, Robertson (structural); Shannan & Wilson (foundation); Jaros, Baum & Bolles (mechanical/ electrical). Landscape architects: Charles Wood & Associates. General contractor: Knutson Construction Co.

Honors: AISC Architectural Award of Excellence, 1974.

See: Architectural Record 154 (November 1973): 105–16. *Bauen + [und] Wohnen* 30 (April 1975): 170–76. Y. Futagawa, ed., *Gunnar Birkerts & Associates: IBM Information Systems Center . . . Federal Reserve Bank . . . ,* Global Architecture, no. 31 (Tokyo: A. D. A. Edita, 1974).

14

■ 38

Fisher Administrative Center, University of Detroit; Detroit, MI; 1967 (see Illus. 15).
Three architecturally contrasting areas of this building house distinctly different activities. Its rambling podium of a ground floor is devoted to direct services to students; above this base, a lozenge-shaped structure with windows shaded by ranks of vertical fins contains four floors of offices and, in turn, is topped by an executive penthouse, which offers views unimpeded by fins.
Principal, project administrator: Almon Durkee; associate for design: Keith Brown. Engineers: Holforty, Widrig, O'Neill Associates (structural); Siegel, Swiech & Associates (mechanical). Landscape architects: Johnson, Johnson & Roy. General contractor: Utley-James Corporation.

See: Architectural Record 142 (July 1967): 109–14. *Progressive Architecture* 46 (April 1965): 224–27. *Lotus* 4 (1967/68): 28–35.

■ 39

IBM Corporate Computer Center (also known as IBM Information Systems Center); Sterling Forest, NY; 1972 (see Illus. 16).
Designed to house computer operations for IBM's internal control and planning, this facility contrasts sharply with its woodland setting. A "piece of minimal graphic sculpture," its smooth skin is a combination of polished aluminum panels and glass separated by bands of red-orange enameled metal.
Designers: Algimantas Bublys and D. Bartley

15

16

Guthrie. Engineers: Skilling-Helle-Christiansen-Robertson (structural); Hoyem Associates (mechanical/electrical).

Honors: PA Design Citation, 1971.

See: Progressive Architecture 53 (December 1972): 50–55. *Domus,* no. 529 (December 1973): 29–32. Y. Futagawa, ed., *Gunnar Birkerts & Associates: IBM Information Systems Center*

. . . Federal Reserve Bank . . . , Global Architecture, no. 31 (Tokyo: A. D. A. Edita, 1974).

■ **40**

Legal Research Building addition, University of Michigan; Ann Arbor, MI; 1981 (see Illus. 17).
This library has been called "the most

esthetically satisfying large underground building to have penetrated American soil." Its three levels all look up through a reflective glass moat at the tall collegiate Gothic structure it supplements. Glass baffles on the interior of the tilted skylight break the view into cubist patterns.
Project director: Kenneth Rohlfing. Engineers: Robert Darvas Assoc. (structural); Joseph R. Loring & Assoc. (mechanical/electrical). General contractor: J. A. Fredman, Inc.

See: AIA Journal 72 (January 1983): 50–55 and cover. *Architectural Record* 170 (March 1982): 77–85. *A + U,* no. 142 (July 1982): 21–33.

■ **41**

Library and two dormitories, Tougaloo College; Tougaloo, MS; 1973 (see Illus. 18).
Built on shifting clay, these trim, modular buildings rest on columns well above the ground and are supported on deep foundations of drilled and belled concrete caissons. They were designed in the 1960s as part of an ambitious master plan for this small black college, but, as of 1988, no further expansion of the campus had taken place.
Project director: Charles Fleckenstein. Engineers: Robert M. Darvas & Associates (structural); Hoyem Associates (mechanical/electrical). Contractor: Frazier-Morton Construction Company.

See: Architectural Record 144 (October 1968): 129–44; 154 (November 1973): 105–16. *Lotus* 4 (1967/68): 24–27.

17

18 Library and two dormitories, Tougaloo College; Tougaloo, MS; 1973. *See* Entry 41. (Courtesy Gunnar Birkerts and Associates; Birmingham, MI. Photographer: Balthazar Korab.)

18

■ 42

Lincoln Elementary School; Columbus, IN; Building: 1967; landscaping, 1968? (see Illus. 19).
A compact, beautifully detailed school, hidden from sight behind a circle of trees, it can be used after school hours for community programs and as a public park.
Associate for design: Harold Van Dine. Supervising architects: Siece, Inc. Landscape architects: Johnson, Johnson & Roy. Engineers: Holforty, Widrig, O'Neill & Assoc. (structural); Hoyem, Basso & Adams (mechanical). General contractor: Dunlap Construction Co.

Honors: AIA Honor Award, 1970; Bartlett Award, 1970.

See: AIA Journal 53 (June 1970): 82. *Architectural Forum* 127 (November 1967): 48–53. *Architectural Record* 140 (August 1966): 95–97.

William N. BREGER

■ 43

Civic Center Synagogue; New York, NY; 1967.
Three boldly curving concrete shells shape this small yet striking downtown synagogue. The windowless front wall of its sanctuary seems to float above its quiet entrance court.
Engineers: Paul Gugliotta (structural); Batlan & Oxman (mechanical). Landscape architect: M. Paul Friedberg. Contractor: Sherry Construction Corporation.

Honors: AIA Honor Award, 1968.

See: AIA Journal 49 (June 1968): 103. *Architectural Forum* 127 (October 1967): 64–69.

BREGMAN & HAMANN *see* ZEIDLER PARTNERSHIP; BREGMAN & HAMANN *and* John B. PARKIN ASSOCIATES

Marcel BREUER

Winner, AIA Gold Medal, 1968.

■ 44

Dormitory, Vassar College; Poughkeepsie, NY; 1950.
Designed for cooperative living and supplied with ample kitchen facilities, its bedrooms are elevated above ground, giving them privacy and providing covered outdoor areas for Ping-Pong tables, bikes, and unimpeded views.

See: Architectural Record 107 (June 1950): 118–19; 111 (January 1952): 127–34. Henry-Russell Hitchcock and Arthur Drexler, eds., *Built in USA: Post-War Architecture* (New York: Museum of Modern Art, 1952), 50–51.

■ 45

Priory of the Annunciation; Bismarck, ND; 1963 (see Illus. 20).
A distinctive geometric, 100-foot-high bell tower sets off a complex of fieldstone, brick, and concrete buildings—linked by walkways—housing a Benedictine convent and a preparatory school for girls. Of particular interest: the starkly striking main chapel.
Associated local architects: Traynor & Hermanson. Structural engineers: Johnston-Sahlman Co. Structural consultant for chapel: Paul Weidlinger. Mechanical engineers:

19 Lincoln Elementary School; Columbus, IN; 1967. *See* Entry 42. (Courtesy Gunnar Birkerts and Associates; Birmingham, MI. Photographer: Orlando Cabanban.)

19

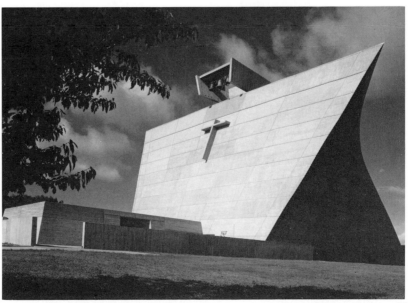

■ **47**

St. John's Abbey; Collegeville, MN; various dates (see Illus. 22).
Breuer submitted the master plan for this Benedictine monastery-campus in 1954. By 1961, three buildings were complete: one student dormitory, a monastic wing, and a monumental church, one of the finest religious structures of modern times, its baptistery surmounted by a high, bannerlike bell tower. Added subsequently were a library, science center, more dorms, and an ecumenical visitors center.
Engineers: Johnston-Sahlman Co. (structural); Gausman & Moore (mechanical).

Honors: AIA Merit Award, 1962.

See: Architectural Forum 128 (May 1968): 40–57. *Architectural Record* 130 (November 1961): 132–42. *L'Architecture d'Aujourd'hui,* no. 100 (February–March 1962): 38–45. *Arts + Architecture* 79 (February 1962): 18–20, 28–29.

20 Priory of the Annunciation; Bismarck, ND; 1963. *See* Entry 45. (Courtesy Hamilton Smith, FAIA; New York, NY. Photographer: Shin Koyama.)

20

Gausman & Moore. General contractors: Meisner Anderson Co., first stage; Anderson, Guthrie & Carlson, second stage.

See: Architectural Record 134 (December 1963): 95–102. *L'Architecture d'Aujourd'hui,* no. 122 (September 1965): 74–75. *Arts + Architecture* 81 (November 1964): 16–19.

Honors: AIA Honor Award, 1973; AIA Bicentennial List, one nomination.

See: Architectural Record 142 (November 1967): 130–37. *L'Architecture d'Aujourd'hui,* no. 108 (June–July 1963): 16–18. *Architect and Building News* 7 (September 1968): 62–67.

■ **48**

Whitney Museum of American Art; New York, NY; 1966 (see Illus. 23).
This distinctive museum makes the most of its small corner site. Upper floors, affording maximum gallery space within, cantilever outward importantly over its shadowy forecourt; seven windows—

Marcel BREUER and Herbert BECKHARD (name of successor firm: Herbert Beckhard Frank Richlan & Associates)

■ **46**

St. Francis de Sales Church; Muskegon, MI; 1967 (see Illus. 21).
Striated concrete walls that swoop into surprising trapezoids and curves shape the exterior of this church. The sanctuary, spanned by a system of rigid concrete arches, seats 1,200 and features a chapel which, when specially lit, can serve as a second altar.
Engineers: Paul Weidlinger (structural); Stinard, Piccirillo & Brown (mechanical). Acoustical consultants: Goodfriend, Ostergaard Associates. General contractor: M. A. Lombard & Son.

21 St. Francis de Sales Church; Muskegon, MI; 1967. *See* Entry 46. (Courtesy Herbert Beckhard, Frank Richlan & Associates; New York, NY. Photographer: Bill Hedrich, Hedrich-Blessing; Chicago, IL.)

21

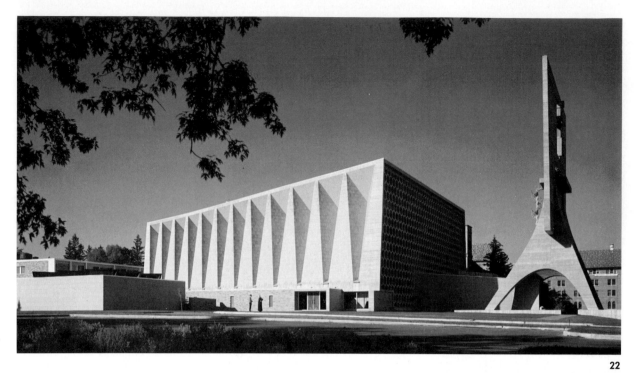

22 St. John's Abbey; Collegeville, MN; various dates. *See* Entry 47. (Courtesy Hamilton Smith, FAIA; New York, NY. Photographer: Bill Hedrich, Hedrich-Blessing; Chicago, IL.)

irregularly spaced trapezoids that vary in size—mark its granite facade like symbolic eyes.

Consulting architect: Michael Irving. Engineers: Paul Weldlinger (structural); Werner, Jensen & Korst (mechanical). General contractor: HRH Construction Corporation.

Honors: Bard Award, 1968; AIA Honor Award, 1970; Bartlett Award, 1970.

See: AIA Journal 67 (September 1978): 40–47. *Architectural Forum* 125 (September 1966): 80–85. *Architect's Journal* 144 (September 1966): 768, 780–81.

BRODSKY, HOPF & ADLER see **HELLMUTH, OBATA & KASSABAUM; BRODSKY, HOPF & ADLER**

BROOKS, BARR, GRAEBER & WHITE see **SKIDMORE, OWINGS & MERRILL; BROOKS, BARR, GRAEBER & WHITE**

John **BURGEE ARCHITECTS** with Philip **JOHNSON**

■ **49**

PPG Place; Pittsburgh, PA; 1984 (see Illus. 24).

Built for a company formerly known as Pittsburgh Plate Glass, this 5½-acre office complex comprises four 6-story structures, one 14-story building, and one 40-story building (PPG Tower) arranged around a formal plaza edged with covered arcades and shops. Its curtain walls are "pleated" into multifaceted, glittering facades and topped with rows of small neo-Gothic spires.

Associate: Glenn Garrison; project architect: Anne Asher. Consultants: Robertson, Fowler (structural); Cosentini Associates (mechanical); Zion & Breen (landscape). General contractor: Mellon Stuart/Blount.

23 Whitney Museum of American Art; New York, NY; 1966. *See* Entry 48. (Courtesy of Hamilton Smith, FAIA; New York, NY.)

24

See: Architectural Record 172 (October 1984): 192–99. *Architecture* 73 (May 1984): 242–51. *A+U: Architecture and Urbanism,* no. 172 (January 1985): 27–34. *GA Document,* no. 12 (January 1985): 66–71.

Jerome R. BUTLER, Jr.
City Architect, Chicago Department of Public Works

■ 50

Navy Pier Restoration; Chicago, IL; 1976.

Fronting on Lake Michigan and originally built (1916) to the design of Charles S. Frost, in the 1920s it not only accommodated pleasure boats and outdoor amusements but boasted a 3,500-seat concert hall. Much deteriorated thereafter, its massive restoration involved structural repair, unsealing and expansion of skylight areas, landscaping, and construction of a solar space- and water-heating system.

Engineers: Bureau of Engineering (Louis Koncza, chief engineer). Consultants: Environmental Systems Design, Inc. (mechanical); Robert H. Samuel & Associates (plumbing). General contractor: Bureau of Construction.

Honors: Chicago AIA Distinguished Buildings

Award, 1976; AIA Honor Award for Extended Use, 1977; Bartlett Award, 1977.

See: AIA Journal 66 (May 1977): 44. *Architectural Record* 161 (March 1977): 107–14. *Inland Architect* 20 (September 1976): 14–17.

CRS see CAUDILL ROWLETT SCOTT and CRSS/CRS SIRRINE

CRSS/CRS SIRRINE

■ 51

Carver-Hawkeye Arena; Iowa City, IA; 1982.

Because it's sited in a ravine, this covered stadium, which seats 15,000, looks smaller than it is. The steel space truss that supports its roof allows clear spans underneath of 300 by 340 feet. Inside, structural and mechanical systems are exposed; curving perimeter walls are made of glass block. Many features of this arena's design save energy.

For CRSS: Paul Kennon, design principal; Wallie Scott, partner in charge. Associate architects: The Durrant Group. Consultants: Geiger Associates (structural); Crose-Gardner Assoc. (landscape). Construction management: CRSS/CRS Sirrine.

Honors: Midwest Regional Design Award, 1984; AIA Honor Award, 1984; Owings-Corning Energy Conservation Award.

See: Architecture 73 (May 1984): 194–99. *Progressive Architecture* 65 (August 1984): 94–99. *Building Design and Construction* 24 (June 1983): 118–20.

CAMBRIDGE SEVEN ASSOCIATES

■ 52

National Aquarium in Baltimore; Baltimore, MD; 1981. (see Illus. 25).

A curious mix of boxy concrete shapes brightened by a colorful mural and topped by off-center glass pyramids set at rakish angles, this recreational building, which rides a pier in Baltimore's Inner Harbor, has a playful air and has proved enormously popular. An array of ramps and escalators transit its central atrium, giving visitors views of a simulated rain forest, a dolphin/sea lion pool, and many other exhibits.

Principal in charge: Peter Chermayeff; Frank Zaremba, principal exhibit designer. Consultants: LeMessurier Associates/SCI (structural); Francis Associates/SCI (mechanical/electrical). General contractor: Whiting-Turner.

Honors: PA Citation for Architectural Design, 1979.

See: AIA Journal 71 (mid-May 1982): 170–75. *Architectural Record* 170 (May 1982): 83–91. *Architecture* 74 (June 1985): 60–69.

■ 53

San Antonio Museum of Art; San Antonio, TX; 1981? (Original architects of brewery complex, 1895–1904: E. Jungerfeld & Co.)

A Romanesque Revival complex designated a historic landmark in 1972, then transformed into a handsome museum. Exterior changes included sealing off some windows, adding color in bright entrance awnings and painted details, and supplying a footbridge between two towers. Inside, colorful sun baffles partly screen new skylights, and "magical" elevators—fancifully lit and mostly transparent, their moving parts chromed and visible—are a delight to watch.

Principal in charge: Peter Chermayeff; principals: Charles Redmon, Ivan Chermayeff.

24 PPG Place; Pittsburgh, PA; 1984. *See* Entry 49. (Courtesy John Burgee Architects; New York, NY. Photographer: © Richard Payne, AIA 1988.)

25

Associated architects: Chumney, Jones and Kell. Consultants: LeMessurier Assoc./SCI (structural); Galson & Galson (mechanical/electrical). General contractor: Guido Brothers.

Honors: PA Award for Architectural Design, 1979.

See: Architectural Record 169 (June 1981): 92–99. *Progressive Architecture* 62 (November 1981): 30. *Interior Design* 52 (July 1981): 194–203.

CAMBRIDGE SEVEN ASSOCIATES; LLOYD JONES FILLPOT

■ 54

INNOVA (formerly Houston Design Center); Houston, TX; 1984.
Spectacular quarters for designer showrooms and offices. Ten stories high, windowless for the most part, and containing 500,000 square feet of space, it's faced with alternating bands of black and gray granite, "like a pin-stripe suit." Its longest facade is gashed by a diagonal sequence of 2-story-high rectangular terraces incised into the building. These terraces, glazed within, afford views of the center's complex interior, where escalators glide through wells that look into glass-walled display areas.
Principal in charge: Charles Redmon; project architect: Gary Johnson. Engineers: Walter P. Moore & Assoc. (structural); I. A. Naman & Assoc. (mechanical). General contractors: Brunel Construction/Texas Construction.

See: Architecture 75 (March 1986): 76–79. *GA Document,* no. 14 (December 1985): 62–73. *Interiors* 144 (March 1985): 124–39.

CARSON, LUNDIN & SHAW (subsequent name of firm: CARSON, LUNDIN & THORSON)

■ 55

Manufacturers Hanover Trust Company Operations Building; New York, NY; 1968.
Behind an intriguing facade that with only the narrowest slits for windows suggests an IBM card, this building accommodates computers and other business machines that process paperwork for New York's financial district.
Partner in charge of design: Arvin Shaw III. Engineers: Edwards & Hjorth (structural); Meyer, Strong & Jones (mechanical). General contractor: George A. Fuller Co.

Honors: AISC Architectural Award of Excellence, 1970.

See: Architectural Forum 132 (January–February 1970): 62–67. *Architectural and Engineering News* 9 (May 1967): 152–53.

CAUDILL ROWLETT SCOTT (subsequent name of firm: CRSS/CRS SIRRINE; see entry no. 51)

Winner of the AIA's Architectural Firm Award, 1972. In 1985, William Wayne Caudill was posthumously awarded the AIA Gold Medal.

■ 56

Fodrea Community School; Columbus, IN; 1973.
Parents and children, administrators and teachers helped design this school. Ramps, slides, and tunnels are incorporated in its two-level open plan; its exposed structural and mechanical systems, painted in bright colors, form major design elements.
Project manager: Truitt B. Garrison; director of design: Paul A. Kennon; technologist: D. Wayne McDonnell. General contractor: Repp & Mundt.

Honors: AISC Architectural Award of Excellence, 1975.

See: Progressive Architecture 55 (May 1974): 84–87. *Baumeister* 70 (August 1973): 994–95. G. E. Kidder Smith, *A Pictorial History of Architecture in America* (New York: American Heritage, 1976), 2: 496–97.

■ 57

Jesse H. Jones Hall for the Performing Arts; Houston, TX; 1966.
This theater's superb acoustics, movable ceiling, and formidably flexible seating arrangements have led it to be called "the most sophisticated building of its kind." It can seat as many as 3,000, but for chamber music and plays, its balcony and rear orchestra areas can be screened off and the orchestra pit and orchestra shell can be repositioned.
Engineers: Walter Moore (structural); Bernard Johnson Engineers, Inc. (mechanical/electrical). Acoustical consultants: Bolt, Beranek & Newman. Theater design–engineering consultant: George C. Izenour. General contractor: George A. Fuller Co.

Honors: AIA Honor Award, 1967.

See: AIA Journal 47 (June 1967): 57. *Architectural Record* 141 (February 1967): 114–21. *L'Architecture Française* 30 (January–February 1969): 7–9.

■ 58

San Angelo Central High School; San Angelo, TX; 1958.
A big school housed in a dozen buildings, all but one air-conditioned, on an ample campus, it is graced by a man-made lake, a large swimming pool, snack bars, and appealing walks—yet it was constructed on a minimal budget.
Associate architect: Max D. Lovett. Engineers: Edward F. Nye (structural); J. W. Hall, Jr. (mechanical/electrical). Landscape architect: Robert F. White. General contractor: Rose Construction Co.

Honors: AIA Merit Award, 1959; AIA Bicentennial List, one nomination.

See: *Architectural Forum* 107 (November 1957): 150–51, 168; 109 (November 1958): 110–23. *Bauen-Wohnen* 14 (November 1959): 378–82.

CAUDILL ROWLETT SCOTT; DALTON, VAN DIJK, JOHNSON

■ 59

Edwin J. Thomas Hall of Performing Arts, University of Akron; Akron, OH; 1973.

By movement of its ceiling alone, this hall can shrink in space from 3,000 seats to 2,400 to 900 and still retain its fine acoustics. Outside, framed by garden terraces and angular, many-leveled hard landscaping, it is "an insistently abstract arrangement of geometric shapes."
Job captain: Charles Lawrence. Associated architects: R. M. Ginsert & Assoc. Engineers: Dick Ginsert (structural); Scheeser & Buckley (mechanical). Theater design consultant: George C. Izenour Associates; acoustical consultant: Vern O. Knudsen. General contractor: Mosser Construction.

Honors: AIA Bicentennial List, one nomination; CRSI Design Award, 1975.

See: *Architectural Forum* 139 (December 1973): 58–65. *Architectural Record* 155 (March 1974): 143–48. George C. Izenour, *Theatre Design* (New York: McGraw Hill, 1977), 317–18, 374–83.

CENTERBROOK

■ 60

Hood Museum of Art, Dartmouth College; Hanover, NH; 1985 (see Illus. 26).

Set between two sharply differing buildings, this low, rambling museum relates remarkably well to its campus neighbors, echoing—in modified form and often in differing elements such as sandblasted concrete in place of stone—such features of older buildings as arches, columns, patterned brickwork, and a cupola while asserting an ageless, sharply etched look all its own. Its varied, pitched copper roofs are outlined in the green to which the copper will oxidize.
Partners in charge: Charles Moore and Chad Floyd. Engineers: Besier Gibble Norden (structural); Helenski-Zimmerer (mechanical/electrical). General contractor: Jackson Construction.

Honors: AIA Honor Award, 1987.

See: *Architectural Record* 174 (February 1986): 108–19. *Architecture* 75 (January 1986): 32–39 and cover. *Abitare,* no. 247 (September 1986): 378–79.

Victor CHRIST-JANER

■ 61

James F. Lincoln Library, Lake Erie College; Painesville, OH; 1966/67.
There are many cubist touches here. Outside, a variety of aluminum-faced regular polyhedrons seem to float over the recessed concrete base; inside, both natural and artificial illumination come from blocky skylight boxes supplemented by light wells.
Engineers and general contractor: The Austin Co.

Honors: R. S. Reynolds Memorial Award.

See: *Architectural Forum* 113 (December 1960): 77–83; 127 (July–August 1967): 46–75, 78–85, 90–97. *L'Architecture d'Aujourd'hui,* no. 137 (April–May 1968): 29.

Mario CIAMPI

■ 62

Fernando Rivera Elementary School; Daly City, CA; 1960.
A small, 1-story school that nestles under a sawtoothed roof of angled plywood plates. Its twelve classrooms, kindergarten,

26 Hood Museum of Art, Dartmouth College; Hanover, NH; 1985. *See* Entry 60. (Courtesy Dartmouth College; Hanover, NH. Photographer: Stuart Bratesman/Dartmouth College © 1988 Dartmouth College.)

library, and related facilities are dispersed into five clusters bounded by courts of varying size.

Associate: Paul Reiter. Engineers: Isadore Thompson (structural); Van Dament & Darmsted (mechanical). General contractor: Midstate Construction Co.

Honors: AIA Honor Award, 1961.

See: *AIA Journal* 35 (April 1961): 72–73. *Architectural Forum* 114 (April 1961): 114–17. *Arts + Architecture* 77 (August 1960): 16–17.

■ 63

University Art Museum, University of California; Berkeley, CA; 1970.
When completed, it was the country's largest university art museum. Located just off campus, its casual concrete ramps lure the passerby into its galleries; its terraces overlook a sunny sculpture garden.

Design associates: Richard L. Jorasch and Ronald E. Wagner. Engineers: Isadore Thompson (structural); K. T. Belotelkin & Assoc. (mechanical). Landscape architects: Mario J. Ciampi & Associates. General contractor: Rothschild & Rahn, Inc.

See: *Architectural Record* 152 (July 1972): 104–7. *Architettura* 18 (December 1972): 526–27. *Arts + Architecture* 82 (October 1965): 26–27.

■ 64

Westmoor High School; Daly City, CA; 1957/58.
Lively metal sculpture and a colorful porcelain enamel mural adorn this inexpensively built high school—designed, factory style, in low, 30-foot-square bays—which also features glass-walled perimeter corridors and a pleasantly landscaped central mall.

Associates: Allyn C. Martin, Paul Reiter. Engineers: Isadore Thompson (structural); Buonaccorsi & Murray (mechanical). Landscape architect: Lawrence Halprin. General contractor: Theodore G. Meyer & Sons.

Honors: AIA Honor Award, 1958.

See: *Architectural Forum* 102 (February 1955): 142–43; 108 (May 1958): 120–25; 115 (November 1961): 152–57.

CORLETT & SPACKMAN

■ 65

Blyth Arena; Squaw Valley, CA; 1959.
Tent shaped, this stadium built for the 1960 Winter Olympics is open on one side to sunshine and the ski-jumping hill. Its roof is suspended, like a bridge, from cables strung over tapered steel masts and tied down to concrete piers.

Associated architects: Kitchen & Hunt. Engineers: H. J. Brunnier, John M. Sardis (structural); Vandament & Darmsted (mechanical/electrical); Punnett, Parez & Hutchinson (civil). Contractors: Diversified Builders, Inc.; York Corp.; Independent Iron Works, Inc.

Honors: PA Design Award, 1958; AIA Honor Award, 1960.

See: *AIA Journal* 33 (April 1960): 76–77. *Architectural Forum* 112 (February 1960): 104–6. *Arts + Architecture* 74 (January 1957): 12–13.

COSSUTA & PONTE see I. M. PEI; COSSUTA & PONTE

CRAIG, ZEIDLER, STRONG

■ 66

Korah Collegiate and Vocational School; Sault Ste. Marie, Ontario; 1969/70 (see Illus. 27).
Flexible in layout and designed for easy expansion, this brick-clad school for 1,200 to 1,800 students is built around a pleasantly detailed pedestrian street, which runs between two bordering public streets. Classrooms look out onto this central space through a 3-foot-high band of windows at eye level. At the second- and third-floor levels, glazed bridges connect the school's two wings.

Partner in charge: Eberhard H. Zeidler. Engineers: G. Dowdell & Assoc. (structural); W. Hardy Craig & Assoc. (mechanical/electrical). General contractor: R. Sampson Construction.

See: *Architectural Forum* 132 (June 1970): 50–55. *Deutsche Bauzeitung* 104 (June 1970): 398–401. *Canadian Architect* 16 (February 1971): 46–51.

■ 67

McMaster University Health Sciences Centre; Hamilton, Ontario; 1972 (see Illus. 28).
This innovative and controversial combination teaching hospital, nursing school, and regional health-care facility was erected with a system of 21-foot-high steel towers above its main roof, supplied to accommodate mechanical and electrical services for possible expansion thereafter. As originally built, it was 4 stories high and encompassed nearly 10 acres on each floor. Inside, pedestrian circulation was designed to save steps; mosaics, inexpensive regional artwork, and fanciful graphics lent warmth and variety to public areas.

Partner in charge: Eberhard H. Zeidler. Engineers: John Maryon & Partners (structural); G. Granek & Assoc. (mechanical). Project manager: Doyle-Hinton Contract Services Ltd.

27 Korah Collegiate and Vocational School; Sault Ste. Marie, Ontario; 1969/70. *See* Entry 66. (Courtesy Zeidler Roberts Partnership/Architects: Toronto, Canada. Photographer: Jones & Morris Photography Ltd.)

Honors: PA Award Citation, 1956; AIA Merit Award, 1958.

See: *AIA Journal* 30 (July 1958): 44–45. *Progressive Architecture* 39 (June 1958): 119–36. *Architect and Building News* 221 (February 7, 1962): 199–204.

■ 70

New Orleans Public Library; New Orleans, LA; 1958.
Here's a library that, like a department store, invites the patron to come in and shop around! Inside, thanks to lavish use of glass, the eye is led from one area to another while enjoying views of the sky and attractive outdoor terraces. Outside, above ground level, the glass structure is enveloped by a lacy sunscreen that reduces glare and heat.
Associated architects: Goldstein, Parham & Labouisse; Fravrot, Reed, Mathes & Bergman Mechanical engineer: Joseph Pazon. General contractor: R. P. Farnsworth & Co.

28 McMaster University Health Sciences Centre; Hamilton, Ontario; 1972. *See* Entry 67. (Courtesy Zeidler Roberts Partnership/Architects; Toronto Canada. Photographer: Panda Associates.)

Honors: PA Design Award, 1957.

See: *AIA Journal* 31 (June 1959): 106–11. *Architectural Forum* 110 (April 1959): 128–29. *Progressive Architecture* 41 (April 1960): 152–55. *Interiors* 126 (February 1967): 100–47.

■ 71

Superdome; New Orleans, LA; 1975.
Thanks to a unique system of movable stands, this giant stadium in the heart of the city can be used not only for sports and cultural events but also for trade shows and conventions. Built on a 55-acre

Honors: Canadian Architect Award, 1969.

See: *Architectural Forum* 138 (June 1973): 30–37; 139 (October 1973): 54–57. *Canadian Architect* 17 (September 1972): 30–48. *L'Architecture Française* 34 (November–December 1973): 37–40. Leon Whiteson, *Modern Canadian Architecture* (Edmonton: Hurtig, 1983), 160–63.

■ 68

Ontario Place; Toronto, Ontario; first phase, 1971; subsequently expanded (see Illus. 29).
Here's a lively recreational complex that hovers causewaylike over Lake Ontario, incorporating three islands. It comprises a permanent exhibition building (the Ontario Pavilion), an 800-seat triodetic domed theater (the Cinesphere), an outdoor amphitheater that seats 8,000, an inventively equipped Children's Village, three "villages" of shops, discos, and restaurants, a large marina, and other appealing features.
Partner in charge: Eberhard H. Zeidler; project architect: Allan M. Young. Engineers: Gordon Dowdell & Assoc.; W. Hardy Craig & Assoc. (mechanical). Landscape architects: Hough Stanbury & Assoc. Contract management: J. L. Neilson Management.

Honors: Canadian Architect Award, 1969.

See: *Architectural Forum* 135 (July–August 1971): 30–37. *Design (England),* no. 290 (February 1973): 48–51. *Canadian Architect* 16 (June 1971): 38–48; 18 (April 1973): 52–55. Leon Whiteson, *Modern Canadian Architecture* (Edmonton: Hurtig, 1983), 156–59.

CURTIS & DAVIS

■ 69

Immaculate Conception Church, Marrero, LA; 1957.
The steeply vaulted nave and unusual, undulating ceiling of this concrete-and-steel Roman Catholic church focus attention on the sanctuary and main altar. A double prizewinner, its design was modified substantially after it won its award from *Progressive Architecture*.
Associate in charge: Walter J. Rooney, Jr. Associated architect: Harrison Schouest. Engineers: Walter E. Blessey, Jr. (structural); Favrot, Guillot, Sullivan & Vogt (mechanical/electrical). General contractor: Gervais F. Favrot.

29 Ontario Place; Toronto, Ontario; 1971. *See* Entry 68. (Courtesy Zeidler Roberts Partnership/Architects; Toronto, Ontario. Photographer: Balthazar Korab.)

site, its golden dome covers 10 acres and rises to a height of 25 stories.
Associated Architects: Edward B. Silverstein & Associates; Nolan, Norman & Nolan. Engineers: Sverdrup & Parcel.

Honors: AIA Bicentennial List, one nomination.

See: Interiors 133 (August 1973): 94–99. *Baumeister* 69 (August 1972): 905. *Indian Institute of Architects Journal* 40 (April–June 1974): 16–19.

DALTON, VAN DIJK, JOHNSON *see* CAUDILL ROWLETT SCOTT; DALTON, VAN DIJK, JOHNSON

DANIEL, MANN, JOHNSON & MENDENHALL

■ 72

Comsat Laboratories; Clarksburg, MD; 1970 (see Illus. 30).
In this building complex with glittering aluminum exteriors, sited on 210 rolling acres, Communications Satellite Corporation employees perform research and produce prototype satellites. Facilities include labs, offices, an auditorium, cafeteria, library, and satellite assembly area.
Director of design: Cesar Pelli; design associate: Philo Jacobsen; partner in charge: S. Kenneth Johnson. Landscape architect: Lester Collins. General contractor: J. W. Bateson.

Honors: PA Design Citation, 1968.

See: Progressive Architecture 51 (August 1970): 70–75. *Architect & Engineering News* 10 (December 1968): 76–77. *Domus,* no. 496 (March 1971): 7–10. John Pastier, *Cesar Pelli* (New York: Whitney Library of Design, 1980).

Richard DATTNER *see* DAVIS, BRODY; Richard DATTNER

DAVIS, BRODY

In 1975, this firm won the AIA's Architectural Firm Award; in 1977, it won the AIA's Louis Sullivan Award.

■ 73

Riverbend Houses; New York, NY; 1969.
Here, despite a tight budget, 624 apartments, 2 spacious playgrounds, and 10,000 square feet of commercial space have been stylishly fitted into a small, awkward site on the banks of the Harlem River. Ribbons of walkways and platforms bridge intervening streets; high-rise towers alternate with medium-rise duplex blocks.
Senior associate in charge: Brian Smith; project coordinator: Walter Beattie. Engineers: Wiesenfeld & Leon (structural); Wald & Zigas (mechanical/electrical). Site work: Coffey & Levine and M. Paul Friedberg & Assoc. Builder-sponsor: HRH Construction Corp.

Honors: Bard Award, 1969.

See: Architectural Forum 131 (July–August

1969): 44–55. *Architectural Record* 152 (August 1972): 97–102. *House and Home* 40 (October 1971): 106–7.

■ 74

W. C. Decker Engineering Building, Corning Glass Works; Corning, NY; 1981 (see Illus. 31).
Designed to accommodate 900 employees and to encourage face-to-face communication among colleagues, this oblong, 3-story administrative and engineering headquarters features a skylighted atrium, alive with stairs and ramps, which runs lengthwise to triangular indoor courtyards at either end. Its curtain walls, alternating strips of clear glass and black-finished glass, harmonize with those of earlier buildings nearby.
Partner in charge: Lewis Davis; associate in charge: Anthony Louvis. Engineers: Wiesenfeld & Leon (structural); Cosentini Assoc. (mechanical). Landscape architects: Peter Rolland & Assoc. General contractor: John W. Cowper Co.

See: AIA Journal 71 (July 82): 75–77. *Architectural Record* 169 (September 1981): 79–85. *A+U: Architecture and Urbanism,* no. 143 (August 1982): 22–28. *Architettura* 29 (May 1983): 358–61.

■ 75

Waterside; New York, NY; 1975 (see Illus. 32).
Comprising high-rise, brick-sheathed apartment buildings with 1,440 housing units built over the East River on specially designed piles, this development also features 4 acres of neatly detailed plazas, a river-edge promenade, ample commercial space, and a 900-car garage.

30 Comsat Laboratories; Clarksburg, MD; 1970. *See* Entry 72. (Courtesy Daniel, Mann, Johnson & Mendenhall; Los Angeles, CA.)

31

Associate: John Lebduska; project architect: Herbert Levine; project designer: Ian Ferguson. Engineers: Robert Rosenwasser (structural/soils); Cosentini Associates (mechanical/electrical). General contractor: HRH Construction Corp.

Honors: Bard Award, 1975; AIA Honor Award, 1976; Bartlett Award, 1976.

See: AIA Journal 65 (April 1976): 46–47. *Architectural Record* 159 (March 1976): 119–24. *Architecture Plus* 1 (November 1973): 66–67.

DAVIS, BRODY with Giorgio CAVAGLIERI

■ 76

New York Public Library restoration and renovation; New York, NY; 1983–. (Original architects: Carrère and Hastings, 1897–1911.)
This ongoing project is re-creating the majesty of a massive Beaux Arts masterpiece that over many years had suffered neglect, deterioration, and defacing modifications. Its original grand galleries, sumptuous with elaborate chandeliers, murals, and a wealth of marble and fine woods, often richly carved, are being restored to their intended glory while gaining air-conditioning and humidity controls, flexible lighting, and smoke detectors— all inconspicuously added.

Honors: AIA Honor Award, 1986; for Phase II: AIA Honor Award, 1987.

See: Architectural Record 171 (August 1983): 74–79. *Architecture* 75 (May 1986): 218–21. *Progressive Architecture* 67 (August 1986): 88–95. *Interior Design* 57 (January 1986): 232–37.

DAVIS, BRODY; Richard DATTNER

■ 77

Estée Lauder Laboratories; Melville, NY; first stage: 1967; second stage: 1971 (see Illus. 33).
Plans for this streamlined cosmetics plant situated alongside the Long Island Expressway allowed for expansion. In 1971, when its size was doubled, it

31 W. C. Decker Engineering Building, Corning Glass Works; Corning, NY; 1981. *See* Entry 74. (Courtesy Davis, Brody & Associates; New York, NY. Photographer: Robert Gray.)

32 Waterside; New York, NY; 1975. *See* Entry 75. (Courtesy Davis, Brody & Associates; New York, NY. Photographer: Robert Gray.)

32

became longer and sleeker—and a top prizewinner.

Project architect: Richard L. Carpenter. Engineers: Goldreich, Page & Thropp (structural); Wald & Zigas (mechanical). Landscape architect: A. E. Bye & Associates. General contractor: W. J. Barney Corp.

Honors: AIA Honor Award, 1971.

See: AIA Journal 55 (June 1971): 51. *Architectural Forum* 126 (March 1967): 76–83; 134 (April 1971): 30–31.

Jorge DEL RIO and Eduardo LOPEZ

■ 78

Housing for the Elderly; Cidra Municipality, 1968 (see Illus. 34).
Sixteen residential units—concrete plastered with white stucco—cluster around small, vehicle-free plazas on a tropical hillside. Farther down the hill, garden lots are provided for the use of the residents.

Project architect: Eduardo Lopez. Engineers: Narcisco Padilla (structural); Jorge del Rio (mechanical). Landscape architect: Jorge del Rio. General contractor: Alverez & Zabala.

Honors: PA Design Citation, 1967; AIA Honor Award, 1977.

See: AIA Journal 66 (May 1977): 47. *Progressive Architecture* 48 (January 1967): 124–25; 54 (June 1973): 120–21.

Vernon DEMARS see Joseph ESHERICK; Donald OLSEN; Vernon DEMARS

DESMOND & LORD see Paul RUDOLPH; DESMOND & LORD

34

DIAMOND, MYERS and WILKIN

■ 79

Housing Union Building (Students' Union Housing), University of Alberta; Edmonton, Alberta: 1972 (see Illus. 35).
On-campus apartments of varying sizes for 1,000 students are supplied by this extraordinary "HUB" which, when completed, was the world's longest skylighted galleria. Well suited to the region's sub-Arctic climate, the 957-foot-long complex, which also contains its own shops, sidewalk cafés, lounges, and a day-care center, is sited along a preexistent street. Cheerful and briskly functional, it was built inexpensively; ductwork is boldly exposed and painted in primary colors.

Partner in charge: Barton Myers. Engineers: Read, Jones, Christofferson (structural); Reid, Crowther (mechanical/electrical). Landscape architects: Hough Stanbury & Assoc. General contractor: Poole Construction.

See: Progressive Architecture 55 (February 1974): 46–51. *L'Architecture d'Aujourd'hui,* no. 179 (May–June 1975): 87–92. *Design Quarterly,* no. 90/91 (1974): 62–63. Leon Whiteson, *Modern Canadian Architecture* (Edmonton: Hurtig, 1983), 82–85.

Walt DISNEY COMPANY
Creator of concept and developer

■ 80

Disney World; near Orlando, FL; 1982.
A gigantic (28,000-acre) theme park à la

residences and rediscovers the virtues, often abandoned in suburbia, of streets on a grid, a central square, ample walkways for pedestrians, and public buildings located at the culminations of major streets, thereby creating meaningful vistas. Leading younger architects—e.g., Leon Krier, Steven Holl, Deborah Berke, and Robert A. M. Stern—are designing these buildings and individual homes in Seaside.

Honors: PA Urban Planning Citation, 1984; American Wood Council 1985 Design Award for Rosewalk Cottage Court, designed by Orr & Taylor.

See: Progressive Architecture 66 (July 1985): 77, 111–18. *Lotus,* no. 50 (1986): 6–29. *Baumeister* 83 (September 1986): 60–67. *Architectural Design* 55, no. 1/2 (1985): 70–77.

Charles DUBOSE

■ 83

Constitution Plaza; Hartford, CT; 1963 (see Illus. 36).
This downtown business center built on the site of a former slum comprises several imposing office buildings, a shopping mall, a hotel, and two garages, all set around a handsomely landscaped plaza. DuBose's responsibilities included site planning, basic design of the overall project, and general design coordination. He also served as architect for the North and South garages, East and West commercial buildings, Research Center, and Brokerage House.
Associated architects for 100 Constitution Plaza: Charles DuBose and Emery Roth & Sons. Associated architects for Hotel America: Charles DuBose and Curtis & Davis. Architects for Broadcast House: Fulmer & Bowers. Architects for One Constitution Plaza (Connecticut Bank and Trust Co. Building): Kahn & Jacobs (for the owner) and Carson, Lundin & Shaw (for the bank).

Honors: AIA Merit Award, 1964.

See: AIA Journal 42 (July 1964): 35. *Architectural Record* 135 (March 1964): 178–87. *Arts + Architecture* 81 (August 1964): 24–25, 32. *See also:* Phoenix Mutual Life Insurance Co. building, by Harrison & Abramovitz (no. 152). (Though not controlled by DuBose's site plan, this nearby office tower coordinates well with it.)

35 Housing Union Building (Students' Union Housing), University of Alberta; Edmonton, Alberta; 1972. *See* Entry 79. (Courtesy A. J. Diamond and Partners.)

Disneyland, it also features EPCOT (the Experimental Prototype Community of Tomorrow), reached by monorail and designed to put to use the most advanced technology in many areas including energy generation, communications, and data processing. It features industry pavilions sponsored by major corporations and, in World Showcase, nine national pavilions that simulate scenes in England, China, Mexico, France, Japan, and elsewhere.
Designed by anonymous "Imagineers."

See: Planning 45 (February 1979): 17–21. *Industrial Design* 30 (March–April 1983): 34–39. *Architect's Journal* 177 (January 12, 1983): 18–19. *Architettura* 29 (June 1983): 450–51.

■ 81

Disneyland; Anaheim, CA; 1955.
Visitors to this 160-acre recreational complex find themselves first in the Main Street of a dream American town of the 1890s, reproduced in loving detail at five-eighths scale. Nearby are other idealized settings: Tomorrowland, Fantasyland, Frontierland, and Adventureland. In a wry

1965 article, Charles Moore (see entries 238–239, 266–268, 323–324) called Disneyland "the most important single piece of construction in the West in the past several decades."
Engineering firm: J. S. Hamel. Landscape development: Evans & Reeves Nurseries.

Honors: AIA Bicentennial List, one nomination.

See: Travel 104 (July 1955): 16–19. *Landscape Architecture* 46 (April 1956): 125–36. *Perspecta,* no. 9/10 (1965): 57–106. *Landscape* 21 (Spring–Summer 1977): 18–22.

Andres DUANY and Elizabeth PLATER-ZYBERK

■ 82

Seaside, FL, master plan, zoning code, etc. Overall design, 1983; development in progress.
This is a planned resort community that strictly controls the architecture of its

86–89. *Domus*, no. 588 (November 1978): 10–14.

■ 86

Scientific Data Systems, Inc.; El Segundo, CA; 1966.

A sprawling computer plant (560 by 464 feet), it has been hailed as a distinguished piece of architecture that was built quickly and cheaply. Clever engineering makes optimal use of steel trusses; steel columns are left freestanding outside the perimeter of the building.
Engineers: Mackintosh & Mackintosh (structural); Stanley Feuer (mechanical). General contractor: C. L. Peck. Landscape architect: Warren Waltz.

See: *Architectural Forum* 125 (November 1966): 70–77. *Lotus* 4 (1967/68): 88–97. *Arts + Architecture* 83 (November 1966): 28–31.

---

36 Constitution Plaza; Hartford, CT; 1963. *See* Entry 83. (Courtesy DuBose Associates, Inc., Architects; Hartford, CT.)

36

EDWARDS & PORTMAN *See also* John PORTMAN

■ 84

Hyatt Regency Hotel; Atlanta, GA; 1967.

The breathtaking 21-story, skylighted atrium/lobby of this 800-room hotel has set the fashion for many other hotels—some designed by Portman, some by others. This giant courtyard, 140 feet across, has vine-covered, cantilevered balconies on all four sides; they serve as corridors for the guest rooms, all of which also have outside balconies.
Designer: John Portman.

Honors: AIA Bicentennial List, three nominations.

See: *Architectural Forum* 130 (April 1969): 42–51. *Interior Design* 38 (September 1967): 136–49. *L'Architecture Française,* no. 303–4 (November–December 1967): 12–14.

Craig ELLWOOD

37 Art Center College of Design; Pasadena, CA; 1976. *See* Entry 85. (Photographer: Sylvia D. Wright; Los Angeles, CA.)

■ 85

Art Center College of Design; Pasadena, CA; 1976 (see Illus. 37).

This 1- and 2-story steel and glass

structure, with exposed steel columns and beams, spans 192 feet across a ravine. On either side, where it rises 2 stories, much of its first floor lies below ground level, so the center looks like a 1-story pavilion on a raised platform.
Consultant: Norman Epstein (structural); Eli Silon & Associates (mechanical/electrical); Alfred Caldwell/Erik Katzmaier (landscape). General contractor: Swinerton & Walberg.

Honors: PA Design Citation, 1976.

See: *Progressive Architecture* 58 (August 1977): 62–65. *Architectural Review* 164 (August 1978):

Arthur ERICKSON

Winner, AIA Gold Medal, 1986.

■ 87

Mass transit design (Yorkdale and Eglinton West stations); Toronto, Ontario; 1978?

These two stunning stations, both aboveground, are skylighted and enhanced by specially commissioned art. Yorkdale's exuberantly arched skylight extends some 700 feet over the center

37

platform and the escalators and stairs at either end. Neon tubes in the skylight produce computerized displays of changing lights whenever trains are nearby or in the station. At Eglinton West, transfer between buses and subways is eased by a 40,000-square-foot coffered roof, much of it cantilevered, that serves as a huge umbrella.

For Yorkdale: Project team: James C. Strasman, Michael Jones, Myron Boyko. Contractors: Janin Building and Civil Works Ltd. *For Eglinton West:* Project team: James C. Strasman, Wayne A. Cybulski, Khaja Vicaruddin. Contractors: E. G. M. Cape & Co. and Folco Construction Equipment. Engineers for both stations: M. S. Yolles & Partners (structural); Tamblyn, Mitchell & Partners (mechanical); Kalns Associates (electrical).

Honors: Governor General's Medal, 1982.

See: Architectural Record 164 (mid-August 1978): 72–77. *Canadian Architect* 21 (May 1976): 31–40; 23 (August 1978): 36–45.

■ 88

Museum of Anthropology, University of British Columbia; Vancouver, British Columbia; 1976, artificial lake on site added later.
Home to a collection of Canadian Indian artifacts, this sternly monumental building mimics in sandblasted precast concrete the timber post and crossbeam construction of a Kwakiutl longhouse; its post-tensioned crossbeams, however, extend over spans of up to 180 feet. Within stand huge totem poles, as tall as 45 feet, some behind windows 40 feet high. Outside stand other poles set in re-created Indian villages, all looking out over a cliff edge to the Pacific.
Consultants: Bogue Babicki and Assoc. (structural); Mechanical Consultants Western (mechanical); Cornelia Oberlander (landscape). General contractor: Grimwood Construction.

Honors: Governor General's Medal, 1983.

See: Architectural Record 161 (May 1977): 103–10 and cover. *Process: Architecture,* no. 5 (1978): 58–63. *Canadian Architect* 22 (May 1977): 54–62. Leon Whiteson, *Modern Canadian Architecture* (Edmonton: Hurtig, 1983), 32–35.

■ 89

Robson Square and the Law Courts Complex; Vancouver, British Columbia; 1980.
A 3-block-long complex whose concrete construction and geometric lines are softened by lots of plantings—even on roofs—plus a pool, waterfalls, and intricate patterns of stairs and ramps. Included are a 7-story Law Courts Building with a tilted glass roof and exposed structural framing, a lower-rise government office building, an indoor mall, outdoor plazas, and an old courthouse transformed into the Vancouver Art Gallery.
Principal: Arthur Erickson; planning coordinators: Bing Thom, James K. Wright, Rainer J. Fassler. Project architects for Robson Square: Junichi Hashimoto, James K. Wright; project architect for the Law Courts: Rainer J. Fassler. Consultants: Bogue Babicki & Assoc. (structural); Reid Crowther & Partners (mechanical); Cornelia Hahn Oberlander, Raoul Robillard (landscape). Construction manager: Concordia Management Co.

Honors: Governor General's Medal, 1982.

See: Architectural Record 168 (December 1980): 65–75. *Progressive Architecture* 62 (March 1981): 82–87. *Architectural Review* 167 (June 1980): 346–53. *GA Document,* no. 1 (Summer 1980): 110–24. *Canadian Architect* 24 (November 1979): 34–41.

ERICKSON/MASSEY

■ 90

Expo '67 theme buildings; Montreal, Quebec; 1967.
Designed to show advanced technology in wood, the exhibit's central building, "Man in the Community," was a pagoda-style pyramid constructed of thirty-seven layers of composite Glulam and plywood beams, combined to give the effect of a giant lattice. A smaller building nearby, housing "Man and His Health," echoed the central building's lines.
Engineers: Janos J. Baracs (structural); Bouthiellette & Parizeau (mechanical/electrical). Special consultant in structural systems: Jeffrey Lindsay.

Honors: Massey Medal, 1970.

See: Architecture Canada 43 (July 1966): 29–52. *Architectural Design* 37 (July 1967): 333–47. *Interiors* 126 (June 1967): 77–119.

■ 91

Simon Fraser University; Burnaby, British Columbia; 1965.
Sited atop a mountain just outside Vancouver, a series of harmonizing concrete buildings are linked by wide, weather-protected spaces. Axial to the campus, designed for up to 18,000 students, is a huge, multipurpose covered mall.
Planning, design concept of all buildings, design coordination, site development and landscaping: Erickson/Massey. Within this framework, the following architects prepared preliminary designs and working drawings and supervised individual buildings: Zoltan S. Kiss (academic quadrangle); Duncan McNab (theater, gymnasium, and swimming pool); Rhone & Iredale (science complex); Robert F. Harrison (library).

Honors: Massey Medal, 1967.

See: Architectural Forum 123 (December 1965): 13–21. *Canadian Architect* 11 (February 1966): whole issue. Leon Whiteson, *Modern Canadian Architecture* (Edmonton: Hurtig, 1983), 24–27.

Joseph ESHERICK (see also entry no. 267)

Winner, AIA Gold Medal, 1988.

■ 92

Adlai E. Stevenson College, University of California; Santa Cruz, CA; residence and academic buildings, 1966; library 1968; music practice rooms, 1975.
There's a "hang loose" look to this campus within a campus: three complexes of white-walled, red-roofed buildings with lots of unexpected juts and angles, amiably tucked into a wooded site. It has won high honors for its "playful forms set with variety in a handsome grove of trees."
Engineers: Rutherford & Chekene (structural); G. L. Gendler & Assoc. (mechanical/electrical). Landscape architects: Lawrence Halprin & Assoc. General contractor: Williams & Burrows.

Honors: AIA Honor Award, 1968; Award of Merit, Library Buildings 1970 Award Program, conferred by the AIA et al.

See: AIA Journal 49 (June 1968): 104; 54 (August 1970): 31–33. *Progressive Architecture* 48 (November 1967): 138–45.

38

■ 93

The Cannery: San Francisco, CA; 1968 (see Illus. 38).

This clever renovation created a mecca for tourists and other shoppers. The old, brick Del Monte Cannery, conveniently located near Fisherman's Wharf, was gutted and entirely rebuilt inside, transformed into three levels of varied commercial space served by elevators, an escalator, and seven different staircases—all arranged, says Esherick, with "enough turns, zigzags and corners . . . to offer at least some hint of a maze."
Engineers: Rutherford & Chekene (structural); K. T. Belotekin & Assoc. (mechanical). Landscape architect: Thomas Church. General contractor: Greystone Builders.

Honors: AIA Honor Award, 1970; Bartlett Award, 1970.

See: *AIA Journal* 53 (June 1970): 93; 67 (July 1978): 50–59. *Architectural Forum* 128 (June 1968): 74–79. *Architectural Review* 145 (March 1969): 161–63.

Joseph ESHERICK; Donald OLSEN; Vernon DEMARS

■ 94

Wurster Hall, College of Environmental Design, University of

California; Berkeley, CA; 1965 (see Illus. 39).

Designed jointly by three members of Berkeley's architecture faculty, this bluntly detailed building with a hatchwork of sun-shading concrete slabs and an assertive tower contrasts boldly with its self-effacing, tile-roofed neighbors. Inside, the ducts and pipes of the mechanical system are left exposed.
Engineers: Isadore Thompson (structural); G. L. Gendler & Assoc. (mechanical). General contractor: Rothschild, Raffin & Weirick.

See: *Architectural Forum* 124 (January–February 1966): 56–63. *Progressive Architecture* 47 (January 1966): 163–67. *Baumeister* 64 (September 1967): 1086–91.

ESHERICK HOMSEY DODGE and DAVIS

Winner, AIA Architectural Firm Award, 1986.

■ 95

Monterey Bay Aquarium; Monterey, CA; 1984 (see Illus. 40).

Nostalgia for the days of Steinbeck's *Cannery Row* dictated much of the design for this deceptively laid-back aquarium. The warehouse and boilerhouse—complete with eye-catching chimneys—of

39

40

40 Monterey Bay Aquarium; Monterey, CA; 1984. *See* Entry 95. (Courtesy Esherick, Homsey, Dodge and Davis; San Francisco, CA. Photographer: Kathleen Olson.)

an abandoned cannery were supplemented by new construction which, though staunchly built of concrete, brashly parades timber framing like the earlier building and looks out on Monterey Bay through window walls of industrial sash. The layout of exhibits is casual and nonrestrictive; 20,000 square feet of decks overlook the water.

Principal in charge: Charles M. Davis; project manager: James W. Hastings. Engineers: Rutherford & Chekene (structural, civil, and marine); Syska & Hennessy (mechanical/electrical). General contractor: Rudolph & Sletten.

See: Architectural Record 173 (February 1985): 114–23. *Architecture* 74 (June 1985): 50–59, 96. *Architectural Review* 177 (March 1985); 22–27. *Connoisseur* 215 (March 1985): 83–89.

FAIRFIELD and DUBOIS

■ 96

Albert Campbell Library; Scarborough, Ontario; 1971 (see Illus. 41).

Long panels of parallel, dull red metal strips, often curving like the rolltop of an old-fashioned desk, lend vivid character inside and out to this public library on a cramped site. This channeled system forms a striking fascia on the outside above a window wall, then reappears to form ceilings and to edge balconies within.

Partner in charge of design: Macy DuBois. Consultants: Sally DuBois (interior design); G. Granek & Assoc. (mechanical); Cazaly-Otter (structural).

See: Progressive Architecture 53 (April 1972): 102–7. *Canadian Architect* 17 (January 1972): 38–47. *Interior Design* 44 (April 1973): 120–23. *Process: Architecture,* no. 5 (1978): 228–34. Leon Whiteson, *Modern Canadian Architecture* (Edmonton: Hurtig, 1983), 144–47.

Edward H. FICKETT see KISTNER, WRIGHT & WRIGHT; Edward H. FICKETT; S. B. BARNES

41 Albert Campbell Library; Scarborough, Ontario; 1971. *See* Entry 96. (Courtesy The DuBois Plumb Partnership, Architects; Toronto, Canada. Photographer: Robert Perron.)

41

O'Neil FORD

■ 97

Tower of the Americas; San Antonio, TX; 1968.
A 622-foot tower with a slender, ribbed stem, it was built as the centerpiece for the San Antonio HemisFair of 1968 and contains a revolving restaurant, a stationary one, and an observation deck.

See: *AIA Journal* 49 (April 1968): 48–58. *Architectural Forum* 129 (October 1968): 84–89. *Progressive Architecture* 49 (April 1968): 49–51.

Ulrich FRANZEN

■ 98

Alley Theatre: Houston, TX; 1968 (see Illus. 42).
Graced with curving parapets and topped by turrets that give it an almost medieval look, this building houses two theaters (one seating 800, the other seating 300), separated by a covered driveway and linked below by shared dressing rooms and areas for the preparation and storage of costumes and sets.
Job captain: Keith Kroeger. Associate architects: MacKie & Kamrath. Engineers: Weiskopf & Pickworth (structural); Cosentini Associates (mechanical). Lighting systems and theater equipment: George Izenour. Acoustical consultants: Bolt, Beranek & Newman. General contractor: W. S. Bellows Construction Corp.

Honors: AIA Honor Award, 1972; Bartlett Award, 1972.

See: *AIA Journal* 57 (May 1972): 31–40. *Architectural Forum* 130 (March 1969): 31–39. *Process: Architecture,* no. 8 (1979): 37–74.

■ 99

Barkin, Levin & Co. factory and office building; Long Island City, NY: 1958.
Comfortable, efficient quarters for all the processes involved in manufacturing a line of quality women's coats. The ultimate design was based on comprehensive research into storage problems, operations flow, and other matters and resulted in a 50 percent savings in space and a 30 percent savings in manufacturing time.
Engineers: Seelye, Stevenson, Value & Knecht. Contractors; Schumacher & Forelle.

See: *Architectural Record* 125 (February 1959): 197–202. *Process: Architecture,* no. 8 (1979): 25–30. *Bauen-Wohnen* 15 (August 1960): 266–69.

■ 100

Bradfield and Emerson Halls, Cornell University; Ithaca, NY: 1968 (see Illus. 43).
A 13-story laboratory tower for agricultural research, also known as the Agronomy Building, plus associated facilities. Built of dark red, hard-surfaced brick and with the striking lines of "a very handsome piece of architectural sculpture," its windows are limited to narrow slots in the stair towers because its interior must be air-controlled.
Project manager: Robert Thorson; project architect: Edward Rosen. Consulting landscape architect: George Swanson. Engineers: Weiskopf & Pickworth (structural); Cosentini Associates (mechanical). General contractor: Irwin & Leighton.

Honors: AIA Honor Award, 1970.

See: *AIA Journal* 53 (June 1970): 79–93. *Architectural Forum* 129 (July–August 1968): 40–53. *Architecture, Formes, Fonctions* 16 (1971): 333–41. David Guise, *Design and Technology in Architecture* (New York: Wiley, 1985), 222–29.

■ 101

Christensen Hall, University of New Hampshire; Durham, NH; 1970 (see Illus. 44).
These clean-cut, brick-faced residence halls aim to provide a sense of privacy and individualized living to occupants sharing double rooms. Floor plans vary from one level to another, L-shaped rooms give each student a distinct "nook," and for every dozen rooms there's a communal study/lounge.
Associate in charge: Samuel E. Nylen. Engineers: Garfinkel, Marenberg & Assoc. (structural); John J. Altieri (mechanical/electrical). Contractor: Harvey Construction.

42 Alley Theatre; Houston, TX; 1968. *See* Entry 98. (Courtesy Ulrich Franzen and Associates; New York, NY. Photographer: Erica Stoller, Esto Photographics.)

Honors: AIA Honor Award, 1971.

See: *AIA Journal* 55 (June 1971): 46.
Architectural Record 142 (October 1967): 133–44; 148 (November 1970): 101–4.

■ 102

Multicategorical and Laboratory Animal Research Wing, College of Veterinary Medicine, Cornell University; Ithaca, NY; 1974 (see Illus. 45).

The two long facades of this brick-clad building differ drastically, expressing their contrasting functions. On one side there's a generously glazed 10-story slab of offices and labs; on the other, blank surfaces worked in starkly geometric fashion and marked by giant stainless steel "nostrils" that exhale air used to ventilate facilities within, where animals to be used for research are bred and housed.

Associate in charge: Edward Rosen; project architect: William Jacquette, Jr. Engineers: Aaron Zicherman & Assoc. (coordinating); Aaron Garfinkel & Assoc. (structural). General contractors: Stewart & Bennett.

See: *A + U: Architecture and Urbanism,* no 56 (August 1975): 109–16. *Process: Architecture,* no. 8 (1979): 111–22. *Architecture Plus* 2 (May–June 1974): 56–63.

■ 103

Philip Morris World Headquarters (120 Park Avenue); New York, NY; 1983 (see Illus. 46).

The two slim facades of this 26-story office building, faced in granite and gray insulating glass and sited on a narrow corner lot, have horizontal strips of windows that contrast sharply with the vertical emphasis of its broader, Park Avenue elevation. At street level, behind a columned entry, an inviting indoor pedestrian plaza is devoted to a 42-foot-high sculpture court and other exhibit space for a branch of the Whitney Museum of American Art.

Associate in charge: Samuel Nylen; project architects: John Kanastab, Steven Lewent. Engineering consultants: Jaros, Baum & Bolles (mechanical); Weiskopf & Pickworth (structural).

See: *Architectural Record* 167 (April 1980): 130–32. *Progressive Architecture* 60 (July 1979): 55–59. *A + U: Architecture and Urbanism,* no. 131 (August 1981): 71–74. *Interior Design* 54 (October 1983): 240–57.

43 Bradfield and Emerson Halls, Cornell University; Ithaca, NY; 1968. *See* Entry 100. (Courtesy Ulrich Franzen and Associates: New York, NY. Photographer: George Cserna.)

43

44 Christensen Hall, University of New Hampshire; Durham, NH; 1970. *See* Entry 101. (Courtesy Ulrich Franzen and Associates: New York, NY. Photographer: George Cserna.)

44

45 Multicategorical & Laboratory Animal Research Wing, College of Veterinary Medicine, Cornell University; Ithaca, NY; 1974. *See* Entry 102. (Courtesy Ulrich Franzen and Associates, New York, NY. Photographer: Norman McGrath.)

45

46 Philip Morris World Headquarters; New York, NY; 1983. *See* Entry 103. (Courtesy Ulrich Franzen and Associates, New York, NY. Photographer: Bill Rothschild.)

In 1980, M. Paul Friedberg won an AIA Medal for inspiring and influencing architectural practice. Credits for his firm's landscape architecture appear in entries 43, 73, 104, 130, 215, 320, 331, and 482.

■ **104**

Bedford-Stuyvesant Superblock; Brooklyn, NY; 1969 (see Illus. 47).
This innovative project transformed much of one street's sidewalk and gutter into a hard landscaped park complete with a fountain, a pool, a small playground, and community seating, while supplying "islands" for diagonal parking and removing no land from the city's tax rolls. M. Paul Friedberg & Assoc., landscape architects in charge of design; associate in charge: James Baisley. Engineers: Robert Silman (structural); I. M. Robbins (mechanical).

See: AIA Journal 65 (May 1976): 40–49. *Architectural Forum* 134 (January–February 1971): 66–68. *Design Quarterly,* no. 77 (1970): 17–18. *Baumeister* 69 (February 1972): 159–61.

FRY & WELCH *see* Paul RUDOLPH; FRY & WELCH

R. Buckminster FULLER

Winner, Royal Gold Medal, 1968; AIA Gold Medal, 1970.

■ **105**

Union Tank Car Repair Facility; Baton Rouge, LA; 1958.
A maintenance and repair facility for railway tank cars, it was built in the round to accommodate circular traffic flow patterns fed by a rotating transfer table. When completed, it was the largest geodesic dome ever built: 120 feet high, with an unobstructed interior diameter of 384 feet.
Creator of fundamental design: R. Buckminster Fuller. Architects and engineers: Battey & Childs. Dome engineers: Synergetics, Inc. Contractor: Nicols Construction Co.

46

47

Honors: Fuller, as designer of both the geodesic dome and the Dymaxion house, received five nominations for the AIA Bicentennial List.

See: Architectural Record 125 (January 1959): 147–70. *Progressive Architecture* 39 (November 1958): 32–33. *Baukunst und Werkform* 13 (January 1960): 23–24.

R. Buckminster FULLER/FULLER & SADAO; GEOMETRICS, INC.

■ 106

U.S. Pavilion, Expo '67; Ile Ste.

Hélène, Montreal, Quebec; 1967 (see Illus. 48).
A giant dome, roughly three-quarters of a sphere, designed to look like a lacy filigree weightlessly poised against the sky. Height: 200 feet; spherical diameter: 250 feet. Construction: a space frame of steel pipes enclosing 1,900 molded acrylic panels.
Interior platforms and exhibit: Cambridge Seven Associates. Structural engineers: Simpson, Gumpertz & Heger. Associated Canadian architect: George F. Eber.

Honors: AIA Honor Award, 1968.

See: Architectural Forum 124 (June 1966): 74 79. *Architectural Design* 37 (July 1967): 333–47. *Japan Architecture* 42 (August 1967): 38–45.

GEDDES, BRECHER & CUNNINGHAM

■ 107

Addition (Pender Laboratory) to Moore School of Electrical Engineering, University of Pennsylvania; Philadelphia, PA; 1958 (see Illus. 49).
This laboratory and classroom wing links two earlier buildings: the Towne School, a turn-of-the-century Jacobean effort, and the Moore School, built along squarer lines in the late 1920s. Vigorous in itself, it also articulates well with its two neighbors of different scale and character.
Engineers: Dorfman & Bloom (structural); J. P. Hartman (mechanical/electrical). General contractor: Joseph R. Farrell, Inc.

Honors: AIA Honor Award, 1960.

See: AIA Journal 33 (April 1960): 78–79. *Architectural Forum* 110 (March 1959): 94–99. *Architectural Record* 122 (August 1957): 172–73.

GEDDES, BRECHER, QUALLS, CUNNINGHAM

Winner, AIA Architectural Firm Award, 1979.

■ 108

Faner Hall, Southern Illinois University; Carbondale, IL; 1975 (see Illus. 50).
A 900-foot-long, spinelike megastructure that serves as Humanities and Social Sciences Center on a sprawling, 21,000-student campus. Colonnades echo a nearby strip of woodland and, along with sun baffles, provide shade in the afternoon.
Design partner: Robert L. Geddes; design associate: M. Neville Epstein; project architect: John R. De Bello. Mechanical engineering consultants: United Engineers. General contractor: J. L. Simmins Co.

Honors: AIA Honor Award, 1977; Bartlett Award, 1977.

See: AIA Journal 66 (May 1977): 42. *Progressive Architecture* 55 (June 1974): 79; 57 (December 1976): 45–49.

48

49 Addition (Pender Laboratory) to Moore School of Electrical Engineering, University of Pennsylvania; Philadelphia, PA; 1958. *See* Entry 107. (Courtesy Geddes, Brecher, Qualls, Cunningham; Philadelphia, PA.)

49

50 Faner Hall, Southern Illinois University; Carbondale, IL; 1975. *See* Entry 108. (Courtesy Geddes, Brecher, Qualls, Cunningham; Philadelphia, PA.)

50

■ 109

Police Headquarters Building; Philadelphia, PA; 1962 (see Illus. 51).
A police office building of remarkable charm and grace, built of precast concrete and shaped in a sequence of arcs inside and out. Public areas at its center curve outward into almost circular security clusters at either side; upper floors cantilever out boldly 12 feet from the base.
Senior staff architect: Roland A. Gallimore. Engineers: David Bloom and Dr. August E. Komendant (structural); Cronheim & Weger (mechanical/electrical). Acoustical consultants: Bolt, Beranek & Newman. General contractor: Sovereign Construction Co.

51 Police Headquarters Building; Philadelphia, PA; 1962. *See* Entry 109. (Courtesy Geddes, Brecher, Qualls, Cunningham; Philadelphia, PA.)

See: Architectural Forum 117 (September 1962): 94–95; 118 (February 1963): 120–25. *Progressive Architecture* 41 (October 1960): 176–91.

■ 110

California Aerospace Museum, Exposition Park; Los Angeles, CA; 1984.
From outside, this 16,000-square-foot museum is an amalgam of diverse sculptural forms that loom, then retreat, then spurt ramps, a shiny globe atop a tower, and—poised on an extruded beam —a Lockheed fighter plane. The 80-foot-high space inside, partly skylighted, accommodates cable-hung exhibits surrounded by an exhilarating mix of soaring footbridges and buttresses. Principal-in-charge: Frank O. Gehry; co-designer: John Clagett. Engineers: Kurily & Szymanski (structural); Store, Matakovich and Wolfberg (mechanical). General contractor: Chartered Construction.

See: Architectural Record 173 (January 1985): 114–23 and cover. *Arts + Architecture,* new series, 3, no. 4 (1985): 74–79. *GA Document,* no. 12 (January 1985): 4–9. *Casabella* 49, no. 514 (June 1985): 52–63.

■ 111

Concord Pavilion; Concord, CA; 1975.
Here's a fan-shaped, open-air performing arts center located in Northern California, at the foot of Mount Diablo. Seating for 3,500 is provided under its roof, and

51

another 4,500 can be accommodated in a raked, grassy bowl—all set in a crater-shaped amphitheater.

Design team: Frank O. Gehry, C. Gregory Walsh, Jr., James F. Porter. Engineers: Garfinkel & Kurily & Assoc. (structural); John Kerr Associates (mechanical); Irving Schwartz Associates (electrical). Landscape architects and civil engineers: Sasaki-Walker & Assoc. Consultant: Christopher Jaffe (acoustics, stage and lighting design). Contractor: F. P. Lathrop Construction Co.

Honors: AIA Honor Award, 1977; AISC Architectural Award of Excellence, 1977.

See: *AIA Journal* 66 (May 1977): 43. *Architectural Record* 159 (June 1976): 95–102. *Baumeister* 74 (April 1977): 338–40.

■ 112

Loyola Law School expansion, Loyola Marymount University; Los Angeles, CA; 1981–84 (see Illus. 52).

Five buildings—three lecture halls, a chapel, and a bookstore/administration/classroom midrise—make up this quirky addition to a campus for 1,300 law students. Inexpensively built and intended to give the school a clear physical identity, it features many allusive columns—which support little or nothing—and fancifully angling exterior stairs that at once provide safety exits, terraces, and bold sculptural accents.

Associate architects: Brooks/Collier. Consultants: Land Images (landscape); Erkel & Greenfield (structural); D. F. Dickerson (mechanical). General contractor: CMC (Phase I); Miano Constructors (Phase II).

Honors: AIA Honor Award, 1986.

See: *Architecture* 74 (May 1985): 202–7, 370. *Progressive Architecture* 66 (February 1985): 67–77 and cover. *GA Document,* no. 5 (1982): 88–91; no. 12 (January 1985): 10–15. *Architectural Design* 55, no. 1/2 (1985): 24–27. *Casabella* 49, no. 514 (June 1985): 52–63.

■ 113

Santa Monica Place; Santa Monica, CA; 1980 (see Illus. 53).

Located in a seaside city, this attractive shopping center ingeniously fits 163 shops and a 500-foot-long central mall into a scant 10-acre urban site. Outside, 10,000 square feet of deck look out to the Pacific; the center's name hangs on one of its two parking structures in chain-link letters 3 stories high.

52 Loyola Law School expansion, Loyola Marymount University; Los Angeles; 1981–84. *See* Entry 112. (Photographer: Sylvia D. Wright; Los Angeles, CA.)

53 Santa Monica Place; Santa Monica, CA; 1980. *See* Entry 113. (Photographer: Sylvia D. Wright; Los Angeles, CA.)

Project manager: Hak Sik Son. Consulting architects: Gruen Associates. Consultants: OMI-Lang Associates, landscape; Johnson & Nielson (structural); Donald F. Dickerson Assoc. and Western Air & Refrigeration (mechanical). General contractor: E. W. Hahn, Inc.

See: *Progressive Architecture* 62 (July 1981): 84–89 and cover. *Domus,* no. 620 (September 1981): 12–18. *GA Document,* no. 5 (1982): 82–87. *A + U: Architecture and Urbanism,* no. 136 (January 1982): 122–28.

GIFFELS & ROSSETTI
(see also entry no. 217)

■ 114

Cobo Hall; Detroit, MI; 1960 (see Illus. 54).

When completed in 1960, this colossus—built to house the annual National Auto Show—was the world's largest exhibit building. It sprawls nearly 1,000 feet over a six-lane expressway, features a rooftop parking lot, and contains 2.2 million square feet of space. Its circular arena was designed to hold up to 12,500 spectators.

Engineers: Giffels & Rossetti, Inc. Contractor: O. W. Burke Co.

See: *Architectural Forum* 113 (October 1960): 98–100. *Michigan Architect and Engineer* 35 (April 1960): 10–13. *(See also entry no. 217.)*

Bertrand GOLDBERG

■ 115

Health Sciences Center, State University of New York at Stony Brook; Stony Brook, NY; 1976 (see Illus. 55).

A steel and concrete megastructure that

54 Cobo Hall; Detroit, MI; 1960. *See* Entry 114. (Courtesy Giffels Associates; Southfield, ML)

54

55 Health Sciences Center, State University of New York at Stony Brook; Stony Brook, NY; 1976. *See* Entry 115. (Courtesy Bertrand Goldberg Associates; Chicago, IL. Photographer: Nathaniel Lieberman.)

55

comprises three huge, connected towers and encloses 2 million square feet of flexible, multipurpose space.

See: *Inland Architect* 18 (January 1974): 20–21. *A + U: Architecture and Urbanism,* no. 55 (July 1975): 73–86. Arthur Drexler, *Transformation in Modern Architecture* (New York: Museum of Modern Art, 1979).

■ **116**

Hilliard Center; Chicago, IL; 1966 (see Illus. 56).
Four 22-story towers, all built of concrete, make up this low-income housing development. Two arc-shaped buildings

contain 346 units for family groups; two cylinders with scalloped exterior walls contain 364 units for the elderly. Floor plans are varied and make optimal use of the limited space permitted by government regulations.
Landscape architect: Alfred Caldwell. General contractor: Paschen Contractors.

See: *Architectural Forum* 125 (November 1966): 25–33. *Architectural Record* 139 (January 1966): 158–59. *Lotus,* no. 6 (1969): 258–63. *Bauwelt* 61 (April 20, 1970): 585–92.

■ **117**

Marina City; Chicago, IL; 1964, plus

additions completed 1967 (see Illus. 57).
When built, this development's two audacious, 60-story, petal-ringed towers were the tallest residential buildings and tallest concrete structures in the world. Twenty stories of parking space are provided on the lower levels of the towers, while space for offices, shops, and a marina are supplied in a complex of facilities nearby.
Structural consultants: Severud-Perrone-Fischer-Sturm-Conlin-Bandel; Mueser, Rutledge, Wentworth & Johnson; Dr. Ralph Peck.
Contractor: James McHugh Construction Co.

Honors: AIA Bicentennial List, one nomination.

See: *Architectural Forum* 122 (April 1965): 68–77. *Architectural Record* 134 (September 1963): 214–16. *L'Architecture d'Aujourd'hui,* no. 117 (November 1964–January 1965): 32–37.

■ **118**

Prentice Women's Hospital and Maternity Center, Northwestern University Downtown Campus; Chicago, IL; 1975 (see Illus. 58).
This medical facility features a 7-story tower, shaped like a four-leaf clover, which contains 264 beds arranged in four patient-care "villages" per floor. Perched atop a striated stem, it is surrounded at its base by a 4-story, rectilinear structure, which accommodates admissions, support services, and several specialized treatment units.
Engineers: Bertrand Goldberg Associates.
Contractor: Paschen-Newburg.

See: *Architectural Record* 160 (July 1976): 109–15. *L'Architecture d'Aujourd'hui,* no. 183 (January–February 1976): 96–97. *Inland Architect* 18 (January 1974): 16–17. *A + U: Architecture and Urbanism,* no. 55 (July 1975): 87–100.

GOLEMAN & ROLFE; PIERCE & PIERCE

■ **119**

Houston Intercontinental Airport, Terminals A and B; Houston, TX; 1968.
The first American airport designed for supersonic travel, its terminals, which offer close, efficient access to both autos and planes, reduce passenger walking to a

minimum and are linked by a completely automated mini-transit loop.

Engineers: Engineers of the Southwest, a joint venture of Lockwood, Andrews & Newman; Bovay Engineers; and Turner, Collie & Braden. Landscape architects: Bishop & Walker and Fred Buxton. Contractor: R. F. Ball Construction Co.

See: *Architectural Record* 144 (August 1968): 134–38. *Progressive Architecture* 50 (September 1969): 96–101. *Architectural Design* 40 (January 1970): 20–25.

John GRAHAM

■ 120

Space Needle; Seattle, WA; 1962 (see Illus. 59).
A 600-foot steel tower built originally for Seattle's World's Fair, Century 21, and retained as part of the civic center. An unmistakable landmark, it features a lofty observation deck and revolving restaurant just under its skyscraper spire.

Engineers: John Graham & Co. Design assistant: Victor Steinbreuck. Structural consultant: John K. Minasian.

Honors: AIA Bicentennial List, one nomination.

See: *Architectural Record* 130 (August 1961): 95–106; 131 (June 1962): 141–48. *Industrial Design* 9 (June 1962): 76–87.

59

Michael GRAVES

■ **121**

Environmental Center, Liberty State Park, Jersey City, NJ; 1983 (see Illus. 60).
This mini-museum is designed to introduce visitors to the flora and fauna of a marshland park. Segmented into three long, parallel spaces and melding timber construction with bleached cedar siding and some stuccoed surfaces, it contains entry areas, an auditorium, and exhibit rooms, all high-ceilinged and lit by small, square clerestory windows. Nearby are a curiously modified entry arch and a pergola that leads to a nature trail.

Associate in charge: Terence W. Smith; production captain: David Teeters. Consultants: Blackburn Engineering Associates (structural); Thomas A. Polise, Consulting Engineers (mechanical). General Contractor: Sempre Construction.

Honors: PA Architectural Design Citation, 1983.

See: Progressive Architecture 64 (January 1983): 97–99; 64 (August 1983): 88–93 and cover. *Connaissance des Arts,* no. 385 (March 1984): 52–61.

■ **122**

Humana Building; Louisville, KY; 1985 (see Illus. 61).
A 27-story office tower set on a massive base that houses an imposing lobby, richly dressed in marble of many hues, as well as a shopping arcade. Its three distinct facades bear extraordinary details, often in contrasting colors. These include a bowed "porch" at its twenty-fifth-floor level, supported by a bridgelike truss and, bisecting the building's opposite facade, a column of dark granite and glass that provides "sun rooms" on the interior. Near the top of the tower, large expanses of glass create lookout areas.
Associate in charge (design and construction): Terence W. Smith; job captain (design): Juliet Richardson-Smith; job captain (interiors): Peter Hague Neilson. Associate architect: Graves/Warnecke, a joint venture of Michael Graves, Architect and John Carl Warnecke & Associates —Lee Hamptian, director; William Collins, project manager. Engineers: DeSimone, Chaplin & Assoc. (structural); Caretsky & Assoc.

(mechanical/electrical). General contractor: Wehr Constructors.

Honors: AIA Honor Award, 1987.

See: Architectural Record 173 (August 1985): 102–13 and cover. *Architecture* 74 (November 1985): 56–63. *GA Document,* no. 14 (December 1985): 12–29. *A + U: Architecture and Urbanism,* no. 183 (December 1985): 19–50. *Architectural Review* 179 (March 1986): 46–51.

■ **123**

Michael C. Carlos Hall, Museum of Art and Archeology, Emory University; Atlanta, GA; 1985.
Adaptive reuse of a landmark building (1916) designed by Palmer, Hornbostel and Jones. Emory's former law school, built in Renaissance Revival style, has been adapted to house in one wing a museum, divided into many small rooms, finished in a broad palette of colors, and embellished with marble, fine woods, and allusions to classical forms. Its other wing, which houses offices and classrooms, has details that recall Egyptian architecture.
Associate in charge: Theodore L. Brown; job captain: Patrick Burke. Consultants: Jack Lynch & Assoc. (structural); Newcomb & Boyd (mechanical). General contractor: Cecil Malone Co.

Honors: AIA Honor Award, 1987; Interiors Institutional Design Award, 1986.

See: Architecture 76 (May 1987): 160–62. *Progressive Architecture* 66 (September 1985): 127–34. *GA Document,* no. 14 (December 1985): 30–35. *Interiors* 145 (January 1986): 178–81.

60

61

62

■ 124

The Portland Building (formerly Portland Public Service Building); Portland, OR; 1982 (see Illus. 62).
When first completed, this postmodern landmark was wildly innovative and controversial. On the varied facades of this chunky 15-story municipal office building, speckled with smallish square windows, masses of deep colors—browns, blues, and a rusty red—make emphatic statements against a sandy background. A stylized garland of blue ribbons (rendered in concrete) decorates one side while a huge statue of a woman, Portlandia, added in 1985, dominates the main entrance.
Principal in charge: Michael Graves; project manager: Lisa F. Lee. Associated architects: Emery Roth & Sons. Engineers: DeSimone & Chaplin (structural); Thomas A. Polise, Consulting Engineer, and Cosentini Assoc. (mechanical/electrical). General contractors: Pavarini Construction Co. and Hoffman Contruction Co. (joint venture).

See: AIA Journal 72 (May 1983): 232–37. *Architectural Record* 170 (November 1982): 90–99. *Architecture* 74 (December 1985): 20, 22. *Architectural Review* 172 (November 1982): 60–67. Paul Goldberger, *On the Rise* (New York: Times Books, 1983), 160–64.

61 Humana Building; Louisville, KY; 1985. *See* Entry 122. (Courtesy Michael Graves, Architect; Princeton, NJ. Photographer: Paschall/Taylor.)

■ 125

San Juan Capistrano Regional Library; San Juan Capistrano, CA; 1984 (see Illus. 63).
A surprisingly homey community library, one-story high, of pale stucco and tile-roofed construction, mission style, with exposed timbers in its varied small galleries and loggias. Inside a courtyard, lattice gazebos like giant trellises are designed to be overgrown with bouganvillea and to provide shaded yet breezy retreats for outdoor reading.
Job Captain: Nicholas Gonser; project managers: David Teeters, Gavin Hogben. Consultants: Woodward Dike (landscape); Robert Lawson, Structural Engineers (structural); Baum & Assoc. and Thomas A. Polise, Consulting Engineer (mechanical). General contractor: Newport Harbor Construction Co.

Honors: AIA Honor Award, 1985.

See: Architecture 73 (May 1984): 258–67. *Progressive Architecture* 65 (June 1984): 69–79. *Architectural Review* 176 (October 1984): 52–57.

62 The Portland Building; Portland, OR; 1982. *See* Entry 124. (Courtesy Michael Graves, Architect; Princeton, NJ. Photographer: Paschall/Taylor.)

63

■ 126

Sunar Showrooms; various locations and dates.

Designing a series of showrooms for a manufacturer of furniture and textiles did much to establish Michael Graves's reputation. Temporary or permanent, located in New York, Chicago, Houston, Dallas, Minneapolis, and Los Angeles, they exhibit the architect's bold use of subtle colors, frankly decorative touches, tendency to break large spaces into several rooms, and assertive sets of columns and other allusions to the ancient world.

See: *Architectural Record* 170 (September 1982): 96–101; *Progressive Architecture* 60 (September 1979): 148–53; 62 (August 1981): 88–93. *GA Document,* no. 5 (1982): 16–35. *Interior Design* 50 (December 1979): 152–55; 52 (November 1981): 324–27.

Victor GRUEN

■ 127

Northland Regional Shopping Center; Southfield Township, near Detroit, MI; 1954.

This was the first shopping center designed as a compact "market town" where shoppers, once they had parked their cars, could browse easily through a series of pedestrian malls. As originally built it boasted space for 12,000 cars, 1,045,000 square feet of rentable area, 80 shops, and one department store. Engineers: Victor Gruen Associates. Associate in charge: Karl van Leuven, Jr. Associated mechanical and electrical engineers: H. E. Beyster & Assoc. Landscape architect: Edward Eichstedt. General contractor: Bryant & Detwiler Co.

Honors: AIA Merit Award, 1954; AIA Bicentennial List, one nomination.

See: *Architectural Forum* 100 (June 1954): 102–23. *Bauen-Wohnen* 13 (August 1956): 267–68. *RAIC Journal* 33 (June 1956): 227–31. *L'Architecture d' Aujourd'hui* 30 (April–May 1959): 38–39.

GRUEN ASSOCIATES

■ 128

Commons and Courthouse Center; Columbus, IN; 1973.

Courthouse Center, privately run, houses a department store and other commercial ventures including twin cinemas; the Commons, city owned, provides quiet seating under trees, a playground, two restaurants, meeting rooms, and a performing stage. Both are contained within a low, 5-acre building, entirely faced with bronze-tinted glass, located on a major shopping street and designed to help revitalize a downtown area.

Partner in charge: Cesar Pelli; project coordinator: Antal Borsa; project designer: Lance Bird. General contractor: F. A. Wilhelm Construction.

See: *Architectural Record* 153 (March 1973): 127–31. *Progressive Architecture* 57 (June 1976): 64–69. *A + U: Architecture and Urbanism,* no. 71 (November 1976): 35–49; (extra edition: July 1985): 54–59. Y. Futagawa, ed., *Cesar Pelli/ Gruen Associates, The Commons and Courthouse Center . . . ,* text by Kenneth Frampton, Global Architecture, no. 59 (Tokyo: A. D. A. Edita, 1981).

■ 129

Pacific Design Center; Los Angeles, CA; 1976.

A six-story, earthquake-resistant, 750,000-square-foot home furnishings market sheathed in vivid blue glass. Though dubbed "the beached whale" and "the blue blimp," it has many attractive features including a barrel-vaulted galleria on its top two floors and a huge, handsome circulation cylinder at its south end.

Partner in charge of design: Cesar Pelli. Partners in charge of project: Edgardo Contini and Allen Rubenstein; project designer: Miloyko Lazovich; construction coordinator: John Friedman. Landscape consultant: Gustav Molnar. General contractor: Henry C. Beck Co.

See: *AIA Journal* 67 (May 1978): 38–45. *Progressive Architecture* 57 (October 1976): 78–83; 68 (January 1987): 92–93. Y. Futagawa, ed., *Cesar Pelli/Gruen Associates . . . Pacific Design Center . . . ,* text by Kenneth Frampton, Global Architecture, no. 59 (Tokyo: A. D. A. Edita, 1981).

■ 130

Rainbow Center Mall and Winter Garden; Niagara Falls, NY; 1977 (see Illus. 64).

A giant, asymmetrical greenhouse, 155 by 175 feet by 107 feet high, sited as a centerpiece for a downtown pedestrian mall. Beneath its airy web of glass and steel lies a lushly landscaped garden crisscrossed by stairs and catwalks that lead to two fanciful observation towers.

Partner in charge: Beda Zwicker; partner in charge of design: Cesar Pelli. Landscape architects: M. Paul Friedberg & Partners. Engineers: DeSimone & Chaplin (structural); Cosentini Assoc. (mechanical/electrical). Contractor: Scrufari-Siegfriend Join Venture. Interior landscape contractor: The Everett Conklin Cos.

Honors: PA Design Award Citation, 1977; AISC Architectural Award of Excellence, 1978.

See: *AIA Journal* 68 (mid-May 1979): 114–17. *Progressive Architecture* 59 (August 1978): 72–81. *A + U: Architecture and Urbanism,* no. 97 (October 1978): 41–48. Y. Futagawa, ed., *Cesar Pelli/Gruen Associates . . . Pacific Design Center . . . Rainbow Mall and Winter Garden,* text by Kenneth Frampton, Global Architecture, no. 59 (Tokyo: A. D. A. Edita, 1981).

GWATHMEY, HENDERSON & SIEGEL

■ 131

Dormitory and dining hall, State University of New York; Purchase, NY; 1973 (see Illus. 65).
An 800-student dormitory with a dramatic dining hall that can serve 400. To provide a sense of intimacy, despite its large size, the U-shaped, 3-story dorm's many entries divide student accommodations into groups of about 60, 20 to a floor; each floor has its own handsome lounge area. Associate in charge: Andrew Pettit. Engineers: Geiger-Berger (structural); William Kaplan with Langer-Polise (mechanical/electrical). Landscape architect: Peter G. Rolland. Contractor: Jos. L. Muscarelle, Inc.

Honors: AIA Honor Award, 1976.

See: *AIA Journal* 65 (April 1976): 36–57. *Architecture Plus* 1 (May 1973): 32–43. *L'Architecture d'Aujourd'hui,* no. 186 (August–September 1976): 61–62.

64 Rainbow Center Mall and Winter Garden; Niagara Falls, NY; 1977. *See* Entry 130. (Courtesy M. Paul Friedberg & Partners; New York, NY.)

GWATHMEY SIEGEL

Winner, AIA Architectural Firm Award, 1982.

■ 132

Whig Hall, Princeton University; Princeton, NJ; 1973 (see Illus. 66).
When this fine old home of a debating society—built in the form of a neoclassical temple—was gutted by fire, Gwathmey Siegel renovated it boldly, inserting new concrete-slab floor levels to supply additional floor space, and removing one entire side wall to expose the new interior in candid contrast to its marble shell.
Job captain: Timothy Wood. Engineers: David Geiger–Horst Berger (structural); Langer-Polise (mechanical).

Honors: PA Design Citation, 1973; AIA Honor Award for Extended Use, 1976.

See: *AIA Journal* 65 (April 1976): 36–57. *Progressive Architecture* 54 (June 1973): 122–25. *Architecture Plus* 1 (May 1973): 32–36.

David HAID

■ 133

Abraham Lincoln Oasis; South Holland, Il; 1968 (see Illus. 67).
Meticulous attention to detail and clarity of line lend distinction to this highway restaurant and rest stop, a weathering steel structure enclosed in bronze-tinted glass. Built directly across the highway—135 feet of clear span plus an additional

65 Dormitory and dining hall, State University of New York; Purchase, NY; 1973. *See* Entry 131. (Courtesy Gwathmey Siegel & Associates; New York, NY. Photographer: Bill Maris.)

66

67

45 feet at each end—it is a calm retreat for travelers going either way.
Engineers: Weisinger-Holland (structural); Wallace-Migdal (mechanical/electrical). Contractor: Leo Michuda & Son.

Honors: AISC Architectural Award of Excellence, 1968.

See: *Architectural Forum* 129 (September 1968): 76–79. *Architectural Design* 38 (April 1968): 185–86. *Arts + Architecture* 84 (January 1967): 16–18.

Lawrence HALPRIN

■ 134

Civic Auditorium Forecourt; (Ira's Fountain) Portland, OR; 1968/70.
A many-leveled, one-block-square extravaganza of waterfalls, stairs that form an irregular outdoor theater, and low mounds planted with maples and oaks—all set off by lighting at night.

Partner in charge: Satoru Nishita; project director: Byron McCulley; designer: Angela Danadjieva Tzvetin. Engineers: Gilbert, Forsberg, Diekmann & Schmidt (structural); Beamer/Wilkinson (mechanical/electrical). General contractor: Schrader Construction Co.

Honors: ASLA Honor Award, 1971; AIA Bicentennial List, two nominations.

See: *Architectural Forum* 133 (October 1970): 56–59. *Process: Architecture,* no. 4 (February 1978): 178–84. *Landscape Architecture* 75 (January–February 1985): 92–95.

Lawrence HALPRIN & ASSOCIATES (landscape architects); NARAMORE, BAIN, BRADY & JOHANSEN; VAN SLYCK, CALLISON, NELSON (architects)

■ 135

Seattle Freeway Park; Seattle, WA; 1976.
Designed to draw together city

neighborhoods divided by a freeway, this 1,300-foot-long park weaves over and alongside that freeway, over a garage, and under a street. Its waterfall masks the din of traffic. Other park delights include trees, flowers, cascading fountains, pools, concrete crags in a "metaphorical landscape," and a gorge.
Project designer: Angela Danadjieva. Consultants: Victor Gray; Washington State Highway Department Bridge Division; Edward McCleod & Assoc.; G.F.D.S. Engineers; Richard Chaix; Engineering Enterprise; Mrs. Pendleton Miller.

Honors: ASLA Merit Award, 1977.

See: *AIA Journal* 72 (June 1983): 43–47. *Progressive Architecture* 58 (June 1977): 86–87. *Process: Architecture,* no. 4 (February 1978): 227–40. *Landscape Architecture* 67 (September 1977): 399–406.

HAMMOND BEEBY BABKA

■ 136

Conrad Sulzer Regional Library; Chicago, IL; 1985 (see Illus. 68).
Neoclassical details and dignity characterize this 2-story, 65,000-square-foot library. The thickened brick facade on its ground-floor level is broken at regular intervals by stately arches while, on the upper level, evenly spaced pilasters mark off bays. The main lobby, an oval rotunda, combines classical columns with postmodern light sconces; its striking

68

glazed ceiling has a framework shaped like a spider web.

Principals: Thomas H. Beeby, Bernard F. Babka, James W. Hammond; project architect: Tannys L. Langdon. Consultants: Gullaksen, Getty & White (structural); H. S. Nachman & Assoc. (mechanical). General contractor: S. N. Nielsen.

Honors: National AIA Honor Award, 1987.

See: *Architecture* 76 (May 1987): 138–43. *Progressive Architecture* 66 (December 1985): 51–61 and cover. *Architectural Review* 170 (August 1981): 71–72.

HARALSON & MOTT see Edward Durell STONE; HARALSON & MOTT

HARDY HOLZMAN PFEIFFER

Winner, AIA Architectural Firm Award, 1981.

■ 137

Best Products Corporate Headquarters; Richmond, VA; 1980 (see Illus. 69).
This large (68,000-square-foot) 2-story office building is wildly innovative yet filled with historical allusions. The approach is guarded by two Art Moderne eagles; entry is over a moat; and the front facade—translucent glass block studded with transparent blocks in a diamond pattern—curves and, at ground and cornice height, is finished with ornamental terra cotta.

Partner in charge: Malcolm Holzman; project manager; Alec Gibson/Associate. Consultants: LeMessurier Associates (structural); Sippican Consultants (civil); Lehr Associates (mechanical/site utilities); Luis Villa/Lois Sherr Associates (landscape). Construction manager: McDonough Construction.

Honors: AIA Honor Award, 1983.

See: *AIA Journal* 72 (May 1983): 250–53. *Progressive Architecture* 62 (February 1981): 66–73; 68 (March 1987): 108–13. *Space Design,* no. 203 (August 1981): 44–48.

■ 138

Brooklyn Children's Museum; New York, NY; 1977 (see Illus. 70).
This underground museum—a four-level,

open-plan facility—offers kids a bounty of hands-on learning experiences in highly original ways. It's topped by a playground that parades highway signage, a silo, and a subway kiosk that serves as the building's entrance. Inside there's a "people tube" that carries sluiceways of water and swirls of neon as well as visitors; there's also a greenhouse of plants, a lucite jungle gym that replicates a molecule's structure, and many other attractions.

Consultants: Hannaham & Johnston (mechanical); Goldreich Page & Thropp (structural); Edwin Schlossberg (exhibition conceptualization). General contractor: D. Fortunato, Inc.

See: *Architectural Record* 151 (April 1972): 114–15. *Progressive Architecture* 59 (May 1978): 62–67. *Design Quarterly,* no. 90/91 (1974): 71–72. *Contract Interiors* 137 (June 1978): 116–19.

■ 139

The Cloisters; Cincinnati, OH; 1970 (see Illus. 71).
A condominium built on a "precipitous, odd-shaped and constricted" 1.4-acre site, it is a wood-framed structure supported on round timber poles, with fire-resistant masonry walls dividing the units. Each of its seventeen units enjoys ample space and an attractive view.

Consultants: WHB Associates (mechanical); Miller, Tallarico, McNinch & Hoeffel (structural).

Honors: First Honor Award, 1973 Homes for Better Living Program, conferred by the AIA et al.

See: *Progressive Architecture* 52 (May 1971): 86–91. *House Beautiful* 114 (June 1972): 50–55. *House & Home* 44 (August 1973): 70–83. *GA Houses,* no. 2 (1977): 44–53.

69   Best Products Corporate Headquarters; Richmond, VA; 1980. *See* Entry 137. (Courtesy Hardy, Holzman, Pfeiffer Associates; New York, NY. Photographer: © Norman McGrath.)

70   Brooklyn Children's Museum; New York, NY; 1977. *See* Entry 138. (Courtesy Hardy, Holzman, Pfeiffer Associates; New York, NY. Photographer: © Norman McGrath.)

71

▪ 140

Columbus Occupational Health Center; Columbus, IN; 1973 (see Illus. 72).

This medical center's interior is enlivened by a colorful display of pipes, coils, bolts, and flanges used both functionally and as architectural ornament. Its exterior is sheathed in two intersecting glazing systems (one black, the other mirrored) while, overhead, light flows in from two long, intersecting mirrored skylights.
Project architects: Michael Ross, Marvin Wiehe, C. E. John Way, Patrick Stanigar. Engineers: Arthur Miller Associates (structural); Ziel-Blossom Associates (mechanical/electrical). Landscape consultant; Dan Kiley. General contractor: Repp & Mundt.

Honors: AIA Honor Award, 1976; Bartlett Award, 1976.

See: Architectural Record 158 (October 1975): 95–102. *Baumeister* 73 (September 1976): 729–33. *A+U: Architecture and Urbanism,* no. 63 (March 1976): 48–55.

▪ 141

Pingry School; Bernards Township, NJ; 1983 (see Illus. 73).

In this symmetrical, 350-foot-long structure for a private school, inexpensive materials come together in startling ways. At the front, rose concrete block —some of it smooth, some rough finished, set in formal patterns—combines with a wavering black granite band between its 2 stories to make it look like a stone building with classical detailing. At the rear, however, corrugated steel forms outer walls and sunshading over continuous strips of windows. An aqua-tiled clock tower straddles both, separating the school's two long wings.
Partner in charge: Norman Pfeiffer; project managers: Stephen Johnson, Victor Gong. Consultants: Stanley H. Goldstein (structural); Jansen & Rogan (mechanical). General contractor: Torcon, Inc.

See: Architecture 74 (May 1985): 192–97, 370. *Progressive Architecture* 65 (August 1984): 65–73 and cover. *Baumeister* 82 (November 1985): 57–59. *GA Document,* no. 13 (September 1985): 100–9.

72

73

■ **142**

Robert S. Marx Theater, the Playhouse in the Park; Cincinnati, OH; 1968 (see Illus. 74).

A 672-seat playhouse set on a grassy knoll in Eden Park, its load-bearing concrete block walls are topped by sloping roofs finished in stainless steel. Inside, stainless steel walls glisten alongside exposed concrete block; the asymmetrical thrust stage boasts a choice of twenty-four entrance points.

Supervising architects: Robert Habel–Hubert M.

Garriot Associates. Engineers: Miller Tallarico McNinch & Hoeffel (structural); Maxfield-Edwards-Backer & Associates (mechanical); Robert A. Hansen Assoc. (acoustical). Contractors: Turner Construction Co.

Honors: AISC Architectural Award of Excellence, 1969.

See: Architectural Forum 129 (September 1968): 65. *Architectural Record* 145 (March 1969): 117–28. *Architettura* 15 (September 1969): 322–23.

■ **143**

WCCO Television Headquarters; Minneapolis, MN; 1984 (see Illus. 75).

Most of this building, which takes up half a city block and is stepped from one to three stories in height, is clad in red variegated sandstone cut in many finishes, shapes, and sizes and arranged in complex patterns. Its largest component, a 100-by-50-foot studio, 30 feet high, is clad in embossed copper shingles. Lots of skylights brighten the interior, which also gains character from mahogany paneling accented with ebony, terrazzo floors, and other craftsmanlike touches.

Project leader: J. Lowery. Architectural field representative: Lindberg Pierce, Inc. Engineers: Meyer, Borgman and Johnson (structural); Michaud, Cooley, Hallberg & Erickson (mechanical/electrical). General contractor: McGough Construction.

See: Architecture 73 (May 1984): 276–83. *Baumeister* 82 (November 1985): 50–51; 82 (December 1985). 41. *Architecture Intérieure Crée,* no. 204 (March–April 1985): 88–91. *Corporate Design and Realty* 4 (March 1985): 58–63.

HARRELL & HAMILTON

■ **144**

2300 Riverside Apartments; Tulsa, OK; 1961.

This 16-story luxury apartment tower features continuous, 6-foot-wide balconies around its rectangular perimeter. Not only does almost every room have direct access to an outdoor space, but the verandas afford good sunshading and make interesting shadow patterns.

Structural engineers: Hunt & Joiner. Landscape

74

75 WCCO Television Headquarters; Minneapolis, MN; 1984. *See Entry* 143. (Courtesy Hardy, Holzman, Pfeiffer Associates; New York, NY. Photographer: © Norman McGrath.)

75

architects: Lambert Landscape Co. General contractor: Centex Construction Co.

Honors: AIA Merit Award, 1963.

See: Architectural Forum 116 (March 1962): 82–85. *Architectural Record* 125 (June 1959): 208–9. *Bauen + [und] Wohnen* 18 (November 1963): 450–53.

Wallace K. HARRISON

Winner, AIA Gold Medal, 1967.

■ **145**

Metropolitan Opera House, Lincoln

Center; New York, NY; 1966 (see Illus. 76).
A home in the grand manner for a time-honored opera company, it combines fine acoustics and highly mechanized stage facilities with a modern baroque ambience rich in flowing lines, repeated curves, gilt, red plush, and a grand staircase reminiscent of an elegant old European opera house.
Planning and architectural liaison: Herman E. Krawitz. Acoustical consultants: Vilhelm L. Jordan and Cyril M. Harris. Engineers: Ammann & Whitney (structural); Syska & Hennessy (mechanical/electrical). General contractor: George A. Fuller Co.

See: Architectural Record 140 (September 1966): 149–60. *Progressive Architecture* 47

(October 1966): 251–53. *Interiors* 126 (September 1966): 93–99.

■ **146.**

United Nations Secretariat; New York, NY; 1950 (see Illus. 77).
This famous marble and glass slab of a building looms importantly over Manhattan's East River. It was designed by Harrison and Max Abramovitz in conjunction with an international "board of design," to provide office space for over 3,500 UN employees and living quarters for the secretary general.
Director of planning: Wallace K. Harrison; deputy director: Max Abramovitz. Associate architects: Gilmore D. Clarke, Louis Skidmore, Ralph Walker. Construction coordinator: James A. Dawson. Engineers: Syska & Hennessy (consulting engineers); Edwards & Hjorth (structural); Madigan-Hyland (structural). Contractor: Fuller-Turner-Walsh-Slattery.

Honors: AIA Bicentennial List, one nomination.

See: Architectural Forum 92 (May 1950): 96–101; 93 (November 1950): 93–112. *Techniques et Architecture* 11 (September 1952): 54–56.

HARRISON & ABRAMOVITZ

■ **147**

ALCOA Building; Pittsburgh, PA; 1952 (see Illus. 78).
A 30-story office building innovatively sheathed in an Oxford gray, waffle-patterned aluminum skin. Other ALCOA-minded features built in included

76 Metropolitan Opera House, Lincoln Center; New York, NY; 1966. *See Entry* 145. (Courtesy Abramovitz-Kingsland-Schiff; New York, NY. Photographer: Joseph W. Molitor.)

76

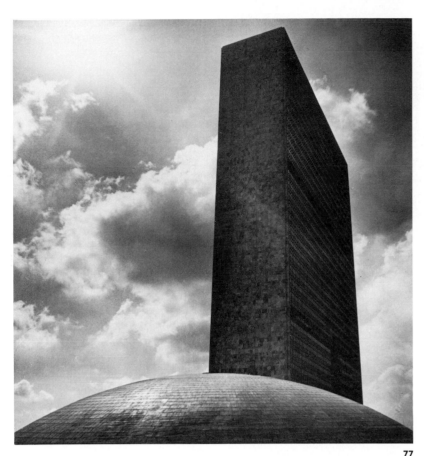

77

78

aluminum plumbing and wiring, and much of the original furniture boasted aluminum frames.

Associate architects: Altenhof & Brown; Mitchell & Ritchey. Consultants: Edwards & Hjorth (structural); Jaros, Baum & Bolles (mechanical); Edward E. Ashley (electrical). General contractor: George A. Fuller Co.

See: *Architectural Forum* 97 (July 1952): 134–35; 99 (November 1953): 124–31. *Architectural Record* 112 (August 1952): 120–27.

■ 148

First Presbyterian Church; Stamford, CT; 1958.

A fish-shaped church on a grassy suburban site, it has an arresting sanctuary enclosed by a patchwork of zigzagging panels of concrete set with irregularly shaped chunks of glass—brightly colored or clear—arranged in abstract patterns.

Associated architects: Sherwood, Mills & Smith. Engineers: Edwards & Hjorth (structural); Fred S. Dubin Assoc. (mechanical/electrical). Consultant: Felix J. Samuely (structural); Bolt, Beranek & Newman (acoustical). Contractor: Deluca Construction Co.

See: *Architectural Forum* 108 (April 1958): 104–7. *Progressive Architecture* 39 (April 1958): 104–7; 40 (May 1959): 152–53.

■ 149

Gov. Nelson A. Rockefeller Empire State Plaza; Albany, NY; 1978 (see Illus. 79).

This headquarters for New York State government, most often referred to as "the Albany Mall," also has been dubbed "Brasilia North" and "the flat Acropolis." The complex, which was Governor Rockefeller's brainchild, occupies almost 100 acres and includes ten monumental buildings sited on a five-level platform; total cost of its construction was over a billion dollars.

Associated architects: James & Meadows & Howard (Legislative Building); Carson, Lundin & Shaw (Swan Street Building); Sargent, Webster, Crenshaw & Folley (Justice Building). Engineers: Ammann & Whitney (structural); Syska & Hennessy (mechanical/electrical). Construction management: George A. Fuller Co.

See: *Architectural Forum* 136 (May 1972): 7. *Progressive Architecture* 60 (May 1979): 106–9. *Architecture Plus* 2 (July–August 1974): 76–81. Carol Krinsky, "St. Petersburg-on-the-Hudson: The Albany Mall," in *Art, the Ape of Nature* (New York: Abrams, 1981). Robert A. M. Stern, *Pride of Place* (Boston: Houghton Mifflin, 1986), 323–24.

77 United Nations Secretariat; New York, NY; 1950. *See* Entry 146. (Courtesy Abramovitz-Kingsland-Schiff; New York, NY. Photographer: Joseph W. Molitor.)

78 ALCOA Building; Pittsburgh, PA; 1952. *See* Entry 147. (Courtesy Abramovitz-Kingsland-Schiff; New York, NY. Photographer: Joseph W. Molitor.)

79

■ 150

Illini Assembly Hall, University of Illinois; Urbana, IL; 1963.
This 16,000-seat bowl for athletic, musical, and theatrical events is housed under a giant concrete dome with sinuously undulating lines. Its acoustics simulate outdoor conditions, and its several interlocking systems of lighting can illuminate a variety of spectacles.
University architect: Ernest L. Stouffer. Engineers: Ammann & Whitney (structural); Syska & Hennessy (mechanical/electrical). Acoustical consultant: Bolt, Beranek & Newman. Lighting consultant: Lighting by Feder. Site landscaping consultants: Clarke & Rapuano. General contractor: Felmley-Dickerson Co.

Honors: AIA Merit Award, 1964.

See: Architectural Record 134 (July 1963): 111–16. *Progressive Architecture* 45 (April 1964): 176–80. *L'Architecture d'Aujourd'hui,* no. 116 (September–November 1964): 42–44.

■ 151

Interfaith Center, Brandeis University; Waltham, MA; 1955.
Three separate chapels—Protestant, Catholic, and Jewish—are grouped harmoniously around a pool on a tree-fringed site. Although their designs vary, they are built of similar materials: pale, glazed brick with large areas of glass.
Engineers: Eipel Engineering (structural); Sears & Kopf (mechanical/electrical); Bolt, Beranek & Newman (acoustical). General contractor: Lilly Construction Co.

Honors: AIA Merit Award, 1956.

See: Architectural Forum 101 (September 1954): 134–35. *Architectural Record* 116 (September 1954): 9–11; 119 (January 1956): 147–53.

■ 152

Phoenix Mutual Life Insurance Company Headquarters; Hartford, CT; 1964.
This office building is situated harmoniously alongside Constitution Plaza, designed by Charles DuBose (see entry no. 83). It consists of a 13-story elliptical tower set on a square, 3-story pedestal. Atop this supporting structure is a trim public plaza complete with reflecting pool.

See: Architectural Record 135 (March 1964): 178–87. *Interior Design* 35 (May 1964): 130ff. *Architect & Building News* 229 (January 12, 1966): 69–70.

HARRISON, ABRAMOVITZ & ABBE

■ 153

Corning Glass Center; Corning, NY; 1951.
This popular showplace—a long, low, glass and marble structure—comprises not only a working factory but also a museum exhibiting fine glass since ancient times, a library, and an area where visitors can view the manufacture of Steuben crystal.
General contractor: George A. Fuller Construction Co.

Honors: AIA Merit Award, 1953.

See: Architectural Forum 95 (August 1951): 125–31; 102 (May 1955): 124–27; 106 (May 1957): 108–13.

■ 154

USX Tower, formerly U.S. Steel Building; Pittsburgh, PA; 1971 (see Illus. 80).
In this 64-story, triangular office tower—topped by a heliport originally designed for use by U.S. Steel executives—weathering steel is used for most of the building's exposed parts. Other unusual structural features include the use of steel columns filled with a salt solution, to provide the building with fireproof support, and an unconventional pattern of wind bracing at every third floor.
Partner in charge: Charles H. Abbe. Engineers: Skilling, Helle, Christianson & Robertson and Edwards & Hjorth (structural); Jaros, Baum & Bolles (mechanical). Landscape architects: Clarke & Rapuano. General contractor: Turner Construction Co.

Honors: AISC Architectural Award of Excellence, 1971.

See: Architectural Forum 135 (December 1971): 24–29. *Interiors* 131 (December 1971); 96–109. *Industrial Design* 18 (December 1971): 62–65. David Guise, *Design and Technology in Architecture* (New York: Wiley, 1985), 146–55.

HARTMAN-COX

■ 155

Florence Hollis Hand Chapel, Mount Vernon College; Washington, DC; 1970 (see Illus. 81).
This nondenominational chapel, sited on a steep slope, is built of red brick and slate and can be used for worship, musical performances, or drama. Its boldly slanting, shedlike roof abounds in skylights, and floods the interior with natural light.
Engineers: James M. Cutts (structural); JEK Associates (mechanical/electrical). Landscape architect: Lester A. Collins. General contractor: Edwin Davis.

80

Honors: AIA Honor Award, 1971; 1971 Community and Junior College Design Award.

See: *AIA Journal* 55 (June 1971): 47. *Architectural Forum* 134 (March 1971): 56–59. *Progressive Architecture* 53 (June 1972): 84–87.

■ 156

National Permanent Building; Washington, DC; 1977 (see Illus. 82).

This 12-story office building, economically built of reinforced concrete, aluminum, and glass, makes the most of a conspicuous site. On two facades, its structural frame of white columns and beams extends 6 feet beyond a wall of gray glass to provide both sunshading and a fascinating play of patterns. Flat black air-conditioning ducts are exposed; at roof level they are huge, but as they descend they get progressively smaller. Conversely, the building's columns get smaller as they rise.

Project assistants: Mario Bioardi, David Jones. Consultants: General Engineering (mechanical); KCE Structural Engineers (structural). General contractor: The Lenkin Company.

Honors: AIA Honor Award, 1981; CRSI Design Award, 1977.

See: *AIA Journal* 70 (mid-May 1981): 238 39. *Progressive Architecture* 58 (December 1977): 54–57. *Architettura* 28, no. 319 (May 1982)· 336–37.

80 USX Tower (formerly U.S. Steel Building); Pittsburgh, PA; 1971. *See* Entry 154.

HAWLEY & PETERSON

■ 157

Qume Corporation Building; San Jose, CA; 1979.

A boldly red, white, and blue facade, exposed and brightly painted structural and mechanical systems, and a skylighted and lushly landscaped central atrium combine to make a surprisingly attractive factory. Two stories high and located in Silicon Valley, it supplies 250,000 square feet of space for offices, an assembly line, and storage.

Design team: John Duvivier and Curtis Snyder; project architect: Wayne Holland; partner in charge: Charles A. Peterson. Engineers; T. T. Siebert (structural); Practicon Associates (mechanical). Landscape architect: Fong & LaRocca. General contractor; Dickman Construction.

81

81 Florence Hollis Hand Chapel, Mt. Vernon College; Washington, DC; 1970. *See* Entry 155. (Courtesy Hartman-Cox Architects; Washington, DC. Photographer: Robert Lautman.)

82

82 National Permanent Building; Washington, DC; 1977. *See* Entry 156. (Courtesy Hartman-Cox Architects; Washington, DC. Photographer: Robert Lautman.)

circular church. In its window areas, no glass is used. Instead they are enclosed with two translucent plastic sheets: the outer sheet a dark gray to contrast with the shell's white exterior, the inner sheet white to glow with diffused natural light. Designer: Gyo Obata. Supervising structural engineer: John P. Nix. Structural engineer: Paul Weidlinger. Mechanical engineer: Harold P. Brehm.

Honors: PA Design Award, 1958.

See: *Architectural Record* 138 (August 1965): 144–45. *Architect & Building News* 222/21 (November 21, 1962): 753–56. *Liturgical Arts* 31 (November 1962): 4–7, 12–25.

■ 160

E. R. Squibb & Sons, Inc. Worldwide Headquarters; Lawrenceville, NJ; 1972 (see Illus. 84).

This headquarters and research facility, set on gently rolling acres, comprises seven brick and limestone buildings linked by glassed-in walkways. Its handsomely designed interiors and other amenities have won much praise; its 662-seat restaurant and an art gallery look out over a man-made lake.

Principal in charge of design: Gyo Obata; principal in charge: Jerome J. Sincoff; interior designer: Michael Willis. Landscape architects: The Office of Dan Kiley. Engineers: Le Messurier Assoc. (structural); Golder, Gass Associates (soils); Joseph R. Loring & Assoc. (mechanical/electrical). Contractor: Huber, Hunt & Nichols.

See: *Architectural Record* 153 (January 1973): 90–91; 153 (June 1973): 139–54. *Interior Design* 43 (September 1972): 132–38.

Honors: AIA Honor Award, 1980.

See: *AIA Journal* 69 (mid-May 1980): 226–27. *Architectural Record* 167 (June 1980): 120–21. *Architectural Review* 169 (May 1981): 283–88. *Interiors* 139 (May 1980): 138–39.

HELLMUTH, OBATA & KASSABAUM
(also known as HOK)

■ 159

Chapel, Priory of St. Mary and St. Louis; near St. Louis, MO; 1962 (see Illus. 83).

Three rings of thin-shell concrete parabolic arches shape this extraordinary

John HEJDUK

■ 158

Foundation Building, Cooper Union; New York, NY; original building, 1858; renovation, 1974.

While the exterior of this Italianate landmark, finished in stone with cast-iron detailing, was respectfully preserved, its interior was gutted and completely rebuilt. The result: immaculate white spaces with refinement and grace to house Cooper Union's School of Art and Architecture.

83 Chapel, Priory of St. Mary and St. Louis; near St. Louis, MO; 1962. *See* Entry 159. (Courtesy Hellmuth, Obata & Kassabaum; St. Louis, MO.)

See: *Progressive Architecture* 55 (July 1974): 96–103; 56 (July 1975): 50–57. *L'Architecture d'Aujourd'hui,* no. 186 (August–September 1976): 50–52.

83

84

■161

Levi's Plaza; San Francisco, CA; 1981.
Set on four blocks between Telegraph Hill and the Embarcadero, these corporate headquarters for Levi Strauss & Co. fit amiably into a largely residential neighborhood. Three new brick-and-glass buildings (the Levi Strauss, Haas, and Koshland buildings), 4 to 7 stories high, and two renovated older ones (Cargo West and the Stern Building) are surrounded by a large public plaza with two wide-ranging, imaginative fountains. Each of the new buildings is stepped, providing terraces with rounded edges that look out to the bay. A striking atrium marks the main building's entrance.
Principal in charge of design: Gyo Obata; project designer: William Valentine. Architects for interiors of new buildings: Gensler & Associates/Architects—Orlando Diaz-Azcuy, design principal. Engineers: Dames & Moore (soils); Cygna Consulting Engineers (structural); Vann Engineering (mechanical). Landscape architects: Lawrence Halprin, and Omi Lang Associates. Contractors: Dinwiddie Construction; Swinerton & Walberg.

See: *AIA Journal* 71 (mid-May 1982): 152–61. *Architectural Record* 170 (May 1982): 114–19. *A + U: Architecture and Urbanism,* no. 145 (October 1982): 111–14. *Landscape Architect* 73 (November–December 1983): 50–53.

■162

National Air and Space Museum; Washington, DC; 1976 (see Illus. 85).
A huge (685-foot-by-225-foot) marble edifice designed to house such twentieth-century wonders as Lindbergh's plane, the *Spirit of St. Louis,* rockets, balloons, and the Apollo 11 lunar module. It features breathtaking interior spaces in which aircraft hang suspended from exposed structural members.
Principal in charge of design: Gyo Obata; principal in charge of project: Jerome Sincoff; project designer: Chih-Chen Jen. Consultants: Le Messurier Associates (structural); HOK Associates (mechanical/electrical/civil). Construction manager: Gilbane Building Co.

Honors: AISC Architectural Award of Excellence, 1977.

See: *AIA Journal* 65 (December 1976): 34–37; 69 (November 1980): 36–45. *Progressive Architecture* 57 (July 1976): 70–75.

85

■163

Neiman-Marcus Store, Galleria Post Oak; Houston, TX; 1968.
A spectacular store in a spectacular shopping mall. The store's precast concrete exterior is accented by translucent onyx panels. Inside, escalators glide, glittering, through an open central well from which riders can see individualized shops all around.
Principal in charge of design: Gyo Obata; project manager: Jon J. Worstell; project design: Alvin Lever. Interior designer: Eleanor LeMaire Associates. Landscape architect: Sasaki, Dawson, DeMay Associates. Engineers: Elmer Ellisor Engineers (structural); Guerrero & McGuire and Leo L. Landauer & Associates (mechanical). Contractors: Henry C. Beck Co. and Linbeck Construction Corp.

See: *Architectural Forum* 136 (April 1972): 24–39. *Architectural Record* 146 (July 1969): 135–50. *Architectural Design* 43 (November 1973): 695–97.

■164

Olympic Center; Lake Placid, NY; 1979 (see Illus. 86).
Built to house the indoor events of the 1980 Winter Olympics, this stadium is connected to the arena where the Winter Games were held in 1932. In 1980 it supplied 5,000 permanent seats plus 3,000 temporary seats in bleachers, all overlooking two giant ice sheets. Its most distinctive feature: the latticework of white trusses that spans its 240-foot-wide south elevation.
Project team: Gyo Obata, Gerald Gilmore, Harry Culpen, John Way, Terry Harkness, Charles Reay. Engineers: Jack D. Gillum & Assoc. (structural); Cosentini Assoc. (mechanical/electrical); Ahrendt Engineering (refrigeration). Construction manager: Gilbane Building Company.

See: *Architectural Record* 167 (February 1980): 120–24. *Techniques et Architecture,* no. 329 (February–March 1980): 136–38. *Architettura* 26 (June 1980): 342–48. *Architect's Journal* 171 (February 13, 1980): 312–14.

■165

St. Louis Science Center (formerly St. Louis Planetarium); St. Louis, MO; 1963 (see Illus. 87).
This planetarium's 408-seat auditorium and dome are sheltered under a graceful parasol of a thin concrete shell. Around the dome, a spectator's ramp winds up to a skylighted penthouse—shielded from

86

87

city lights by the shell's flaring rim—where stars can be observed directly.
Partner in charge of design: Gyo Obata. Engineers: Albert Alper (structural); Harold P. Brehm (mechanical). Structural consultants: Ketchum, Konkel & Hastings. General contractor: Gamble Construction Co.

Honors: PA Design Citation, 1960.

See: *Architectural Forum* 119 (August 1963): 94–97. *Architectural Record* 138 (August 1965): 146–47. *Architectural Review* 133 (June 1963): 406–9, 422.

■166

St. Louis Union Station, renovation and adaptive reuse; St. Louis, MO. Originally completed in 1894 (Theodore C. Link, architect; interior designed by Louis Millet); renovation completed 1985 (see Illus. 88).
A lengthy project costing $140 million restored this mammoth, long-abandoned Romanesque Revival railroad station, with a wealth of Sullivanesque interior ornament, as well as its 11.5-acre train shed and related buildings to their former glory while adapting them to new uses. This complex now contains 150 shops and restaurants—some in kiosks—and a new 546-room luxury hotel, the Omni International, most of it fitted under the train shed's glass and metal canopy.
Consultants for restoration accuracy: Timothy Samuelson, architectural historian; Donna Laidlaw, project coordinator. General contractor: HCB Contractors.

See: *Progressive Architecture* 66 (November 1985): 83–93 and cover. *Historic Preservation* 37 (June 1985): 34–39. *Architektur + Wettbewerbe,* no. 121 (March 1985): 50–53.

88

HELLMUTH, OBATA & KASSABAUM; BRODSKY, HOPF & ADLER

■ **167**

Dallas/Fort Worth Regional Airport; near Dallas, TX; first phase, 1973 (see Illus. 89).

Conceived as a complex of thirteen terminal units to be completed by the year 2000, this airport's first four terminals, constructed of beige concrete, were built as paired horseshoes, each of which gives access to planes on the outside and parking for cars on the inside. Principal in charge of design: Gyo Obata. Associate architects: Preston M. Geren, Jr.; Harrell & Hamilton. Engineers: Le Messurier Associates and Terry-Rosenlund & Co. (structural); Herman Blum Consulting Engineers and Cowan, Love & Jackson (mechanical). Landscape consultants: Richard B. Myrick & Associates. Construction management: Parsons McKee.

See: Architectural Forum 136 (May 1972): 24–31. *Progressive Architecture* 54 (December 1973): 68–73. *Concrete* 8 (February 1974): 22–27.

HELLMUTH, YAMASAKI & LEINWEBER

■ **168**

Lambert–St. Louis Municipal Airport

Terminal Building; St. Louis, MO; 1955 (see Illus. 90).

Intersecting barrel vaults shaped of thin-shell concrete frame a huge interior space: 412 feet long and 120 feet wide with window arches 32 feet high at the center. Plastic skylights set in long sweeping arcs supply additional natural light.

Partner in charge of design: Minoru Yamasaki. Engineers: William C. E. Becker (structural); Ferris & Hamig (mechanical). Shell consultants:

89

90

Roberts & Schaefer. Consultant during preliminaries: Edgardo Contini.

Honors: AIA Honor Award, 1956.

See: *Architectural Forum* 104 (May 1956): 106–15. *Architectural Record* 119 (April 1956): 195–202, 278. *Progressive Architecture* 36 (July 1955): 76.

■169

Pruitt-Igoe; St. Louis, MO; 1955.
Probably the most notorious disaster in the field of public housing. When it opened, this complex of thirty 11-story buildings was hailed for its imaginative design. For economy, elevators stopped only on the fourth, seventh, and tenth floors; these floors featured sunny, 85-foot-long galleries, which were planned for use as indoor playgrounds and "neighborhood gathering places." Instead —in part due to changes in policies regarding tenants admitted—crime mounted and law-abiding tenants fled. In 1974, the federal Department of Housing and Urban Development demolished the project.
Partner in charge of design: Minoru Yamasaki. Engineers: William C. E. Becker (structural); John D. Falvey (mechanical/electrical).

See: *Architectural Forum* 123 (December 1965): 22–25. *Architectural Record* 120 (August 1956): 182–89. *Building Official & Code Administrator* 8 (March 1974): 56–57.

HENRIQUEZ & TODD

■170

Gaslight Square; Vancouver, British Columbia; 1975.
In a historic district, a new building whose height matches existing cornice lines but which boasts lavish and unusual glazing on its two long sides joins with two renovated adjoining buildings to define an inviting courtyard where stepped, open-air walkways provide access to shops on two levels. The complex also provides office space on its upper floors.
Project architect: Glen Cividin; landscape architect: Cornelia Oberlander. Engineers: C. Y. Loh & Assoc. (structural); Park & Djwa (mechanical).

Honors: Canadian Architect Yearbook Award, 1972.

See: *Process: Architecture,* no. 5 (1978): 206–9. *Canadian Architect* 17 (December 1972): 62–63; 21 (August 1976): 46–49. William Bernstein and Ruth Cawker, *Contemporary Canadian Architecture* (Toronto: Fitzhenry & Whiteside, 1982), 154–58.

HERTZKA & KNOWLES; SKIDMORE, OWINGS & MERRILL

■171

Crown Zellerbach Building; San Francisco, CA; 1959/60.
One of San Francisco's first glass-walled office towers, this 20-story building is set in an appealing and imaginative sunken garden. A surprisingly dainty 1-story bank (see entry no. 430) is located at one corner of its plaza.
Structural engineer: H. J. Brunnier. General contractor: Haas & Haynie.

Honors: AIA Merit Award, 1961.

See: *AIA Journal* 35 (April 1961): 87. *Architectural Record* 125 (April 1959): 163–74. *Interiors* 119 (June 1960): 88–99. *Japan Architect* 36 (April 1961): 64–69.

HODNE/STAGEBERG

■172

1199 Plaza Cooperative Housing; New York, NY; 1974 (see Illus. 91).
Sited on 12 acres in East Harlem, this handsome, red brick–faced, middle-income development provides 1,602,000 square feet of residential space, divided into 1,590 desirable units. Each of its four buildings has a 31-story tower plus wings of from six to ten stories.
Engineers: Robert Rosenwasser Associates (structural); Arthur L. Zigas & Associates (electrical/mechanical). Landscape architect: Herb Baldwin. Contractor: Starrett Brothers & Eken, Inc.

91   1199 Plaza Cooperative Housing; New York, NY; 1974. *See* Entry 172. (Courtesy Thomas A. Hodne, Jr., FAIA; Winnipeg, Canada. Photographer: Norman McGrath.)

Honors: Bard Award, 1976; AIA Honor Award, 1977; Bartlett Award, 1977.

See: *AIA Journal* 66 (May 1977): 38–39. *Architectural Forum* 134 (May 1971): 42–45. *Progressive Architecture* 57 (March 1976): 64–69.

HOK see HELLMUTH, OBATA & KASSABAUM

Frank L. HOPE (subsequent name of firm: HOPE CONSULTING GROUP)

■ 173

San Diego Jack Murphy Stadium; San Diego, CA; 1967 (see Illus. 92).
The San Diego River was rerouted to put this 50,000-seat, baseball/football stadium safely above flood level. Its strong, simple design gains added verve from the placement of its transportation facilities—corkscrew ramps and sleek elevator towers—as almost freestanding sculptural elements at its outer margins. In 1985, an expansion designed by Hope added 8,000 new seats.
Principal in charge of architecture: Frank L. Hope, Jr.; principal in charge of engineering: Charles B. Hope; project designer: R. Gary Allen. Civil engineers: City of San Diego. Landscape architects: Wimmer & Yamada. General contractor: Robertson Larsen-Donovan.

Honors: AIA Honor Award, 1969; Bartlett Award, 1969.

See: *AIA Journal* 51 (June 1969): 103. *Progressive Architecture* 48 (December 1967): 98–101. *Arena-Interbuild* (*Arena* 15, *Interbuild* 83) (January 1968): 22–26.

Morton HOPPENFELD, planner for The ROUSE COMPANY

■ 174

Planned community: Columbia, MD.
This is an outstanding example of a successful "new town," a community planned and built from scratch. Plans for Columbia, located between Baltimore and Washington, D.C., stressed a heterogeneous mix of people, a lively

92 San Diego Jack Murphy Stadium; San Diego, CA; 1967. *See* Entry 173. (Courtesy Hope Architects and Engineers; San Diego, CA.)

downtown cultural center, and opportunities for employment nearby. "New town zoning" was granted in 1965. As of mid-1988, there were 25,629 housing units and a population of over 70,000.

Honors: AIA Bicentennial List, one nomination.

See: *Architectural Forum* 127 (November 1967): 42–47. *Architect's Yearbook* 13 (1971): 34–47. *Architectural Design* 39 (November 1969): 585.

Norman HOTSON (subsequent name of firm: HOTSON BAKKER ARCHITECTS)

■ 175

Granville Island Redevelopment; Vancouver, British Columbia; 1977– (see Illus. 93).
An industrial ghost town sprawling on a peninsula has been transformed into a vivid village designed to encourage

93 Granville Island Redevelopment; Vancouver, BC; 1977–. *See* Entry 175. (Courtesy Hotson Bakker Architects; Vancouver, Canada.)

"randomness, curiosity, delight, and surprise." Additions include a seawall, parkland, and distinctive, uniform paving for roadways and sidewalks; areas throughout are defined by brightly colored steel pipes borne by cedar poles. A Public Market complex has been recycled from five old structures. Also on the "Island": an art school, restaurants, theaters, working factories, shops, old railroad tracks and, offshore, a community of houseboats.

Planning project team: Norman Hotson, Joost Bakker, Greg Ball. Consultants: Buckland and Taylor (structural); Don Vaughn Associates (landscape).

Honors: Awards of Excellence from *Canadian Architect,* 1977 (for project design) and 1978 (for project execution).

See: Progressive Architecture 63 (November 1982): 102–9. *Canadian Architect* 22 (December 1977): 43–48; 25 (August 1980): 16–27. Leon Whiteson, *Modern Canadian Architecture* (Edmonton: Hurtig, 1983), 60–63.

HOYLE, DORAN & BERRY see SERT, JACKSON & GOURLEY; HOYLE, DORAN & BERRY

R. E. HULBERT

■ 176

The Fairways; Coquitlam, British Columbia; 1977.

Here's housing with style: fifty-eight condos cleverly fitted into two sloping acres that overlook a golf course. All units have private entrances, some from an attractively landscaped and skylighted pedestrian street reached by elevator. The 3-story complex combines wood-frame construction, metal roofs, and a subterranean concrete garage with 125 spaces.

Design: Eugene V. Radvenis; technical coordination: John C. H. Porter. Engineers: David Nairne & Assoc. (structural); Cook, Pickering, Doyle (foundations); Perelco Design (mechanical). Landscape architects: John Lantzius & Assoc. Contractor: Bidwell Construction.

Honors: AR Award of Excellence for Design, 1978 (Apartments of the Year); *Canadian Architect* Award of Excellence, 1975.

See: Architectural Record 163 (mid-May 1978): 116–19. *Canadian Architect* 23 (February 1978): 14–17. *Housing* 53 (May 1978): 68–71 and cover. *Process: Architecture,* no. 12 (1980): 76–81.

Arata ISOZAKI

Winner, Royal Gold Medal, 1986.

■ 177.

Palladium; New York, NY; 1985.

Funk and pizzazz meet in this disco where a 3-story gridded cage that conceals 10,000 light bulbs, and balcony space modeled after a Greek amphitheater, have been inserted into the shell of a theater built in 1854 and long known as the Academy of Music. Three different sets can descend onto the 3,200-square-foot dance floor; overhead, two arrays of video monitors show varying mixes of images and move up and down. Passageways and stairs are illuminated by lights beneath steel-and-glass-block treads underfoot.

Assistants to Arata Isozaki, architect in charge (design): Shin Watanabe, Ann Kaufman. Associate architect: Bloch, Hesse & Shalat— Daniel L. Beechert, project architect; Michael Overington, project director; Andree Putnam, interior design consultant. Engineers: Lovett & Rozman (structural); Kallen & Lemelson (mechanical). General contractor: Herbert Construction.

See: Architectural Record 173 (mid-September 1985): 126–37 and cover. *Interiors* 145 (October 1985): 128–37. *Japan Architect* 60 (November–December 1985): 17–26. *Interior Design* 56 (October 1985): 230–33.

Arata ISOZAKI; GRUEN ARCHITECTS

■ 178

Los Angeles Museum of Contemporary Art, California Plaza; Los Angeles, CA; 1986.

Though built low on a constricted site with most of its space below grade, embedded in the plaza's parking garage, this museum asserts its presence aboveground with walls of intricately worked red sandstone and with stark geometric forms: the barrel vault of its library, sheathed in copper and set on

square pillars above an entry court, and eleven pyramidal skylights, one especially large. Gallery spaces are of varied sizes and shapes and offer many choices of lighting.

Project designer: Makoto Shin Watanabe. Partners in charge for Gruen Associates: Herman Guttman, Kurt Franzen. Consultants: John A. Martin & Assoc. (structural); Syska & Hennessy (mechanical). General contractor: HCB Contractors.

See: Architecture 76 (February 1987): 40–53 and cover. *Progressive Architecture* 67 (November 1986): 83–95 and cover. *Japan Architect* 62 (February 1987): 14–23 and cover. *A + U: Architecture and Urbanism,* no. 196 (January 1987): 5–9. *Domus,* no. 677 (November 1986): 36–49.

Hugh Newell JACOBSEN

■ 179

Bolton Square; Baltimore, MD; 1967 (see Illus. 94).

This crisply attractive town house complex, built on two inner-city blocks, creates an environment for elegant yet reasonably priced living. Positioned around a central oval, houses are dark burgundy brick with slate roofs and with all trim painted black. Each house also has a private, walled garden.

Engineers: James Salmer; Carl Hansen. Contractor: Ames-Ennis Inc.

Honors: AIA Honor Award, 1969.

See: AIA Journal 51 (June 1969): 95–111. *Architectural Record* 143 (January 1968): 145–60. *House and Home* 34 (October 1968): 88–89.

Charles-Edouard JEANNERET-GRIS see LE CORBUSIER

John M. JOHANSEN

■ 180

Charles Center Theater Building: The Morris Mechanic Theater; Baltimore, MD; 1967.

On the outside it's knobby and roughly circular, modeled of muted golden

94 Bolton Square; Baltimore, MD; 1967. *See* Entry 179. (Courtesy Hugh Newell Jacobsen. Photographer: Robert C. Lautman.)

94

poured-in-place concrete. Inside there's a clean-lined theater where a fan-shaped array of 1,800 seats faces a stage with an extra wide (59-foot) proscenium opening. Associates in charge: Douglas Kingston, Jr., and Robert Kienker. Supervising architects: Cochran, Stephenson & Donkervoet. Engineers: Milo S. Ketchum & Partners (structural); Henry Adams Inc. (mechanical). Theater consultant: Jean Rosenthal. Acoustical consultant: Harold R. Mull. General contractor: Piracci Construction Co.

See: *AIA Journal* 67 (February 1978): 32–37. *Architectural Forum* 126 (May 1967): 72–79. *Japan Architect* 42 (December 1967): 93–102.

■ 181

Mummers Theater; Oklahoma City, OK; 1970 (see Illus. 95).
This fiercely unconventional building—a jazzy assemblage of raw concrete, plain wooden decking, and brightly painted steel ducts and towers—accommodates two shows at once. It contains both an arena theater (240 capacity) and a larger (592 capacity) thrust-stage theater. Associate in charge: Charles A. Ahlstrom. Supervising architects: Seminoff-Bowman-Bode. Engineers: Rudolph Besier (structural); John Altieri (mechanical/electrical). Landscape architect: Thomas Roberts. Stage designer: David Hays. General contractor: Harmon Construction Co.

Honors: AIA Honor Award, 1972.

See: *AIA Journal* 57 (May 1972): 34; 70 (August

95 Mummers Theater; Oklahoma City, OK; 1970. *See* Entry 181. (Courtesy Johansen & Bhavnani; New York, NY. Photographer: Balthazar Korab.)

95

1981); 40–46 and cover. *Architectural Forum* 134 (March 1971): 31–37.

■ 182

Robert Hutchings Goddard Library, Clark University; Worcester, MA; 1968.
Brick, concrete, and lots of glass come together here in a library that is both functional and visually assertive. Unusual touches include cubist-looking cantilevered outcroppings, "reading terraces," and lots of Johansen's characteristic bridges and ramps. Job captain: John Robie. Landscape architect: Corrier Anderson Guida. Engineers: Rudolph Besier (structural); John L. Altieri (mechanical). General contractor: Granger Contracting Co.

Honors: Award of Merit, Library Buildings 1970 Award Program, conferred by the AIA et al.

See: *Architectural Forum* 131 (September 1969): 40–47. *Architectural Record* 137 (June 1965): 151–53. *L'Architecture d'Aujourd'hui,* no. 128 (October–November 1966): 10–11.

Philip JOHNSON

Winner of the AIA Gold Medal, 1978, and the Pritzker Architecture Prize, 1979. (See also entry no. 258.)

■ 183

Amon Carter Museum of Western Art; Fort Worth, TX; 1961 (see Illus. 96).
This dignified, beautifully detailed museum, is faced with hand-carved Texas shellstone and set on a multilevel plaza. Its spectacular main gallery is 24 feet high, 24 feet wide, and 120 feet long.
Supervising architect: Joseph R. Pelich. Engineers: Lev Zetlin (structural); Jaros, Baum & Bolles (mechanical). Interiors and landscaping: Philip Johnson. General contractor: Thomas S. Byrne, Inc.

See: Architectural Forum 114 (March 1961): 86–89. *Aujourd'hui, Art et Architecture* 6, no. 35 (February 1962): 70–71. G. E. Kidder Smith, *A Pictorial History of Architecture in America* (New York: American Heritage, 1976), 2: 616–17.

■ 184

John F. Kennedy Memorial; Dallas, TX; 1970.
A starkly simple, precast concrete structure, which the architect has described as "a pair of magnets about to clamp together." It stands a few hundred yards from where President Kennedy was assassinated.

See: Perspecta, no. 11 (1967): 178–218. *Bauen + [und] Wohnen* 21 (May 1966): 192. G. E. Kidder Smith, *A Pictorial History of*

Architecture in America (New York: American Heritage, 1976), 2: 612.

■ 185

Kneses Tifereth Israel Synagogue; Port Chester, NY; 1956.
A monumental building, it is white inside and out except where rows of slit windows, arrayed from floor to ceiling, are filled with brightly colored stained glass. As many as a thousand worshipers can be seated in the combined sanctuary and social hall area, a giant room 37 feet high.
Structural engineers: Eipel Engineering. Landscape architect: Charles Middeleer. Contractor: Marcello Mezzullo.

See: Architectural Record 117 (June 1955): 177–208; 120 (December 1956): 123–29. *Architect and Building News* 218 (December 28, 1960): 821–22.

■ 186

Munson-Williams-Proctor Institute; Utica, NY; 1960.
A spacious, granite-faced art museum with sharp, square lines and no windows above the ground-floor level. Giant bronze-sheathed girders, two on each face, strike bluntly up the walls, then turn at right angles to crisscross the roof. Unusual facilities inside include a children's gallery and an auditorium that seats 300.
Supervising architects: Bice & Baird. Engineers: Lev Zetlin (structural); Fred S. Dubin Associates (mechanical). Landscaping: Charles Middeleer. General contractor: George A. Fuller Co.

See: Architectural Forum 111 (September 1959): 118; 113 (December 1960): 90–95.

L'Architecture d'Aujourd'hui, no. 100 (February–March 1962): 29–31.

■ 187

Museum of Modern Art Additions and Sculpture Garden; New York, NY; 1953; further changes and additions, 1964.
The main museum building, completed in 1939, was designed by Goodwin & Stone. The added wing designed by Johnson is distinguished by an ambience of tastefully appointed serenity. It comprises classrooms and offices plus a small cafeteria that lets out onto the Abby Aldrich Rockefeller Sculpture Garden. Further additions, designed primarily by Cesar Pelli, are described in entry no. 319.
Associate architect: Landis Gores. Structural engineers: Eipel Engineering Co. Landscape architect: James Fanning.

Honors: Bard Award, 1966.

See: Architectural Forum 102 (May 1955): 146–49. *Progressive Architecture* 45 (July 1964): 65–66. *Interiors* 123 (July 1964): 92–95.

■ 188

Museum Wing for Pre-Columbian Art, Dumbarton Oaks; Washington, DC; 1963.
Each of this mini-museum's eight round, interconnecting rooms, arranged in a tidy square around a central courtyard, was designed to display the art of a different cultural group. Exquisitely detailed, they feature curved glass walls, teak and marble floors, and eight separate domes linked together by a wavy-margined, bronze-trimmed roof.
Engineers: Lev Zetlin & Associates (structural); Jaros, Baum & Bolles (mechanical/electrical). General Contractor: George A. Fuller Co.

See: AIA Journal 69 (July 1980): 44–49. *Architectural Forum* 120 (March 1964): 106–11. *Architectural Record* 132 (July 1962): 120–21.

■ 189

New York State Theater, Lincoln Center; New York, NY; 1964.
The lushly ornamented red and gold interior of this 2,700-seat theater contrasts boldly with its neoclassical, travertine facade. Its three balconies are horseshoe shaped and, at the first balcony level, a spectacular promenade area lures theatergoers at intermission.
Engineers: Severud-Elstad-Krueger Associates

96 Amon Carter Museum of Western Art; Fort Worth, TX; 1961. *See* Entry 183. (Courtesy John Burgee Architects: New York, NY. Photographer: © Richard Payne, AIA 1988.)

96

(structural); Syska & Hennessy (mechanical).
Consultants for theater architecture: Ben
Schlanger and Werner Gabler. Stage consultants:
Donald Oenslager and Walter Unruh.
Contractor: Turner Construction Co.

See: *Architectural Record* 135 (May 1964): 137–
44. *Progressive Architecture* 45 (May 1964): 58–
59. *Interiors* 123 (July 1964): 86–91.

■ **190**

**Sheldon Memorial Art Gallery,
University of Nebraska; Lincoln, NE;
1963 (see Illus. 97).**
This boldly elegant museum contains
two floors of galleries, a 300-seat
amphitheater, offices, and quarters for
technical services. Its central Great Hall,
30 feet high, is glazed on both its outer
walls. Most of the rest of the building is
windowless, adorned by gracefully
curving columns with splayed tops that
trace a series of arches on its travertine
exterior.
Supervising architects: Hazen & Robinson.
Engineers: Lev Zetlin & Associates (structural);
Jaros, Baum & Bolles (mechanical). Contractor:
Olson Construction Co.

See: *Architectural Record* 132 (July 1962): 122–
23; 134 (August 1963): 129–31. *Arts +
Architecture* 80 (August 1963): 18–21, 30–31.

■ **191**

Shrine; New Harmony, IN; 1960.
Built as a memorial to the Rappites who
founded New Harmony as a utopian
religious community in the early 1800s,
the shrine is 50 feet high, with a cedar-
shingled dome that undulates like a not-
quite-fallen parachute. At its center, open
to the air, rests a bronze *Virgin* sculpted
by Jacques Lipchitz.
Structural engineers: Wilcox & Erickson.
General contractor: Traylor Brothers.

Honors: AIA Honor Award, 1961.

See: *AIA Journal* 35 (April 1961): 74–77.
Architectural Forum 111 (September 1959):
115–23; 113 (September 1960): 128.

Philip JOHNSON and Richard FOSTER

■ **192**

**Kline Science Center, Yale University;
New Haven, CT; 1965 (see Illus. 98).**
A complex of buildings erected near

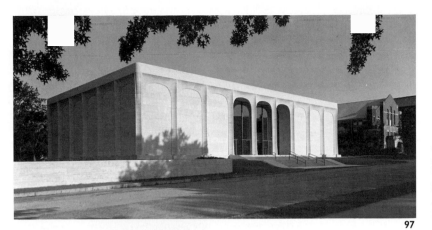

Yale's older facilities for study and
research in the natural sciences, it
provides added space for work in biology,
geology, and chemistry, as well as a
related library. The Kline Biology Tower,
sited on a hill, is its most striking element.
Engineers: Lev Zetlin & Assoc. (structural);
Strong & Jones (mechanical). Landscape
architects: Zion & Breen. General contractor:
E & P Construction.

Honors: PA Design Award, 1964, for Kline
Biology Tower; AIA Bicentennial List, one
nomination.

See: *Architectural Record* 141 (June 1967):
140–45. *Progressive Architecture* 48 (February
1967): 90–97. *Architectural Design* 34 (April
1964): 176–77.

Philip JOHNSON; WITTENBERG, DELONY & DAVIS

■ **193**

**Bailey Library, Hendrix College;
Conway, AR; 1967.**
An unusual 2-story academic library, it is
sited centrally on campus yet built almost

completely underground so as to conserve open space. Ingenious landscaping, which includes many berms, transforms its roof area into a plaza and provides entry to the library from a connecting sunken plaza alongside. Engineers: W. H. Goodman, Jr. (mechanical); Engineering Consultants (structural). Landscape consultant: Joe Lambert.

Honors: Award of Merit, 1972 Library Buildings Award Program, conferred by AIA et al.

See: *AIA Journal* 57 (April 1972): 45. *Architectural Record* 146 (December 1969): 87–96. G. E. Kidder Smith, *A Pictorial History of Architecture in America* (New York: American Heritage, 1976), 2: 604–5.

Philip JOHNSON/John BURGEE

■ 194

AT&T Building; New York, NY; 1984 (see Illus. 99).
This stately 36-story office tower, 647 feet high, is finished in granite and topped by a much-discussed Chippendale-style broken pediment. At street level, a 65-foot-high central arch and three tall oblong entries at either side invite pedestrians into a magnificent vaulted lobby/loggia area shaped by repeats of arches, columns, and oculi. A monumental golden sculpture, *The Spirit of Communication*—sculpted by Evelyn Beatrice Longman in 1914 and nicknamed Golden Boy—dominates the lobby. At the rear of the building there's a Galleria with shops.
Associate: Alan Ritchie; field representative: Rolf Hedlund. Simmons Architects, associates (Harry Simmons, Russell Patterson). Consultants: Robertson & Fowler (structural); Leroy Callender (associate engineers); Cosentini Assoc. (mechanical); Mueser, Rutledge, Johnston & DeSimone (foundations); ISD Inc. (interior design). Construction manager: Frank Briscoe Co., Crow/Briscoe joint venture, HRH Construction.

See: *Architecture* 74 (February 1985): 46–55 and cover. *Progressive Architecture* 65 (February 1984): 70–75. *A + U: Architecture and Urbanism,* no. 172 (January 1985): 19–26.

■ 195

Boston Public Library Addition; Boston, MA; 1972 (see Illus. 100).
The library's original turn-of-the-century building was designed in stately Renaissance Revival style by McKim, Mead & White. The boldly contrasting addition features giant exterior arches and columns that echo the older building's smaller, more conservative ones and a structural system that yields ample unobstructed space within.

Honors: AIA Bicentennial List, four nominations.

See: *Architectural Record* 152 (December 1972): 42. *Progressive Architecture* 54 (February 1973): 32. G. E. Kidder Smith, *A Pictorial History of Architecture in America* (New York: American Heritage, 1976), 1: 92–93.

■ 196

Crystal Cathedral, also known as Garden Grove Community Church; Garden Grove, CA; 1980 (see Illus. 101).

The exterior of this extraordinary church, designed for a television minister who was used to preaching outdoors in a drive-in, is reflective glass supported by a lacy framework of slender white pipe trusses. It's huge—415 by 207 feet by 128 feet high at its apex—and is shaped like an elongated four-pointed star, with stepped concrete balconies in three of its four points. Ventilated by banks of centrally operated windows and 90-foot-high hangerlike doors, it seats almost 3,000.

Field architect and civil engineer: Albert C. Martin. Engineers: Severud-Perrone-Szegezdy-Sturm (structural); Cosentini Assoc. (mechanical/electrical). Acoustical consultants: Klepper-Marshall-King. Joint-venture builder: C. L. Peck, Contractor; Morse-Diesel, Inc.; and Koll Co.

See: *AIA Journal* 70 (mid-May 1981): 148–57. *Architectural Record* 168 (November 1980): 77–85. *Progressive Architecture* 61 (December 1980): 76–85 and cover. *GA Document,* no. 3 (Winter 1981): 22–32.

■ 197

IDS Center; Minneapolis, MN; 1972 (see Illus. 102).

Four buildings, including a 19-story hotel and the 51-story IDS tower, faced with mirror glass and strikingly notched, surround 20,000 square feet of covered mall. This central square, the Crystal Court, is canopied by an exhilaratingly varied grid of metal-framed glass and plastic cubes and is penetrated by four Skyways (glassed-in, second-floor-level pedestrian walkways) that thread into it from adjoining streets.

Associated architects: Edward F. Baker Associates. Engineers: Severud-Perrone-Sturm-Conlin-Bandel (structural); Cosentini Associates (mechanical). General contractors: Turner Construction Co.

Honors: AIA Honor Award, 1975; Bartlett Award, 1975; AIA Bicentennial List, one nomination.

See: *AIA Journal* 68 (June 1979): 52–59. *Architectural Forum* 140 (November 1973): 38–45. *A + U: Architecture and Urbanism,* special issue no. 6, (June 1979): 85–104.

101 Crystal Cathedral (Garden Grove Community Church); Garden Grove, CA; 1980. *See* Entry 196. (Courtesy John Burgee Architects; New York, NY. Photographer: © Richard Payne, AIA 1988.)

102 IDS Center; Minneapolis, MN; 1972. *See* Entry 197. (Courtesy John Burgee Architects; New York, NY. Photographer: © Richard Payne, AIA 1988.)

■ 198

Republic Bank Center; Houston, TX; 1984 (see Illus. 103).

This imposing banking and office complex, granite sheathed and almost 800 feet high, dwarfs and contrasts sharply with the same firm's Pennzoil Place across the street. The stepped roofline of a Dutch Staat house is used four times: first to shape a huge, skylighted banking hall, 125 feet high, then to shape the setbacks—which resemble three stacked towers—of the skyscraper beside it. A dramatic barrel-vaulted arcade runs through both buildings.

Associate: Stephen Achilles; associate architects: Kendall/Heaton. Consultants: CBM Engineers (structural); I. A. Naman & Assoc. (mechanical/electrical). General contractor: Turner Construction.

See: *Progressive Architecture* 65 (February 1984): 86–93. *Domus,* no. 662 (June 1985): 26–27. *A + U: Architecture and Urbanism,* no. 172 (January 1985): 35–42. *GA Document,* no. 12 (January 1985): 80–87.

103 Republic Bank Center; Houston, TX; 1984. *See* Entry 198. (Courtesy John Burgee Architects; New York, NY. Photographer: © Richard Payne, AIA 1988.)

103

■ 199

Pennzoil Place; Houston, TX; 1976 (see Illus. 104).
Here's 1,400,000 square feet of office and commercial space wrapped in a dramatic package: twin 36-story trapezoidal towers that are mirror images of each other. At ground level they define connected triangular plazas enclosed by sloping walls of steel-framed glass.
Engineers: Ellisor Engineers (structural); I. A. Naman & Associates (mechanical/electrical). Contractor: Zapata Construction.

Honors: AIA Bicentennial List, one nomination; AIA Honor Award, 1977; AISC Architectural Award of Excellence, 1977; R. S. Reynolds Memorial Award, 1977.

See: *AIA Journal* 71 (June 1982): 38–43. *Architectural Record* 160 (November 1976): 101–10. *Progressive Architecture* 58 (August 1977): 66–73. *Johnson/Burgee: Architecture,* text by Nory Miller, photographs by Richard Payne (New York: Random House, 1979).

Philip JOHNSON/John BURGEE; S. I. MORRIS ASSOCIATES

104 Pennzoil Place; Houston, TX; 1976. *See* Entry 199. (Courtesy John Burgee Architects; New York, NY. Photographer: © Richard Payne, AIA 1988.)

104

■ 200

Transco Tower; Houston, TX; 1983 (see Illus. 105).
From a distance, this majestic 900-foot-high office building set on an ample grassy site looks as if it's made of stone, but in fact its skin combines two kinds of glass: mirror and gray tinted. Setbacks toward its top recall 1920s Art Deco; long vertical grooves in its facade create a wealth of bay windows; at ground level there's a huge, ceremonial doorway framed in pink granite.
Associate: Stephen Achilles. Consultants: CBM Engineers (structural); I. A. Naman & Assoc. (mechanical); Zion & Breen (landscape). General contractor: J. A. Jones Construction.

Honors: AISC Architectural Award of Excellence, 1985.

See: *Architecture* 74 (May 1985): 182–87. *Progressive Architecture* 65 (February 1984): 94–97. *A + U: Architecture and Urbanism,* no. 172 (January 1985): 43–48. *GA Document,* no. 12 (January 1985): 109–13.

105

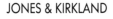

■ 202

Mississauga City Hall; Mississauga, Ontario; 1987 (see Illus. 107).
This 626,000-square-foot complex, clad in yellow brick banded with concrete and designed to resemble a cluster of farm buildings, includes plazas, gardens, and an amphitheater. Among its notable interior spaces are a monumental Great Hall—a square court surrounded by an arcade, richly finished in two kinds of marble, green and coral, accented by black granite —a 5-story Grand Stair, and a handsome, circular council chamber.
Consultants: M. S. Yolles & Partners (structural); Mitchell Partnership (mechanical). Construction manager: Jackson-Lewis.

Honors: PA Architectural Design Citation, 1985.

See: Progressive Architecture 67 (August 1987): 69–79 and cover. *Canadian Architect* 32 (June 1987): 20–35 and cover. *Building Design,* no. 811 (November 7, 1986): 16–19. P. Arnell and T. Bickford, eds., *Mississauga City Hall: A Canadian Competition* (New York: Rizzoli, 1984).

105 Transco Tower; Houston, TX; 1983. *See* Entry 200. (Courtesy John Burgee Architects; New York, NY. Photographer: © Richard Payne, AIA 1988.)

E. Fay JONES (Subsequent name of firm: Fay JONES & Maurice JENNINGS ARCHITECTS)

■ 201

Thorncrown Chapel; Eureka Springs, AR; 1980 (see Illus. 106).
This exquisite chapel in the Ozark woods is small (24 feet by 60 feet by 48 feet high) and walled with glass. It rises from fieldstone floors and two low fieldstone walls; otherwise it is built almost entirely of standard-size lumber worked with the attention to detail of a master cabinet-maker. Repeating diamond shapes loft upward to its overhanging peaked roof. It has been compared to Lloyd Wright's Wayfarers Chapel (see entry no. 500). General contractor: Jerry Labounty.

Honors: AIA Honor Award, 1981; American Wood Council First Honor Award, 1981.

See: AIA Journal 70 (mid-May 1981): 140–47 and cover. *Architectural Record* 169 (March 1981): 88–93 and cover. *Architectural Review* 170 (July 1981): 40–41. *Interiors* 140 (May 1981): 176–77.

106 Thorncrown Chapel; Eureka Springs, AR; 1980. *See* Entry 201. (Courtesy Fay Jones & Associate Architects; Fayetteville, AR. Photographer: © R. Gregg Hursley.)

106

Design and Technology in Architecture (New York: Wiley, 1985), 184–91.

■ **204**

Center for British Art and Studies, Yale University; New Haven, CT; 1977 (see Illus. 108).
Built of subtly detailed reinforced concrete and located across the street from the Yale Art Gallery, which was designed by Kahn in association with Douglas Orr (see entry no. 298), the center's strongly rectilinear exterior is accentuated by dark glass and by panels of gray stainless steel. Its interior features include a cylindrical stair enclosure, a 3-story, skylight-roofed inner court, and exposed satin-finish aluminum ducts. Completed after Kahn's death by Pellechia & Meyers, architects. Engineers: Pfister, Tor & Associates (structural); van Zelm, Heywood & Shadford (mechanical/electrical). General contractor: George B. H. Macomber Co.

Honors: AIA Honor Award, 1978; Bartlett Award 1978 (to Pellechia & Meyers).

See: *AIA Journal* 67 (mid-May 1978): 80–89 and cover. *Architectural Record* 161 (June 1977): 95–104 and cover. *Progressive Architecture* 59 (May 1978): 76–81.

■ **205**

Eleanor Donnelly Erdman Hall, Bryn Mawr College; Bryn Mawr, PA; 1965.
Dark gray slate outlined by white concrete forms the calmly symmetrical facade of this dormitory and dining hall. Its exterior design, marked by regular crenellations and set off by parapets, calls to mind a medieval castle.

107 Mississauga City Hall; Mississauga, Ontario; 1987. *See* Entry 202. (Courtesy Jones/Kirkland Architects; Toronto, Ontario. Photographer: Robert Burley, Design Archive; Toronto, Ontario.)

107

Louis I. KAHN

Winner, AIA Gold Medal, 1971; Royal Gold Medal, 1972. (See also entry no. 298.)

■ **203**

Alfred Newton Richards Medical Research Building, University of Pennsylvania; Philadelphia, PA; 1960.
Three 8-layered towers containing offices and labs cluster around a 10-story central tower housing elevators, lavatories, pens for laboratory animals, and similar "servant areas." Constructed of Kahn's customary reinforced concrete but faced with brick to match the rest of the campus, the building combines a look of "brawny sculpture" with efficient, precise design and economy of construction.
Structural consultant: August E. Komendant. Engineers: Keast & Hood (structural); Cronheim & Weger (mechanical). Landscape architect: Ian McHarg. General contractor: Joseph R. Farrell, Inc.

Honors: AIA Bicentennial List, six nominations.

See: *Architectural Forum* 113 (July 1960): 82–87, 185. *Architectural Record* 128 (August 1960): 149–56. Y. Futagawa, ed., *Louis I. Kahn; Richards Medical Research Building . . . Salk Institute . . . ,* text by Fumihiko Maki, Global Architecture, no. 5 (Tokyo: A. D. A. Edita, 1971). David Guise,

108 Center for British Art and Studies, Yale University; New Haven, CT; 1977. *See* Entry 204. (Courtesy Yale Center for British Art; New Haven, CT. Photographer: Tom Brown.)

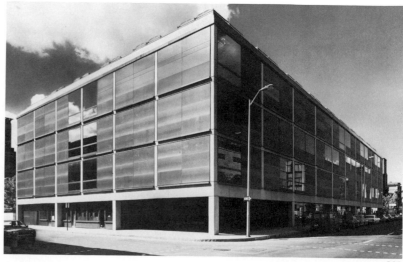

108

Structural consultant: August E. Komendant. Engineers: Keast & Hood (structural); John W. Furlow, Inc. (mechanical/electrical). Landscape architect; George Patton. General contractor: Nason & Cullen.

See: Architectural Forum 123 (November 1965): 58–63. *Zodiac* 17 (1967): 58–117. *Kokusai Kentiku* 34 (January 1967): 62.

■ 206

First Unitarian Church; Rochester, NY; 1967.

A church with the look of a medieval fortress, it is faced with red brick and includes four towers, whose unusual clerestory windows admit light from above into the sanctuary.

Honors: AIA Bicentennial List, two nominations.

See: Kokusai Kentiku 34 (January 1967): 48–50. *Architecture Canada* 45 (February 1968): 31–42. G. E. Kidder Smith, *A Pictorial History of Architecture in America* (New York: American Heritage, 1976), 1: 259.

■ 207

Kimbell Art Museum; Fort Worth, TX; 1972 (see Illus. 109).

A very large museum, 318 by 174 feet, constructed as a series of cycloid, post-tensioned reinforced concrete vaults, each 100 by 22 feet and supported on four corner columns. Natural light flows in through skylights and lunettes; the exterior is enhanced by roofs of lead and infill walls of travertine.
Project manager: Marshall D. Meyers. Resident associate architect: Preston M. Geren & Associates. Structural engineer: August E. Komendant. General contractor: Thos. S. Byrne & Co. Landscape architect: George Patton.

Honors: AIA Honor Award, 1975; Bartlett Award, 1975; AIA Bicentennial List, three nominations.

See: AIA Journal 71 (August 1982): 36–43. *Interiors* 132 (March 1973): 84–91. *Architectural Review* 155 (June 1974): 319–29. Y. Futagawa, ed., *Louis I. Kahn . . . Kimbell Art Museum,* text by Marshall D. Meyers, Global Architecture, no. 38 (Tokyo: A. D. A. Edita, 1976).

■ 208

Phillips Exeter Academy Library; Exeter, NH; 1972 (see Illus. 110).

Brick, concrete, and wood are masterfully

109 Kimbell Art Museum; Fort Worth, TX; 1972. *See* Entry 207. (Courtesy Kimbell Art Museum; Fort Worth, TX. Photographer: Michael Bodycomb.)

109

combined in this large library for a private school. In its brick exterior, windows grow progressively larger from the second to the fifth levels while, at ground level, an arcade welcomes entry from the campus. Inside, the Great Hall features curving concrete stairs and, in powerfully trussed balcony walls, giant circular openings through which stack areas can be seen.
Project manager: Winton F. Scott. Site manager Earle W. Bolton. Engineers: Keast & Hood (structural); Dubin-Mindell-Bloome Associates (mechanical/electrical). Landscape architect: George Patton. Contractor: H. P. Cummings.

Honors: AIA Bicentennial List, one nomination.

See: AIA Journal 74 (February 1985): 74–79. *Architectural Forum* 139 (October 1973): 26–35. *Architectural Review* 155 (June 1974): 336–42. Y. Futagawa, ed., *Louis I. Kahn . . . Exeter Library, Phillips Exeter Academy . . . ,* text by Romaldo Giurgola, Global Architecture, no. 35 (Tokyo: A. D. A. Edita, 1975).

■ 209

Salk Institute for Biological Studies; La Jolla, CA; 1965.

A massive research complex built of elegantly finished reinforced concrete and

sited on the shores of the Pacific. On either side of a garden stand two sternly sculptured laboratory buildings, each 65 feet wide and 245 feet long; individual "studies" for scientists arc in towers facing onto the garden and open to sea breezes as well.
Structural consultant: August E. Komendant. Associated structural engineers: Fervor-Dorland & Associates. Electrical-mechanical engineers: Fred F. Dubin Associates. Landscape architect: Roland S. Hoyt.

See: AIA Journal 66 (March 1977): 42–49. *Architectural Forum* 122 (May 1965): 36–45. Y. Futagawa, ed., *Louis I. Kahn; Richards Medical Research Building . . . ,* Global Architecture, no. 5 (Tokyo: A. D. A. Edita, 1971).

KALLMAN, McKINNELL & KNOWLES

■ 210

Boston City Hall; Boston, MA; 1969.

An extraordinary building like a giant abstract sculpture, it won a design competition in 1962 but also has been compared to a bunker or an egg crate. It is set in City Hall Square—multileveled and brick paved—an exciting open space

110

that reaches out to the Federal Office Building on one side and Faneuil Hall (see entry no. 464), down the hill, on the other.
Associated architects: Campbell, Aldrich & Nulty. Project managers: Robert C. Abrahamson, Henry A. Wood. Design coordinator: Gordon F. Tully. Engineers: Le Messurier Associates (structural); Greenleaf Associates (mechanical). General contractor: J. W. Bateson Co., Inc.

Honors: AIA Honor Award. 1969; Bartlett Award, 1969; AIA Bicentennial List, twelve nominations.

See: *AIA Journal* 69 (September 1980): 46–53. *Architectural Forum* 130 (January–February 1969): 38–53. *Architectural Record* 145 (February 1969): 133–44. *Architectural Review* 147 (June 1970): 398–411.

KALLMAN McKINNELL & WOOD

Winner, AIA Architectural Firm Award, 1984.

■ 211

The American Academy of Arts and Sciences; Cambridge, MA; 1981.
This stately 2-story building, faced in red brick and, behind rows of piers, heavily glazed with small square panes framed in mahogany, combines postmodern and Arts and Crafts design elements and features much interior detailing in mahogany. Pillared arcades edge its central atrium. Its first floor—devoted to a lecture hall, dining facilities, and spaces

for meetings from large to very small—has a deliberately mazelike plan.
Job captain: Hans Huber. Engineers: Le Messurier Assoc. (structural); Thompson Consultants (mechanical/electrical). General contractor: Walsh Brothers.

See: *AIA Journal* 71 (mid-May 1982): 134–44. *Architectural Record* 169 (November 1981): 79–87. *A + U: Architecture and Urbanism*, no. 143 (August 1982): 43–52. *Architectural Review* 170 (October 1981): 215–21.

KAPLAN & McLAUGHLIN

■ 212

Martin Luther King Square; San Francisco, CA; 1969 (see Illus. 111).
This low-income cluster housing development takes advantage of a sloping site to fit 116 relatively spacious units into one city block while providing most apartments with private entrances and many with private gardens. Apartments contain from one to four bedrooms; a typical building contains 3 to 4 apartments.
Engineers: Yanow & Bauer (mechanical); Gilbert, Forsberg, Diekmann, Schmidt (structural). General contractor: Winston A. Burnett.

Honors: 1972 Design Honor Award for Nonprofit-Sponsored Low and Moderate Income Housing.

See: *AIA Journal* 58 (November 1972): 38–39. *Architectural Record* 143 (June 1968): 147–49; 147 (March 1970): 111. *Deutsche Bauzeitung* 105, no. 3 (1971): 273–74.

■ 213

St. Mark's Hospital; Salt Lake City, UT; 1973 (see Illus. 112).
In this 304-bed hospital, thoughtfully designed for easy modification and expansion, nursing units are triangular to shorten walking distances, patients' rooms are generously glazed to give each a fine view of the out-of-doors, and major corridors are glazed either along one side or at one end to enhance the feeling of openness.
Project team: Herbert McLaughlin, James Diaz, and Roy Latke. Associated architects: Snedaker, Budd & Watts. Engineers: H. C. Hughes, Page & Assoc. (structural); Bridgers & Paxton

111   Martin Luther King Square; San Francisco, CA; 1969. *See* Entry 212. (Courtesy Kaplan, McLaughlin, Diaz; San Francisco, CA. Photographer: Joshua Freiwald.)

112   St. Mark's Hospital; Salt Lake City, UT; 1973. *See* Entry 213. (Courtesy Kaplan, McLaughlin, Diaz; San Francisco, CA. Photographer: Noel Barnhurst.)

Honors: American Wood Council Citation Award, 1983.

See: *Progressive Architecture* 62 (April 1981): 118–21; 64 (April 1983): 42. *Space Design,* no. 215 (August 1982): 106. *Techniques et Architecture,* no. 344 (November 1982): 109–13.

KELLY & GRUZEN (subsequent names of firm: GRUZEN & PARTNERS; GRUZEN SAMTON STEINGLASS)

■ **215**

Chatham Towers; New York, NY; 1965 (see Illus. 113).

Inexpensively built yet luxurious in feeling is this 240-unit, reinforced concrete, middle-income housing development in Lower Manhattan. Most apartments have corner exposures; many have terraces. Because the buildings take up just 15 percent of the site, there's room for a sophisticated plaza and a well-equipped playground.

Associate in charge: George G. Shimamota; project architect: Raymond P. Tuccio. Engineers: Weinberger, Frieman, Leichtman & Quinn (structural); Herman Scherr (mechanical). Landscape architects: M. Paul Friedberg & Associates.

Honors: Award of Merit, 1964, New York State Architects Association; Bard Award, 1967.

See: *Progressive Architecture* 47 (February 1966): 132–39. *L'Architecture d'Aujourd'hui,* no. 126 (June–July 1966): 94–95. *Deutsche Bauzeitung* 100 (October 1966): 837–40.

William KESSLER

■ **216**

Center for Creative Studies, College of Art and Design; Detroit, MI; 1975 (see Illus. 114).

Built of precast concrete and featuring innovative cylindrical columns, notched to receive beams, that are both striking and functional, here is an environment for design students that proudly reveals the bare facts about its structure. Modules repeat emphatically, most walls are left unpainted, and pipes are left exposed.

Engineers: Robert Darvas & Associates (structural); Hoyem Associates (mechanical/

(mechanical). General contractor: Tolboe Construction.

See: *AIA Journal* 55 (January 1971): 28–31. *Architectural Record* 154 (September 1973): 156–60. *Modern Hospital* 122 (March 1974): 53–58.

KELBAUGH & LEE

■ **214**

Milford Reservation Environmental Center; Milford, PA; 1981.

This showplace for passive solar technology provides a comfortable setting where inner-city youth visit for two-week stints year-round to study environmental issues. Clad in cedar siding, the lodgelike structure is 225 feet long to maximize its southern exposure where it has Trombe walls, water drums, and other heat-controlling features. Much of its north side is buried. Overhead there's a 160-foot-long double-glazed skylight atop a water-heating pipe. Inside are a dormitory for 117, classrooms, and a dining hall.

Project designer: Douglas S. Kelbaugh; project manager: Sang J. Lee; landscape: Alan Goodheart. Consultants: Raval Engineering (structural); Robert Bennett (mechanical). General contractor: Dorsan.

architect: Eberhard H. Zeidler; project architect: Thomas W. Gunn. *For Giffels Assoc.:* project director: John M. Breed; assistant project director: John Urban. Engineering: A. V. Cornwall, George B. Davidson, Fred L. Lantz, R. M. Patel, H. M. Baghdadi. Landscape architects: Elon Mickels & Assoc. General contractor: Turner Construction.

Honors: AIA Honor Award, 1980; Governor General's Medal, 1982.

See: AIA Journal 69 (mid-May 1980): 214–19. *Architectural Record* 167 (April 1980): 83–90. *Interiors* 140 (January 1981): 70–71. *Architectural Review* 169 (May 1981): 307–8.

113 Chatham Towers; New York, NY; 1965. *See* Entry 215. (Courtesy Gruzen, Samton, Steinglass; New York, NY.)

113

Morris KETCHUM, Jr.

■ 218

Lila Acheson Wallace World of Birds Building, Bronx Zoo; New York, NY; 1972.

Simulated natural environments for various types of birds are provided by "an asparagus-like bunch of cut-off cylinders, ellipses and free forms joined by ramps." Thanks to abundant skylights, natural vegetation thrives within.

Job captain: Paul Palmieri. Engineers: Paul Weidlinger (structural); Wald & Zigas (mechanical/electrical). Contractor: William L. Crow Construction Co.

Honors: Bard Award, 1969.

See: AIA Journal 58 (August 1972): 53–54. *Architectural Forum* 130 (June 1969): 90–91; 137 (September 1972): 62–65.

114 Center for Creative Studies, College of Art and Design; Detroit, MI; 1975. *See* Entry 216. (Courtesy William Kessler; Detroit, MI. Photographer: Balthazar Korab.)

114

electrical). Landscape architects; William Kessler & Associates.

Honors: AIA Honor Award, 1976; Bartlett Award, 1976.

See: AIA Journal 65 (April 1976): 50–51. *Domus,* no. 569 (April 1977): 22–24.

William KESSLER; ZEIDLER PARTNERSHIP; GIFFELS ASSOCIATES

■ 217

Medical complex: Detroit Receiving Hospital and University Health

Center, Wayne State University; Detroit Medical Center Concourse; Detroit, MI; 1979 (see Illus. 115).

This huge (almost 900,000-square-foot) and intricate complex comprises several cruciform structures, each with an atrium at its center. Clad in silver aluminum accented at intervals by red-orange panels and, at ground level, by yellow half vaults over office and public areas, its interior spaces also are enlivened by bright colors and by decorative art. Huge concrete wedges that serve as periscopes and light wells for a futuristic underground concourse sit like abstract sculpture on its lawn.

For William Kessler & Assoc.: architect in charge: William H. Kessler; project designer: James A. Cardoza. *For Zeidler Partnership:* executive

KEYES, LETHBRIDGE & CONDON

■ 219

Tiber Island; Washington, DC; 1965.
Built of reinforced concrete and gray-tan brick, this appealing residential complex near the Potomac River comprises four 8-story apartment buildings, eighty-five row houses with garden areas, a two-level parking garage, and a central plaza with a pool.

Landscape architect: Eric Paepke. Engineers: Carl Hansen (structural); Kluckhuhn & McDavid Co. (mechanical); Eberlin & Eberlin (site).

level and sited atop a handsome plaza. Below street level, under the plaza, there's a huge public concourse where as many as 2,000 people at a time can apply for licenses, pay bills to city bureaus, and the like.
Engineers: McCormick-Taylor Associates (structural); Charles S. Leopold, Inc. (mechanical/plumbing/electrical).

Honors: PA First Design Award, 1962; AIA Honor Award, 1967.

See: AIA Journal 47 (June 1967): 49. *Progressive Architecture* 46 (December 1965): 108–17, 151. *Architettura* 11 (April 1966): 808–9.

115

Honors: AIA Honor Award, 1966.

See: AIA Journal 46 (July 1966): 30–33. *Architectural Forum* 123 (July–August 1965): 48–51. *Architectural Record* 134 (September 1963): 196.

KING & KING *see* I. M. PEI; KING & KING

KISTNER, WRIGHT & WRIGHT; Edward H. FICKETT; S. B. BARNES

■ 220

Passenger-Cargo Terminal Berths 93A–93B; San Pedro, CA; 1963?
A harbor terminal or "transit shed" for the loading and unloading of ships, this building innovatively provides separate facilities for the handling of passengers and of cargo. On the passenger level there are lounges, customs inspection areas, and a "spectators' waving gallery."
Joint venture of Kistner, Wright & Wright and Edward H. Fickett, architects, and S. B. Barnes, structural engineer. Engineers: Los Angeles Harbor Department. Landscape architects: Armstrong & Sharfman. General contractor: L. C. Dunn, Inc.

Honors: AISC Architectural Award of Excellence, 1963.

See: Architectural Record 134 (September 1963): 163–68. *Arts + Architecture* 80 (August 1963): 26–27, 30. *Baumeister* 61 (January 1964): 8–12.

Vincent G. KLING (subsequent name of firm: THE KLING PARTNERSHIP)

■ 221

Municipal Services Building; Philadelphia, PA; 1965 (see Illus. 116).
A 16-story municipal office building largely elevated on columns above street

■ 222

Penn Center Transportation Building and Concourse; Philadelphia, PA; total Penn Center redevelopment, including City Hall West Plaza, completed 1976 (see Illus. 117).
Linked by a four-block underground concourse and shopping promenade, here subways, a railroad, and intercity buses come together. Aboveground there's a 1,000-car parking garage, the Greyhound bus terminal, and an 18-story office tower, the Transportation Building.

116

Lipshutz. Engineers: Souza & True (structural); Shooshanian Engineering Associates (mechanical). Contractors: Kirkland Construction Co.

See: AIA Journal 53 (February 1970): 37–45. *House and Home* 45 (February 1974): 88–93. *Architecture Plus* 2 (March–April 1974): 45–48.

117

117 Penn Center Transportation Building and Concourse; Philadelphia, PA; 1976. *See* Entry 222. (Courtesy The Kling-Lindquist Partnership; Philadelphia, PA. Photographer: Lawrence S. Williams, Inc.)

Engineers: McCormick & Taylor Associates (structural); Robert J. Siegel, Inc. (mechanical/electrical).

Honors: PA Award Citation, 1955.

See: Architectural Record 118 (August 1955): 169–72; 121 (May 1957): 190–96. *Progressive Architecture* 38 (June 1957): 168.

■ 223

Westinghouse Molecular Electronic Laboratory; Elkridge, MD; 1963 (see Illus. 118).
This facility was designed with elaborate air-conditioning and purification equipment to provide superclean atmospheric conditions for the manufacture of tiny, highly sophisticated electronic devices. Offices look out on a pleasant courtyard enhanced by a pool in which are stored 50,000 gallons of water needed for fire protection.
Engineers: Allabach & Rennis (structural);

Charles S. Leopold, Inc. (mechanical/electrical). General contractor: Kirby & McGuire.

Honors: AIA Merit Award, 1964; AISC Architectural Award of Excellence, 1964.

See: Architectural Record 136 (July 1964): 163–78. *Progressive Architecture* 45 (November 1964): 158–60; *L'Architecture Française* 31 (November–December 1970): 16–17.

Carl KOCH

■ 224

Lewis Wharf Rehabilitation; Boston, MA; 1973.
An attractive and popular complex of housing, offices, shops, restaurants, and recreational facilities recycled from what formerly was a rundown waterfront area.
Associates in charge: Margaret M. Ross, Leon

KOHN PEDERSON FOX

■ 225

Proctor & Gamble General Offices; Cincinnati, OH; 1985 (see Illus. 119).
The fenestration and cladding (limestone with accents in marble and granite) of this 800,000-square-foot, basically **L**-shaped building echo those of P&G's earlier headquarters nearby. Where its two wings meet, two octagonal 17-story towers rise, each topped by a pyramid; glass bridges connect them. Low, multifaceted structures—an entry pavilion and an auditorium—fit between them. Interiors are adorned in Art Deco style.
Partner in charge: A. Eugene Kohn; partner in charge of design: William Pederson; managing partner: Robert Cioppa; partner in charge of interior design: Patricia Conway of Kohn Pederson Fox Conway. Consultants: Bentley-Meisner (landscape); Weiskopf & Pickworth (structural); Syska & Hennessy (mechanical). General contractor: Huber, Hunt & Nichols.

Honors: AIA Honor Award, 1987.

See: Architectural Record 173 (June 1985): 162–69. *Architecture* 74 (November 1985): 34–39. *Progressive Architecture* 66 (October 1985): 71–87 and cover. *Inland Architect* 29 (September–October 1985): 33–36.

118 Westinghouse Molecular Electronic Laboratory; Elkridge, MD; 1963. *See* Entry 223. (Courtesy The Kling-Lindquist Partnership; Philadelphia, PA. Photographer: Lawrence S. Williams, Inc.)

118

Associated architects: Perkins & Will Group; partner in charge: A. Eugene Kohn; partner in charge, design: William Pederson, senior designer: Alexander Ward. Consultants: Gillum-Colaco (structural); Environmental Systems Design (mechanical/electrical). General contractor: Inland Construction.

Honors: AIA Honor Award, 1984.

See: *Architecture* 73 (May 1984): 186–93. *Progressive Architecture* 64 (October 1983): 78–83 and cover. *GA Document,* no. 9 (February 1984): 84–89.

Ernest J. KUMP; MASTEN & HURD

In 1970, Ernest J. Kump, Associates, won the AIA's Architectural Firm Award.

119

■ 227

Foothill College; Los Altos Hills, CA; 1961.
Some forty buildings, on a 122-acre campus, all designed and built as a unit. Though these buildings vary widely in size and purpose, they were constructed of the same materials (redwood, brick, and concrete) and are sited tastefully to achieve a calm and gracious whole.
Engineers: Huber & Knapik, Earl & Wright (structural); Keller & Gannon (mechanical/electrical). Landscape architects: Sasaki, Walker & Associates. General contractors: Williams & Burrows; O. E. Anderson; Carl N. Swenson Co.

Honors: PA Design Citation, 1960; AIA Honor Award, 1962; AIA Bicentennial List, one nomination.

See: *Architectural Forum* 116 (February 1962): 52–57. *Progressive Architecture* 41 (January 1960): 146–47; 43 (September 1962): 136–45.

LANGDON and WILSON (Subsequent name of firm: LANGDON WILSON MUMPER ARCHITECTS)

■ 228

J. Paul Getty Museum; Malibu, CA; 1974 (see Illus. 121).
Almost inadvertently, this museum foreshadowed the postmodern movement. When first opened, this richly decorated replica of an ancient Roman estate, designed to house a collection of

119 Procter & Gamble General Offices; Cincinnati, OH; 1985. *See* Entry 225. (Courtesy Kohn, Pedersen, Fox Associates; New York, NY. Photographer: Tim Hursley.)

■ 226

333 Wacker Drive; Chicago, IL; 1983 (see Illus. 120).
One facade of this 35-story office/commercial building fronts on a bend of the Chicago River and echoes that bend in a taut curve of its own; other exterior walls rise rectilinearly in harmony with the grid of the Loop. Cladding is green reflective glass banded at 6-foot intervals by horizontal stainless steel strips. Pedestrian arcades at ground level are defined by elegantly detailed marble and granite colonnades.

120

120 333 Wacker Drive; Chicago, IL; 1983. *See* Entry 226. (Courtesy Kohn, Pedersen, Fox Associates; New York, NY. Photographer: Barbara Karant.)

Greek and Roman art, was derided for having "turned its back upon the ideology and imagery of 'Modern Architecture.'" It comprises a peristyle garden with a central reflecting pool and a 2-story villa with thirty-eight galleries arranged around an atrium. Its many ornamental features include trompe l'oeil paintings, mosaics, and elaborately coffered ceilings.
Historian-archaeologist: Norman Neuerberg. Landscape architects: Emmet L. Wemple, ASLA & Assoc.; Denis L. Kurutz, project landscape architect.

See: *Architecture Plus* 2 (September–October 1974): 56–61, 122. *Archeology* 27 (July 1974): 175–81. Charles A. Jencks, *The Language of Post-Modern Architecture,* 4th revised and enlarged ed. (New York: Rizzoli, 1984), 82–83, 94–95.

LE CORBUSIER

Winner, Royal Gold Medal, 1953; AIA Gold Medal, 1961. (His real name was Charles-Edouard Jeanneret-Gris.)

■ 229

Carpenter Center for the Visual Arts, Harvard University; Cambridge, MA; 1963.
This, Le Corbusier's only major building in the United States—designed to house classes in architecture, film, and other arts —has struck some critics as surprisingly "modest and accommodating." Its concrete exterior has a smooth, precise finish; tall, thin columns break up its interior spaces. A great curvilinear ramp

bisects the structure and connects with the main stair and an exhibition space. Collaborating architects: Sert, Jackson & Gourley. Structural engineer: William Le Messurier. General contractor: George A. Fuller Co.

Honors: AIA Bicentennial List, one nomination.

See: *Architectural Forum* 119 (October 1963): 104–7. *Architectural Record* 133 (April 1963): 151–58. Y. Futagawa, ed., *Le Corbusier: Millowners Association Building . . . Carpenter Center . . . ,* text by Kenneth Frampton, Global Architecture, no. 37 (Tokyo: A. D. A. Edita, 1975).

Maya Ying LIN

■ 230

Vietnam Veterans Memorial; Washington, DC; 1982 (see Illus. 122).
This eloquent memorial, designed by a 21-year-old female architecture student, won a national competition. Recessed into the lawn of the Mall, two black granite walls, 220 feet long—one pointing to the Washington Monument, the other to the Lincoln Memorial—form a V. At their intersection they're 10 feet high, but the ground before them rises gradually toward the two ends till they disappear. The names of all those killed in Vietnam are carved on them in chronological order. To satisfy critics, a statue and a flag have been added nearby.

Detailing by Cooper-Lecky Partnership with the collaboration of Ms. Lin.

Honors: AIA Honor Award, 1984; Henry Bacon Medal for Memorial Architecture, 1984.

See: *AIA Journal* 71 (November 1982): 17; 72 (May 1983): 150–51 and cover. *Landscape* 28, no. 2 (1985): 1–9. *Landscape Architecture* 72 (March 1982): 54–56.

LOEBL SCHLOSSMAN BENNETT & DART (subsequent name of firm: LOEBL SCHLOSSMAN & HACKL)

■ 231

St. Procopius Abbey Church and Monastery; Lisle, IL; 1972.
Common brick, wood framing, and concrete, combined with originality and a strong sense of geometry, provide living and working quarters for a community of 100 Benedictine monks. The abbey's centerpiece, a church that seats 700, has neither statuary nor stained glass nor elaborate altar; its ambience is one of "inspired simplicity" conducive to meditation.
Partner in charge: Edward D. Dart. Associate architect: Paul Straka. Engineers: Eugene A. Dubin & Associates (structural); William T. Brookman & Assoc. (mechanical). General contractor: McCarty Brothers, Inc.

Honors: AIA Honor Award, 1973.

See: *AIA Journal* 59 (May 1973): 42–43.

Architectural Forum 137 (December 1972): 40–45. Progressive Architecture 52 (December 1971): 50–51.

LOEBL, SCHLOSSMAN, BENNETT & DART; C. F. MURPHY ASSOCIATES

■ 232

Water Tower Place; Chicago, IL; 1976 (see Illus. 123).
The base of this midtown complex contains a seven-level shopping mall with

123

two department stores and over a hundred shops and other attractions, centering around a Grand Atrium with a spectacular "cascading garden" escalator. Above this base rises a tower with 44 stories of luxury condominiums and 22 stories of hotel space.
Consulting architect: Warren Platner Associates.

See: Architectural Record 159 (April 1976): 136–40; 162 (October 1977): 99–104. Inland Architect 20 (October 1976): 6–13. Building Design & Construction 26 (September 1985): 95.

Eduardo LOPEZ see Jorge DEL RIO and Eduardo LOPEZ

Charles LUCKMAN

■ 233

Prudential Center; Boston, MA; 1965 (see Illus. 124).
Located on a spacious 31-acre site adjacent to downtown Boston, this complex comprises a 52-story office building, the Prudential Tower, for Prudential Insurance; the 29-story Sheraton-Boston Hotel; and, linked to the hotel by a

covered bridge, the multipurpose War Memorial Stadium.
Overall planning: Charles Luckman Associates. Architects for tower and hotel: Charles Luckman Associates. Architects for stadium: Hoyle, Doran & Berry.

See: Architectural Forum 122 (May 1965): 24. Architectural Record 135 (March 1964): 190–91.

Victor A. LUNDY

■ 234

Church of the Resurrection, East Harlem Protestant Parish; New York, NY; 1964.
This small, inexpensively built but dramatically angled church is surrounded by medium-rise public housing and, according to the architect, was "designed as a piece of sculpture to be looked down upon from above."
Engineers: Severud Associates (structural); Fred S. Dubin Assoc. (mechanical). General contractor: Thompson Brinkworth, Inc.

Honors: AIA Merit Award, 1966.

See: AIA Journal 46 (July 1966): 42–43. Architectural Forum 124 (January 1966): 48–53. L'Architecture d'Aujourd'hui, no. 125 (April–May 1966): 68–69.

■ 235

Florida's Silver Springs; Silver Springs, FL; 1957.
This complex of airy 1- and 2-story buildings was designed to serve a popular tourist resort that offers rides in glass-bottomed boats; it includes a restaurant, a boat dock, and a structure that houses shops and offices and curves harmoniously along the banks of the Silver River. In recent years its original flat roofs and simple lines have been modified to give it a Victorian look.
General contractor: John Rasmussen.

Honors: PA Award Citation, 1956; AIA Merit Award, 1959.

See: AIA Journal 31 (June 1959): 85. Progressive Architecture 39 (April 1958): 146–48.

■ 236

Unitarian Meetinghouse, Hartford, CT; 1964.
A ground-hugging church whose outline

122 Vietnam Veterans Memorial; Washington, DC; 1982. See Entry 230. (Courtesy U.S. Dept. of the Interior, National Park Service; Washington, DC. Photographer: Bill Clark.)

123 Water Tower Place; Chicago, IL; 1976. See Entry 232. (Courtesy Loebl, Schlossman & Hackl; Chicago, IL.)

124

is defined by a circle of spiky reinforced concrete fins, which support a system of concentric steel cables. Outside, roofs of heavy wooden decking span the spaces between the concrete fins while, inside, the central sanctuary boasts a remarkable ceiling that looks like a billowing web.

See: *Architectural Forum* 121 (August–September 1964): 126–29. *Architectural Record* 131 (February 1962): 118–20. *L'Architecture d'Aujourd'hui* 35, no. 122 (September 1965): 72–73.

■ 237

Warm Mineral Springs Inn; Venice, FL; 1958.
A single-story, L-shaped motel, it has a sprightly feeling all its own. Taller and shorter roofs—each a concrete shell on a stem, like a squared-off mushroom—alternate, checkerboard style. Inside, the checkerboard theme is repeated: ceilings over dining and sleeping areas are dark and low, over cooking and lounge areas pale and high.
Consulting engineers: Donald A. Sawyer (structural); Louis H. V. Smith (mechanical). General contractor: Spear, Inc.

Honors: PA Award Citation, 1958; AIA Merit Award, 1958.

See: *AIA Journal* 30 (July 1958): 52. *Architectural Forum* 108 (May 1958): 114–17. *Architectural Record* 123 (January 1958): 141–46.

MLTW/MOORE TURNBULL see also MOORE, LYNDON, TURNBULL, WHITAKER, the firm from which this one evolved, and entry nos. 266, 323, and 324.

■ 238

Faculty Club, University of California; Santa Barbara, CA; 1968.
Standard components of a faculty club—dining facilities, guest rooms, meeting rooms, and a swimming pool—are plunked into a whimsically theatrical setting complete with hanging neon lights, Pop Art graphics, and other ostentatiously neo-roadhouse touches.
Partner in charge: Charles W. Moore. Consulting architect: Thore H. Edgren. Engineers: Davis & Moreau (structural); Archer-Spencer Engineering (mechanical). General contractor: James I. Barnes Construction Co.

See: *Architectural Forum* 130 (March 1969): 78–85. *Architettura* 15 (August 1969): 256–57. *L'Architecture d'Aujourd'hui,* no. 145 (September 1969): XX.

■ 239

Kresge College, University of California at Santa Cruz; Santa Cruz, CA; 1973.
A compact campus set among redwoods and modeled after a Mediterranean hillside village. Its stuccoed wood-frame

buildings—painted white with accents of bright colors—are arranged along a curving, 1,000-foot-long "street" complete with a "triumphal arch" and a couple of plazas.
Principals in charge: Charles W. Moore, William Turnbull, Jr., Robert Simpson. Engineering consultants: Steve H. Sassoon & Assoc. (structural); Loran A. List (mechanical). General contractor: Bogard Construction, Inc.

Honors: PA Design Citation, 1970.

See: *AIA Journal* 68 (August 1979): 48–55, 70 and cover. *Progressive Architecture* 55 (May 1974): 76–83; 68 (February 1987): 76–79. *Architectural Review* 156 (July 1974): 28–31. *Process: Architecture,* no. 3 (1977): 135–49.

■ 240

Sea Ranch Swim and Tennis; Sonoma County, CA; 1967.
An amenity of the Sea Ranch condominium (see entry no. 267), it was designed to blend into a sweep of rugged hills while shielding a pool and tennis court from chilly north winds. A 2-story unfinished redwood wall with attendant buttresses serves as a windbreak and sun reflector. Inside, white plywood walls sport boldly oversized, multicolor graphics.
Structural engineers: Davis & Moreau and Gilbert, Forsberg, Diekmann & Schmidt. Landscape architects: Lawrence Halprin & Assoc. Graphic design: Barbara Stauffacher. General contractor: Matthew Sylvia.

Honors: PA Design Citation, 1966; AIA Honor Award, 1968.

See: *AIA Journal* 49 (June 1968): 84–104. *Architecture* 73 (December 1984): 56–63. *Zodiac,* no. 17 (1967): 136–37. *MLTW/Moore, Lyndon, Turnbull and Whitaker; The Sea Ranch . . . ,* edited and photographed by Y. Futagawa, text by W. Turnbull, Jr., Global Architecture, no. 3 (Tokyo: A. D. A. Edita, 1970).

John H. MACFADYEN and Alfredo DE VIDO

■ 241

Mann Music Center (formerly Robin Hood Dell West), Fairmont Park; Philadelphia, PA; 1976.
This inexpensively built concert hall for a great symphony orchestra's summer

performances seats 5,000 indoors with minimally obstructed sight lines and accommodates another 10,000 outside. Its irregularly shaped exterior, made of stainless steel terne-coated to a shimmery gray, suggests a tent. Inside, for acoustical reasons, there are a wood ceiling and wood baffles.

Job captain: Hans-Jeorg Baehler. Associate architect: Israel Demchick. Engineers: Charles H. Thornton, The Office of Lev Zetlin (structural); M. Michael Garber & Assoc. (mechanical); Heinrich Keilholz (acoustical). Contractor: McCloskey & Co.

Honors: AISC Architectural Award of Excellence.

See: Architectural Record 161 (January 1977): 129–32. *A+U: Architecture and Urbanism,* no. 75 (March 1977): 29–36. *Architettura* 23 (July 1977): 176–77.

MANN & HARROVER

■ 242

Memphis Metropolitan Airport; Memphis, TN; 1963.
About a third of the passengers who use this busy inland airport have to change planes here. Arrival/departure gates are arranged efficiently along a Y-shaped concourse, the stem of which leads into the monumental central hall of the concrete-and-masonry terminal.

Engineers: S. S. Kenworthy & Assoc. (structural); Allen & Hoshall (mechanical/electrical). Landscape architects: Ewald Associates. General contractor: J. A. Jones Construction Co.

Honors: PA Design Citation, 1961; AIA Merit Award, 1964.

See: AIA Journal 42 (July 1964): 30. *Architectural Record* 134 (October 1963): 165–72. *Progressive Architecture* 42 (January 1961): 112–15.

MARQUIS & STOLLER

■ 243

St. Francis Square; San Francisco, CA; 1963.
A low-rise development of 299 co-op apartments in an urban renewal area.

Along with a YMCA, it occupies an attractively landscaped L-shaped mega-block put together from three city blocks and the streets that used to divide them. Residents enjoy tree-lined walks and spacious recreational areas.

Engineers: Eric Elsesser (structural); K. S. Oliphant (mechanical/electrical). Landscape architects: Lawrence Halprin & Assoc. General contractor: Jack Baskin.

Honors: AIA Merit Award, 1964; AIA Design Award for Nonprofit-Sponsored Low and Moderate Income Housing, 1970.

See: AIA Journal 42 (July 1964): 34. *Arts + Architecture* 81 (August 1964): 14–16. *L'Architecture d'Aujourd'hui,* no. 120 (April–May 1965): 77–79.

Gerald McCUE

Winner, Kemper Award, 1971.

■ 244

Research Laboratory D, Chevron Research Company; Richmond, CA; 1967 (see Illus. 125).
As part of a Standard Oil of California installation, this lab, equipped with an

elaborate ventilation system, flaunts a phalanx of vertical exhaust flues on one long side and horizontal rows of air supply ducts on the other. Bluntly rectilinear, it is an economically built yet handsome example of "no-nonsense architecture."

Engineers: John Blume & Assoc. (structural); Sanford Fox (mechanical). General contractor: Barrett Construction Co.

Honors: AIA Honor Award, 1968.

See: AIA Journal 49 (June 1968): 85. *Architectural Forum* 124 (April 1966): 40–47. *Lotus* 4 (1967/68): 58–65.

Richard MEIER

Winner, Pritzker Architecture Prize, 1984.

■ 245

The Atheneum; New Harmony, IN; 1980 (see Illus. 126).
This orientation center for visitors to a historic town contains a 180-seat auditorium, four galleries, and observation terraces. Its exterior—which combines surprising juts with sinuous curves—gleams with white porcelain

125 Research Laboratory D, Chevron Research Company; Richmond, CA; 1967. *See* Entry 244. (Courtesy MBT Associates; San Francisco, CA. Photographer: Morley Baer.)

125

126 The Atheneum; New Harmony, IN; 1980. *See* Entry 245. (Photographer: Ezra Stoller © Esto.)

panels; delicately worked white pipe railings edge ramps, terraces, and stairs inside and out. Indoors, a recurring skew of 5 degrees off the rectangular grid creates intriguing tensions in plan and details.

Consultants: Severud-Perrone-Sturm, Bandel (structural); Flack & Kurtz (mechanical); Kane & Carruth (landscape architects). General contractor: Peyronnin Construction.

Honors: PA Award for Architectural Design, 1979; AIA Honor Award, 1985.

See: *AIA Journal* 69 (mid-May 1980): 126–37 and cover. *Progressive Architecture* 61 (February 1980): 67–75 and cover. *GA Document,* no. 1 (Summer 1980): 27–65. *Richard Meier & Associates. The Atheneum . . . ,* edited and photographed by Y. Futagawa, text by Paul Goldberger, Global Architecture, no. 60 (Tokyo: A.. D. A. Edita, 1981).

■ **246**

Bronx Developmental Center; New York, NY; 1976 (see Illus. 127).
An arresting U-shaped complex, four stories high, this 384-bed residential and outpatient treatment center for the mentally retarded features small units where residents are trained to live outside in the community. Faced with aluminum panels and finished on the interior with a wide range of colors, it has been hailed as virtually "pure architecture"—but by the same token has been criticized for its perhaps inappropriately abstract, unhomelike quality.

Architects: Richard Meier, Gerald Gurland, Sherman Kung, Henry Smith-Miller. Engineering consultants: Severud-Perrone-Sturm, Bandel (structural); Caretsky & Assoc. (mechanical). Landscape architects: Gangemi & De Bellis.

Honors: AIA Honor Award, 1977; Bard Award, 1977; Bartlett Award, 1977; 1977 Reynolds Memorial Award; AISC Architectural Award of Excellence, 1978.

See: *Progressive Architecture* 58 (July 1977): 43–54. *A + U: Architecture and Urbanism,* no. 64 (April 1976): 96–115. *L'Architecture d'Aujourd'hui,* no. 186 (August–September 1976): 66–67. Paul Goldberger, *On the Rise* (New York: Times Books, 1983), 168–71.

■ **247**

Des Moines Art Center Second Addition; Des Moines, IA; 1985 (see Illus. 128).
To expand a museum designed by Eliel Saarinen, then added to by I. M. Pei (entry no. 302), Meier devised three separate wings: a courtyard pavilion with a restaurant/meeting room; a north addition with extensive gallery space, much of it below grade; and a west addition

127 Bronx Developmental Center, New York, NY; 1976. *See* Entry 246. (Photographer: Ezra Stoller © Esto.)

128

providing both gallery and service space. The exteriors of these intricately curving and angling additions combine Meier's signature white porcelain-enamel panels with pinkish granite that blends with the masonry of the Saarinen building.
Design team: Richard Meier, Gerald Gurland, Michael Palladino. Engineers: Severud-Perrone-Szegezdy-Sturm (structural); John L. Altieri, P. E. (mechanical). General contractor: Ringland, Johnson, Crowley.

See: Architecture 74 (October 1985): 32–41 and cover. *Architectural Design* 55, no. 1–2 (1985): 64–69. *GA Document,* no. 13 (September 1985): 4–21. *A + U: Architecture and Urbanism,* no. 180 (September 1985): 49–70. *Domus,* no. 671 (April 1986): 36–43.

■ 248

Hartford Seminary; Hartford, CT; 1981.
This L-shaped building, 2 to 3 stories high, designed to house an interdenominational center for religious education and research, is clad in white porcelain-enamel; its facade is as complex yet balanced as an abstract sculpture. Inside, multidirectional light comes from side windows, clerestories, and skylights. Spaces within include a dramatic 3-story-high meeting room, a 2-story chapel, a bookstore, and a library on the ground floor, and numerous offices and seminar rooms upstairs.
Principals in charge: Richard Meier, Gerald Gurland. Engineers: Severud-Perrone-Szegezdy-Sturm (structural); Cosentini Assoc. (mechanical/electrical). Landscape architects: The Office of P. DeBellis. General contractor: Charles Jewett Corporation.

Honors: AIA Honor Award, 1983.

See: Architectural Record 169 (April 1981): 96–97 and cover; 170 (January 1982): 65–73 and cover. *GA Document,* no. 4 (1981): 50–67. *L'Architecture d'Aujourd'hui,* no. 219 (February 1982): 64–68.

■ 249

The High Museum of Art; Atlanta, GA; 1983 (see Illus. 129).
A fan-shaped atrium—skylighted, heavily glazed along its arc, and surrounded on three sides by roughly cubic forms—dominates the lines of this stunning, sparkling white museum. Visitors approach it via a welcoming ramp; inside, other ramps climb the quarter-circle wall of the atrium to reach galleries arranged on an open plan, with many dividing walls omitted or merely suggested.

129

Principals in charge: Richard Meier and Gerald Gurland. Engineers: Severud-Perrone-Szegezdy-Sturm (structural); John L. Altieri (mechanical/electrical). General contractor: Beers Construction.

Honors: AIA Honor Award, 1984.

See: Architectural Record 172 (January 1984): 118–31 and cover. *Architecture* 73 (May 1984): 222–29. *L'Architecture d'Aujourd'hui,* no. 219 (February 1982): 59–63. *Casabella,* no. 485 (November 1982): 50–61.

■ 250

Twin Parks Northeast, The Bronx; New York, NY; 1972/74.
Tastefully designed limited-income housing ingeniously fitted into an irregular site on parts of three adjacent blocks. The 7-story and 16-story brick-

faced concrete buildings frame sharply defined and handsomely detailed public spaces.

Structural engineer: Robert Rosenwasser. Landscape architect: Joseph Gangemi. General contractor: Leon D. De Matteis & Sons.

Honors: Bard Award, 1973; AIA Honor Award, 1974.

See: Architectural Forum 138 (June 1973): 54–67. *Architectural Record* 154 (July 1973): 89–98. *L'Architecture d'Aujourd'hui,* no. 186 (August–September 1976): 4–7.

■ 251

Westbeth Artists Housing; New York, NY; 1970.

A stunning example of adaptive reuse: a block-square complex of eleven buildings formerly used by Bell Telephone rehabilitated and transformed into dramatically high-ceilinged yet moderately priced loft-style housing exclusively for artists. Provision was made for a communal gallery and other unusual amenities.

Associates in charge: Murray Emslie, Gerald Gurland, Carl Meinhardt. Engineers: Felcher Atlas Associates (structural); Wald & Zigas (mechanical). General contractor: Graphic-Starrett Co.

Honors: AIA Design Award for Nonprofit-Sponsored Low and Moderate Income Housing, 1970; AIA Honor Award, 1971.

See: Architectural Forum 133 (October 1970): 44–49. *Architectural Record* 147 (March 1970): 103–6. *House and Home* 40 (October 1971): 104–5.

Erich MENDELSOHN

■ 252

Maimonides Health Center; San Francisco, CA; 1950.

As originally built, this hospital for the chronically ill had a lighthearted, tonic look, largely due to blithely curving balconies with feathery white railings. Unfortunately, modifications made some years later detracted from its airy charm.

Consulting engineer: Isadore Thompson. Contractor: Barrett & Hilp.

See: Architectural Forum 94 (February 1951): 92–99. *L'Architecture d'Aujourd'hui,* no. 38 (December 1951): 36–40. *Architect and Engineer* 176 (January 1949): 26–27.

■ 253

Mount Zion Temple and Center; St. Paul, MN; 1954.

This synagogue was completed after the architect's death in September 1953. Its richly decorated interior hides behind a spartan facade and contains interesting symbolic touches such as ten ribbed sections, recalling the Ten Commandments, in both the chapel and sanctuary and twelve steps, representing the Twelve Tribes of Israel, rising to the ark.

Associate architect: Michael Gallis. Architects for completion: Bergstedt & Hirsch. Mechanical consultant: Clyde E. Bentley. Structural consultant: Isadore Thompson. General contractor: Naugle-Leck.

See: Architectural Forum 102 (February 1955): 106–15. *L'Architecture d'Aujourd'hui* 28 (April–May 1957): 73–77. G. E. Kidder Smith, *A Pictorial History of Architecture in America* (New York: American Heritage, 1976), 2: 490.

Ludwig MIES VAN DER ROHE

Winner, AIA Gold Medal, 1960; Royal Gold Medal, 1959.

■ 254

Federal Center; Chicago, IL; overall plan and courthouse completed 1964, remainder completed subsequently.

Less than half of the center's 1½-block area in the heart of the Loop is taken up by its three buildings: a 42-story office building, a 30-story office building/courthouse, and a 1-story, glass-walled post office, all marked by Mies's characteristic serenity of line and meticulous detailing.

Architects: Chicago Federal Center Architects, a joint venture of Schmidt Garden & Erikson, Ludwig Mies van der Rohe, C. F. Murphy Assoc. and A. Epstein & Son.

Honors: AIA Bicentennial List, one nomination.

See: Architectural Record 137 (March 1965): 125–34. *Architectural Design* 34 (January 1964): 18–19. G. E. Kidder Smith, *A Pictorial History of Architecture in America* (New York: American Heritage, 1976), 2: 520.

■ 255

Illinois Institute of Technology; Chicago, IL; various dates.

In 1939 Mies designed the entire campus, but not all its buildings were ultimately built to his design. Those that are his display in common a regularly repeated standard unit, a steel-framed structural bay 24 feet wide by 24 feet deep by 12 feet high. In 1956 Crown Hall was completed; Reyner Banham has called it "his masterpiece, the holy of holies, the architecture school."

Honors: AIA Bicentennial List, six nominations.

See: Architectural Forum 97 (November 1952): 93–111; 105 (August 1956): 104–111. *Domus,* no. 346 (September 1958): 1–3. Reyner Banham, *Guide to Modern Architecture* (London: Architectural Press, 1962). Y. Futagawa, ed., *Mies van der Rohe: Crown Hall, ITT, Chicago . . . ,* text by Ludwig Glaeser, Global Architecture, no. 14 (Tokyo: A. D. A. Edita, 1972).

■ 256

Lafayette Park; Detroit, MI; 1963.

A residential complex on 78 acres, it comprises the 20-story Pavilion Apartments, a number of town houses, and Lafayette Towers, a pair of 21-story apartment buildings, each of which contains 300 units. Curtain walls here were among the first designed with sleeves for individual air conditioners.

Engineers for Pavilion Apartments: Frank Kornacker (structural); William Goodman (mechanical/electrical). Engineers for Lafayette Towers: Nelson, Ostrom, Berman, Baskin & Assoc. (structural); William Goodman (mechanical/electrical).

See: Architectural Forum 119 (September 1963): 80–91. *Architectural Record* 127 (April 1960): 170–73. *Architectural Design* 34 (April 1964): 164–66.

■ 257

860–880 Lake Shore Drive; Chicago, IL; 1951.

Two clean-lined, 26-story residential towers set at right angles to each other in a fashionable lakefront setting. Black-painted structural steel combines with floor-to-ceiling glass walls to create a "tower of glass" innovatively adapted to apartment living.

Associated architects: Pace Associates; Holsman, Holsman, Klekamp & Taylor; Ludwig Mies van der Rohe.

Honors: AIA Bicentennial List, five nominations; AIA Twenty-Five Year Award, 1976.

See: *Architectural Forum* 97 (November 1952): 93–111. *Arts + Architecture* 69 (March 1952): 16–31. *L'Architecture d'Aujourd'hui,* nos. 50–51 (December 1953): 30–33. *Architect & Building News* 205 (April 8, 1954): 402–9.

Ludwig MIES VAN DER ROHE and Philip JOHNSON

■ 258

Seagram Building; New York, NY; 1958 (see Illus. 130).
An office tower designed less for profit than to heighten the prestige of its namesake firm. Its sleek facade of bronze, travertine, and tinted glass overlooks Park Avenue; it soars straight up for over 500 feet from a serene and spacious plaza paved with pink granite and inlaid with two symmetrical pools set with rows of fountains.

Associate architects: Kahn & Jacobs. Engineers: Severud-Elstad-Kreuger (structural); Jaros, Baum & Bolles (mechanical). Landscape consultants: Karl Linn & Charles Middeleer. General contractor: George A. Fuller Co.

Honors: AIA Bicentennial List, fifteen nominations; AIA Twenty-Five Year Award, 1984.

See: *Architectural Forum* 109 (July 1958): 66–77. *Arts + Architecture* 77 (January 1960): 14–15. *Bauen + [und] Wohnen* 14 (January 1959): 1–8. David Guise, *Design and Technology in Architecture* (New York: Wiley, 1985), 92–99.

MILLER HANSON WESTERBECK BELL

■ 259

Butler Square; Minneapolis, MN; 1975.
Here's a huge landmark warehouse, occupying a full city block, which has been recycled into a multiuse center with retail shops and office space in one half and a hotel in the other. Most of its original structural system of heavy Douglas fir columns and beams was retained and exposed.

Collaborating project architect: Arvid Elness. Structural engineers: Frank Horner. TAC Engineering (electrical/plumbing). Contractor: Knutson Co.

Honors: AIA Honor Award for Extended Use, 1976.

See: *AIA Journal* 65 (April 1976): 42–43. *Architectural Record* 158 (December 1975): 108–112. *Progressive Architecture* 56 (October 1975): 74–78.

MITCHELL/GIURGOLA

Winner of the AIA's Architectural Firm Award, 1976. In 1982, Ronaldo Giurgola won the AIA Gold Medal.

■ 260

Columbus East Senior High School; Columbus, IN; 1973 (see Illus. 131).
This long, low-lying high school of over 2,000 students has a crisp high-tech look about it. There are lots of aluminum panels and glass here and thoughtful, energy-efficient design—all set off by a whimsical triumphal arch.

Engineers: Keast & Hood (structural); Paul H. Yoemans, Inc. (mechanical/electrical); Geiger-Berger & Assoc. (air structure). Landscape architects: Clark & Rapuano. Contractor: Geupel-Demares, Inc.

Honors: AIA Honor Award, 1975.

See: *AIA Journal* 63 (May 1975): 34–35. *Architectural Record* 159 (April 1976): 107–18. *A + U: Architecture and Urbanism,* no. 12 (1975): 61–82.

■ 261

Penn Mutual Tower; Philadelphia, PA; 1975 (see Illus. 132).
Located directly behind Independence Hall at a transition point between tall new buildings and more historic low ones, this 22-story office building has four differing facades, each keyed to harmonize amiably with its neighbors. On one side, the 4-story facade of an 1838 Egyptian Revival building has been erected as a freestanding sculptural wall that relates

130

130 Seagram Building; New York, NY; 1958. *See* Entry 258. (Courtesy Joseph E. Seagram & Sons, Inc.; New York, NY. Photographer: Ezra Stoller.)

131

131 Columbus East Senior High School; Columbus, IN; 1973. *See* Entry 260. (Courtesy Mitchell/Giurgola Architects; Philadelphia, PA. Photographer: Rollin R. Lia France.)

132 Penn Mutual Tower; Philadelphia, PA; 1975. *See* Entry 261. (Courtesy Mitchell Giurgola Architects; Philadelphia, PA. Photographer: Rollin R. Lia France.)

132

well to its vintage neighbors while it defines the tower's entrance plaza. Engineers: Skilling, Helle, Christiansen, Robertson (structural); Robert J. Sigel, Inc. (mechanical/electrical). General contractor: Turner Construction Co.

Honors: AIA Honor Award for Extended Use, 1977.

See: *AIA Journal* 66 (May 1977): 32. *Progressive Architecture* 57 (April 1976): 72–75. *Process: Architecture,* no. 2 (October 1977): 183–96. *Fortune,* (March 1966): 161–62.

MITCHELL & RITCHEY

■ **262**

The Auditorium; Pittsburgh, PA; 1961.

A huge circular arena, 417 feet in diameter, with a retractable dome—the first of its kind in the world. At the press of a button, it can open or close in 2½ minutes.
Consulting engineers: Ammann & Whitney. Engineers: Robert A. Zern (structural); Carl J. Long (electrical); Dzubay & Bedsole, John W. Mullin (mechanical). Landscape architects: Simonds & Simonds. General contractor: Dick Corporation.

Honors: PA Award Citation, 1954.

See: *Architectural Record* 125 (May 1959): 250–52; 130 (November 1961): 165–68. *L'Architecture d'Aujourd'hui,* no. 100 (February–March 1962): 23–27.

MOODY, MOORE, DUNCAN, RATTRAY, PETERS, SEARLE, CHRISTIE

■ 263

Centennial Hall, University of Winnipeg; Winnipeg, Manitoba; 1972.
To add needed space to a crowded campus while disturbing ongoing activities as little as possible, this 300,000-square-foot, 5 story structure was built over and between a varied mix of existing buildings. It rests on a series of square steel towers connected by full-story, square-tube trusses that span 40 to 120 feet. Clad in dark steel panels outside, spiced with primary colors inside, it has a high-tech, industrial look.
Partner in charge: James Christie.

See: *Canadian Architect* 18 (March 1973): 32–41. *Detail,* (July–August 1974): 689–96. Leon Whiteson, *Modern Canadian Architecture* (Edmonton: Hurtig Publishers, 1983), 114–17. W. Bernstein and R. Cawker, *Contemporary Canadian Architecture* (Toronto: Fitzhenry & Whiteside, 1982), 166–71.

Arthur Cotton MOORE

■ 264

Canal Square, Georgetown; Washington, DC; 1971 (see Illus. 133).
Shops, offices, and restaurants enjoy a lively home in what formerly was a warehouse on the banks of a barge canal. Original timber columns, wood planking, and exposed brick walls lend flavor to its renovated interiors; a contemporary addition in brick and glass helps enclose —and enhance the square.
Consultants: Cotton & Harris (mechanical); Milton Gurewitz (structural).

Honors: AIA Honor Award for Extended Use, 1977.

See: *Progressive Architecture* 52 (April 1971):

133

66–73. *Baumeister* 69 (February 1972): 149–51. *L'Architecture d'Aujourd'hui,* no. 157 (August–September 1971): 44–46.

■ 265

Science Building, The Madeira School; Greenway, VA; 1976 (see Illus. 134).
The angular shape of this building at a private girls' school is largely determined by its solar collector roof. The collector is designed to provide 60 percent of the building's heat; in spring and fall it also heats an adjacent swimming pool.
Consultants: James Madison Cutts (structural); Flack & Kurtz Consulting Engineers (mechanical/electrical). General contractor: Commercial Industrial Construction, Inc.

133   Canal Square, Georgetown; Washington, DC; 1971. *See* Entry 264. (Courtesy Arthur Cotton Moore/Associates P.C.; Washington, DC. Photographer: Jim Berkon.)

Honors: AIA Bicentennial List, one nomination.

See: *Progressive Architecture* 57 (February 1976): 54–57. *Domus,* no. 560 (July 1976): 9–11. *L'Architecture d'Aujourd'hui,* no. 192 (September 1977): 12–13.

MOORE GROVER HARPER; has also been attributed to MLTW/MOORE-TURNBULL

■ 266

Whitman Village Housing; Huntington, NY; 1975.
This deceptively simple low- to moderate-

134

134   Science Building, The Madeira School; Greenway, VA; 1976. *See* Entry 265. (Courtesy Arthur Cotton Moore/Associates P.C.; Washington, DC. Photographer: Jim Berkon.)

income development makes the most of a grassy 12-acre site with beautiful old trees to accommodate 260 units including 88 town houses with two to five bedrooms, 21 four-family houses, and 88 one-bedroom units. Houses located near a busy highway face inward toward the green. Most construction, in harmony with the neighborhood, is shingled woodframe.
Construction administrator: Edward Johnson & Co. Owner/contractor: Melville Industrial Associates.

See: Architectural Record 175 (March 1975): 152–53. *L'Architecture d'Aujourd'hui,* no. 184 (March 1976): 43–46. *Harvard Architecture Review* 1 (Spring 1980): 207–9, 214–17. *Baumeister* 74 (January 1977): 40–41.

MOORE, LYNDON, TURNBULL, WHITAKER; Joseph ESHERICK *see also* MLTW/MOORE TURNBULL

■ 267

Sea Ranch Condominium; Sonoma County, CA; 1966 (similar clusters of homes were added subsequently).
A second-home community, largely unpainted and of wood-frame construction, built along a wild, windy, and almost treeless stretch of the Pacific Coast. The main condominium building has ten ample rooms ranged around two courtyards. In its lee nestle jagged, almost shedlike dwelling units, each composed of a single great room imaginatively broken into smaller areas by painted enclosures and lofts. A group of less unconventional homes on the huge property, formerly a sheep ranch, was designed by Esherick.
Structural engineers: Davis & Morreau. Landscape architects: Lawrence Halprin & Assoc. General contractor: Matthew D. Sylvia.

Honors: PA Design Citation, 1965; AIA Honor Award, 1967. Special Citation, Homes for Better Living Program, 1967, for house designed by Esherick.

See: Progressive Architecture 47 (May 1966): 120–37. *House & Home* 32 (September 1967): 90–101. Charles Moore et al., *The Place of Houses* (New York: Holt, Rinehart & Winston, 1974). Y. Futagawa, ed., *MLTW/Moore, Lyndon, Turnbull & Whitaker: The Sea Ranch Condominium and Athletic Club #1 & #2,* text

by William Turnbull, Jr., Global Architecture Detail, no. 3 (Tokyo: A. D. A. Edita, 1976).

MOORE RUBLE YUDELL

■ 268

St. Matthew's Parish Church; Pacific Palisades, CA; 1983.
This understated, informal-looking church was designed with the participation of about 200 members of its congregation. Modifications to its traditional cruciform shape allow semicircular seating. There is no air-conditioning; instead, operable skylights and windows provide cross ventilation.
Project designers: Charles W. Moore, John Ruble, Buzz Yudell. Engineers: Kurily & Szymanski (structural); Sullivan & Assoc. (mechanical). General contractor: Meskell & Sons.

Honors: AIA Honor Award, 1984.

See: Architectural Record 172 (February 1984): 94–103 and cover. *Architecture* 73 (May 1984): 178–85. *Architectural Design* 54, no. 11–12 (1984): 53–55.

Luigi W. MORETTI

■ 269

The Watergate; Washington, DC; 1965/70.
This waterfront complex has considerable distinction—aside from its historic notoriety! Located on the Potomac, its five buildings—each significantly different from its neighbors—describe long free-form curves while their facades are marked irregularly with sweeping ranges of terraces. Included are 683 luxury apartments, offices, a hotel, and a shopping center.
Associated architects: Fischer-Elmore.

See: Domus, no. 419 (October 1964): 1–22. *Bauwelt* 61, no. 16 (April 20, 1970): 593–94. *Interiors* 127 (August 1967): 110–13.

William MORGAN

■ 270

Dunehouse; Atlantic Beach, FL; 1975 (see Illus. 135).
Two mirror-image one-bedroom

135 Dunehouse; Atlantic Beach, FL; 1975. *See* Entry 270. (Courtesy William Morgan Architects; Jacksonville, FL. Photographer: Creative Photographic Services [CPS].)

apartments are set deep in a grassy mound in a steel-reinforced concrete bubble, built in part by spraying gunite onto steel mesh. Thanks to its underground location in a preexistent dune, this house requires little heating or cooling.
Engineer: Geiger Berger Assoc.; partner in charge: Horst Berger.

See: *AIA Journal* 67 (April 1978): 38–39. *Architectural Record* 162 (mid-August 1977): 74–75. *Interior Design* 48 (January 1977): 128–31. *Process: Architecture,* no. 7 (1978): 136–39; special issue (September 1985): 72–74. *House and Garden* 148 (April 1976): 122–25.

■ 271

Pyramid Condominium; Ocean City, MD; 1975 (see Illus. 136).

The unusual V-shaped plan of this 20-story beachfront condo gives every apartment cross ventilation, a terrace, and an ocean view. From the front, its striking geometric lines suggest a pyramid.
Project manager: Thomas A. McCrary. Project architect: Theodore C. Strader. Consultants: Sherrer-Bauman & Assoc. (structural); Geiger-Berger Associates (special structural); Archison & Keller (mechanical).

Honors: PA Design Citation, 1975.

See: *Progressive Architecture* 56 (January 1975): 62; 57 (September 1976): 64–67. *A+U: Architecture and Urbanism,* no. 82 (September 1977): 37–48.

Raymond MORIYAMA

■ 272

Centennial Centre of Science and Technology; Toronto, Ontario; 1969.

This huge museum complex, built primarily of concrete and designed to welcome up to 10,000 visitors daily, including 3,000 students arriving in school buses, comprises three buildings: a long Entrance Building with coat-checking, orientation, and restaurant facilities; a triangular Core Building with a Great Hall for science fairs and similar large functions, a 500-seat auditorium, and lecture rooms; and a sprawling Exhibition Building where some 450 exhibits designed to arouse visitor curiosity and participation are displayed.
Project manager: David Vickers; project

construction manager: John Snell; assistant construction manager: Thomas Motomochi; design coordinator: Donald Cooper. Landscape: Bon W. Mueller. Engineers: M. S. Yolles Assoc. (structural); Nicholas Fodor & Assoc. (mechanical). Contractor: Pigott Construction.

See: *Architectural Record* 148 (August 1970): 103–9. *Canadian Architect* 14 (September 1969): 38–53. *L'Architecture d'Aujourd'hui,* no. 154 (February–March 1971): 92–93.

■ 273

Metropolitan Toronto Library; Toronto, Ontario; 1977.

The heart of this central reference facility, designed for a 1.2-million-book collection, is a 5-story atrium rimmed with balconies. Sinuously winding ramps and two curved glass elevators link floors. The library's almost windowless brick exterior is relieved at two opposite corners by huge sloping Vs, heavily glazed with skylights and side windows that open reading lounges to views of the city.
Engineers: Robert Halsall & Assoc. (structural); G. Granek & Assoc. (mechanical). Contractors: The Charles Nolan Co.

Honors: Governor General's Medal, 1982.

See: *Process: Architecture,* no. 5 (1978): 74–79. *Canadian Architect* 23 (January 1978): 20–29. *Artscanada* 35, no. 218/19 (February–March 1978): 18–31. *Architectural Review* 165 (May 1979): 286–89. *Architettura* 27 (June 1981): 340–48.

■ 274

Scarborough Civic Centre; Scarborough, Ontario; 1973.

This sleekly modeled, 336,000-square-foot civic center, which contains borough offices for a Toronto suburb and for its boards of education and health is bowtie shaped in plan. A circular central atrium, 67 feet high, is ringed with asymmetrically hung balconies that reach into it from wedge-shaped office wings at either side. Exterior cladding is white aluminum and dark reflective glass. Imaginative landscaping includes a waterfall and reflecting pools indoors and out.
Associates in charge: James Wilkinson and Ted Tashima. Consultants: Robert Halsall & Assoc. (structural); G. Granek & Assoc. (mechanical). Construction management: McDougall Construction Management.

See: *Architectural Record* 156 (July 1974): 91–98. *Process: Architecture,* no. 5 (1978): 80–85. *Canadian Architect* 18 (November 1973): 32–47. *A+U: Architecture and Urbanism,* no. 54 (1975): 79–88.

Eric Owen MOSS with James STAFFORD

■ 275

Morgenstern Warehouse; Los Angeles, CA; 1978 (see Illus. 137).

This small (13,000-square-foot)

136 Pyramid Condominium; Ocean City, MD; 1975. *See* Entry 271. (Courtesy William Morgan Architects; Jacksonville, FL. Photographer: Bob Lautman.)

136

137

warehouse/office facility, built of concrete block finished in two contrasting ways, brightens its dour downtown neighborhood by sporting oversize green and yellow graphics, and selected mechanicals exposed and arranged with decorative flair.

Project team: Eric Moss, James Stafford, George Elian. Consultants: Hugh Weber, mechanical; Dimitry Vergun, structural. General contractor: J. F. Baden.

Honors: PA Design Citation, 1978.

See: Progressive Architecture 60 (June 1979): 66–69. *Domus,* no. 598 (September 1979): 18–21. *A + U: Architecture and Urbanism,* no. 102 (March 1979): 51–56.

William C. MUCHOW *see also* ARCHITECTURAL ASSOCIATES COLORADO

■ **276**

First Federal Savings and Loan Association of Denver; Denver, CO; 1954.
A small local bank that uses simple lines, lots of glass, and custom-designed furnishings to create a sense of spaciousness.

Engineers: Ketchum & Konkel (structural); M. S. Wilson (mechanical). General contractor: Olson & Hart.

Honors: PA Award Citation, 1954; AIA Merit Award, 1954.

See: Architectural Record 125 (February 1959):

179–81. *Progressive Architecture* 35 (January 1954): 90; 36 (September 1955): 110–13.

MUCHOW ASSOCIATES

■ **277**

Park Central; Denver, CO; 1974.
A downtown banking, shopping, office, and garage complex that pulls together into one unified whole elements of varying heights and depths. Local authorities had imposed different height limitations on different parts of the site; this megastructure's disparate elements gain unity from its striking dark exterior of black anodized aluminum and solar bronze glass, and from the skillful balancing of its masses.

Project designer: George Hoover. Engineers: Ketchum, Konkel, Barrett, Nickel, Austin (structural); Hadji & Associates (mechanical/electrical). Landscape architect: Chris Moritz. General contractor: C. H. Leavell & Co.

Honors: AIA Honor Award, 1975; Bartlett Award, 1975.

See: AIA Journal 63 (May 1975): 30–31; 69 (February 1980): 30–37 and cover. *Architectural Record* 155 (April 1974): 107–12.

C. F. MURPHY ASSOCIATES (subsequent name of firm: MURPHY/JAHN. See also entry no. 232.)

■ **278**

Auraria Learning Resources Center; Denver, CO; 1976 (see Illus. 138).
Aluminum sun screens on two sides work

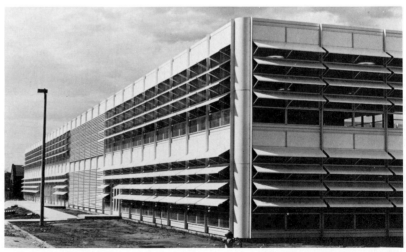

138

together with floor-to-ceiling glass to make the most of Denver's sunny climate for this 2-story library and media center shared by Denver Community College, Metropolitan State College, and the University of Colorado. Inside are 184,000 square feet of flexible loft space without suspended ceilings; structural, mechanical, and electrical systems are left exposed overhead.

Partner in charge: Helmut Jahn; project architect: David Hovey. Engineers: Zeller & Grey (structural); C. F. Murphy Associates (mechanical/electrical). General contractor: Martin K. Eby Construction Co.

Honors: Chicago AIA Distinguished Building Award, 1976.

See: *Architectural Record* 162 (November 1977): 109–24. *A + U: Architecture and Urbanism,* no. 10 (October 1978): 55–62. *Domus,* no. 572 (July 1977): 26–29.

■ 279

Crosby Kemper Memorial Arena; Kansas City, MO; 1974 (see Illus. 139).

This multipurpose indoor arena seats 16,000 to 18,000 people for sports events, theatrical spectacles, and conventions. Its enclosure, clad in metal panels, is dramatically framed by three gigantic exposed roof trusses, meticulously scaled and detailed.

Partner in charge: Helmut Jahn; project architect: James Goettsch. Landscape architects: Parks and Recreation, Kansas City. Acoustical consultants: Coffeen, Gatley & Assoc. Contractor: J. E. Dunn Construction Co.

Honors: AISC Architectural Award of Excellence, 1975; AIA Honor Award, 1976; Bartlett Award, 1976.

See: *AIA Journal* 65 (April 1976): 36–57. *Architectural Record* 159 (March 1976): 109–14. *Domus,* no. 557 (April 1976): 21–24. *A + U: Architecture and Urbanism,* no. 94 (July 1978): 19–26.

■ 280

McCormick Place–On–The–Lake; Chicago, IL; 1970.

A huge, glass-walled convention center on the banks of Lake Michigan, it was built to replace the McCormick Place complex destroyed by fire in 1967. Its two companion structures—one housing a 4,451-seat theater plus restaurants and meeting rooms, the other providing over 300,000 square feet of exhibition space— share a single, dramatically steel-trussed roof.

Engineers: C. F. Murphy Associates. Consultants: John W. Ditamore (theater); Bolt, Beranek & Newman (acoustics). General contractors: Gust K. Newberg Construction and Paschen Contractors (joint venture).

Honors: AIA Honor Award, 1972; AISC Architectural Award of Excellence, 1972; Bartlett Award, 1972.

See: *Architectural Forum* 135 (November 1971): 36–57. *Architectural Record* 149 (May 1971): 95–106. *Architectural Review* 151 (April 1972): 211–15.

■ 281

Michigan City Public Library; Michigan City, IN; 1977 (see Illus. 140).

This 1-story, 35,000-square-foot high-tech library built of prefab, industrial materials has been dubbed a reading factory. In plan it's a hollow square of virtually undivided loft space with an off-center courtyard for outdoor reading. Natural light flows inward through its side walls of translucent fiberglass panels and its unusual sawtooth roof, where rows of skylights are arranged on a diagonal grid oriented toward northern light.

Design principal: Helmut Jahn; administrative principal: Carter H. Manny; project architect: Dennis Recek. General contractor: Larson-Danielson.

See: *Progressive Architecture* 59 (July 1978): 62–65. *A + U: Architecture and Urbanism,* no. 94 (July 1978): 12–18. *Detail* (May–June 1980), 367–70.

■ 282

O'Hare International Airport, Chicago, IL: 1963, plus subsequent additions by this firm and Murphy/Jahn.

The C. F. Murphy firm inherited an existing runway, control tower, and partly finished terminal built according to an earlier plan; then the firm had to negotiate with thirteen airlines and arrive at a compromise design. A striking circular restaurant building with a skylighted central hall is one of the most appealing elements of this sprawling, often modified airport.

Partner in charge, 1963: Carter H. Manny, Jr.

See: *Architectural Record* 152 (October 1972): 127–42; 173 (May 1985): 132–39. *Progressive Architecture* 44 (August 1963): 102–11. *Inland Architect* 17 (August 1973): 18–22.

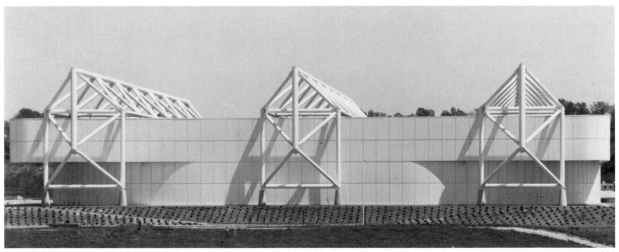

139 Crosby Kemper Memorial Arena; Kansas City, MO; 1974. *See* Entry 279. (Courtesy Murphy/Jahn; Chicago, IL. Photographer: Keith Palmer/James Steinkamp.)

140

140 Michigan City Public Library; Michigan City, IN; 1977. *See* Entry 281. (Courtesy Murphy/Jahn; Chicago, IL. Photographer: Keith Palmer/James Steinkamp.)

■ 283

Richard J. Daley Center (formerly Chicago Civic Center); Chicago, IL; 1966 (see Illus. 141).
A 648-foot-high tower set on a 2½-acre plaza, it was designed to house offices and courtrooms. Faced with oxidizing steel and glass, it has no major interior columns, just twelve huge cruciform exterior columns with 87-foot steel trusses running lengthwise and 48-foot spans running crosswise.

Design architect: Jacques Brownson. Associate architects: Skidmore, Owings & Merrill and Loebl, Schlossman, Bennett & Dart. Consulting engineers: Severud-Elstad-Kreuger Associates (structural). General contractor: Gust K. Newberg Construction Co.

Honors: AISC Architectural Award of Excellence, 1966; AIA Honor Award, 1968; AIA Bicentennial List, one nomination.

See: Architectural Forum 125 (October 1966): 33–37. *Progressive Architecture* 47 (October 1966): 244–47. *Casabella,* no. 309 (September 1966): 48–55.

141 Richard J. Daley Center (formerly Chicago Civic Center); Chicago, IL; 1966. *See* Entry 283. (Courtesy Murphy/Jahn; Chicago, IL. Photographer: Keith Palmer/James Steinkamp.)

141

■ 284

St. Mary's Angela Athletic Facility, St. Mary's College; Notre Dame, IN; 1977 (see Illus. 142).
This is a stripped-down, colorful, high-tech gymnasium that matches the high spirits of athletes at this small women's college. Fiberglass used in translucent wall panels and in transparent, curved clerestory windows combines with exposed red trusses, blue pipes, and yellow ducts to fashion its light and lively good looks.

Design principal. Helmut Jahn; project architect: James Goettsch. General contractor: The Hickey Co.

Honors: AIA Honor Award, 1979; Chicago AIA Distinguished Building Award, 1977; AISC Architectural Award of Excellence, 1978.

See: Progressive Architecture 59 (July 1978): 58–61. *A + U: Architecture and Urbanism,* no 94 (July 1978): 3–11. *Domus,* no. 581 (April 1978): 24–26.

143

MURPHY & MACKEY
(subsequent name of firm:
MURPHY DOWNEY WOFFORD &
RICHMAN)

■ 285

Climatron, Botanical Garden; St. Louis, MO; 1960 (see Illus. 143).
This climate-controlled greenhouse is topped by a giant, aluminum-framed geodesic dome. A range of climates can be simulated at the same time, unusual displays such as a waterfall and a bog can be presented, and, at night, dramatic illumination sets the dome glowing like an incandescent globe.
Dome consultant: Synergetics, Inc. Mechanical engineer: Paul Londe.

Honors: R. S. Reynolds Memorial Award, 1961; AIA Bicentennial List, one nomination.

See: AIA Journal 35 (May 1961): 27–32. *Architectural Record* 129 (April 1961): 12–13. *Progressive Architecture* 42 (April 1961): 174–78.

MURPHY/JAHN

■ 286

Xerox Centre; Chicago, IL; 1980 (see Illus. 144).
Sited next to a plaza in the Loop, this 42-story speculative office building is graciously set back from it and gracefully curved at the corner from ground level to roof, where a teardrop-shaped "penthouse" for mechanicals forms an eye-catching embellishment. Horizontal ribbons of silver reflective glass and off-white aluminum panels make up its skin. Diagonal detailing predominates in the lobby and is repeated by rows of asphalt pavers on the roof.
Partner in charge: Helmut Jahn; project architect: James Goettsch; manager of production: Bill McLenahan. Consultants: Cohen, Barretto, Marchertas (structural); CFMA (mechanical/electrical). General contractor: Turner Construction.

See: AIA Journal 70 (mid-May 1981): 208–14. *Progressive Architecture* 61 (December 1980): 58–63. *Architectural Review* 169 (April 1981): 230–33. *GA Document,* no. 3 (Winter 1981): 80–87.

MURPHY/JAHN; Lester B. KNIGHT

■ 287

State of Illinois Center; Chicago, IL; 1985 (see Illus. 145).
Central to this immense building is a 17-story atrium, 160 feet in diameter, ringed near ground level by shops and

142 St. Mary's Angela Athletic Facility, St Mary's College; Notre Dame, IN; 1977. *See* Entry 284. (Courtesy Murphy/Jahn; Chicago, IL. Photographer: Keith Palmer/James Steinkamp.)

143 Climatron, Botanical Garden; St. Louis, MO; 1960. *See* Entry 285. (Courtesy Murphy, Downey, Wofford & Richman/Architects.)

restaurants, with 1 million square feet of office space for state agencies above. On most of three sides, its exterior walls—entirely glazed in vertically striped patterns of different kinds of glass—rise straight up, but one huge corner is sliced away in a back-sloping curve.

Project principals: Helmut Jahn, James Goettsch, Thomas O'Neill, and Donald Hitchcock; principal in charge of design; Helmut Jahn; project architect: James Goettsch; project manager: David Sauer; structural engineer: Lou Moro; mechanical engineer: Shepard Eisenberg. General contractors: Newberg/Paschen Joint Venture; Walsh Construction Co. of Illinois; A. N. Ebony Co.

See: *Architecture* 74 (November 1985): 40–45 and cover. *Progressive Architecture* 66 (December 1985): 72–79. *GA Document,* no. 13 (September 1985): 42–61. *A+U: Architecture and Urbanism* no. 184 (January 1986): 77–96.

144 Xerox Centre; Chicago, IL; 1980. *See* Entry 286. (Courtesy Murphy/Jahn; Chicago, IL. Photographer: Keith Palmer/James Steinkamp.)

144

Barton MYERS

■ 288

Seagram Museum; Waterloo, Ontario; 1983 (see Illus. 146).

Dedicated to the science and history of preparing alcoholic beverages, this museum is set among Victorian industrial buildings that are still in use. Visitors enter through a former warehouse—now converted to a spacious atrium bordered by racks of barrels. The new museum, attached, is faced with brick–buff striped with rust—that helps to integrate it with its older neighbors. Inside it's a hall 120 feet by 120 feet by 50 feet high, with a grid of large coffered skylights and exposed ceiling trusses. Exhibits are mounted in two interior mini-buildings and in pavilions along the sides.

Associate in charge: Donald Clinton. Engineers: Read Jones Christoffersen (structural); ECE Group (mechanical/electrical). Contract manager: Grahame Vincent (Joseph E. Seagram & Sons).

Honors: Governor General's Medal, 1986.

145 State of Illinois Center; Chicago, IL 1985. *See* Entry 287. (Courtesy Murphy/Jahn; Chicago, IL. Photographer: Keith Palmer/James Steinkamp.)

See: *Architectural Record* 173 (April 1985): 138–45 and cover. *GA Document,* no. 13 (September 1985): 114–19. *Architectural Review* 178 (November 1985): 64–67.

145

146

efficient, cast-in-place concrete, mixed-occupancy building is underground; yet, thanks to clerestory windows and an interior courtyard, it's a bright and cheerful place.

Engineers: Meyer, Borgman & Johnson, Inc. (structural); Oftedal, Locke, Broadston & Assoc. (mechanical/electrical). General contractor: Lovering Associates.

Honors: PA Design Award, 1975; CRSI Design Award, 1977; Merit Award, Minnesota AIA, 1977.

See: *AIA Journal* 67 (April 1978): 34–51. *Progressive Architecture* 56 (January 1975): 52–53. *Architecture Minnesota* 3 (November–December 1977): 19–27.

NARAMORE, BAIN, BRADY & JOHANSON (subsequent name of firm: The NBBJ GROUP; see also entry no. 459)

■ 291

1001 Fourth Avenue Plaza (formerly known as Seafirst National Bank Building and Seattle–First National Bank); Seattle, WA; 1969 (see Illus. 148).

This 50-story office tower, sheathed in bronze anodized aluminum, was erected on a very steep site; downhill it has four more levels than on its uphill side! Uphill there's a gracious plaza with trees and sculpture. Unusual and attractive public banking facilities, located partly below grade, are reached by escalator from the plaza lobby. In 1986 the same firm retrofitted this building, adding retail space and public amenities to the street-level plaza.

Barton MYERS in association with R. L. WILKIN

■ 289

Citadel Theatre; Edmonton, Alberta; 1976 (see Illus. 147).

This community resource, built for a popular repertory company, houses three performance spaces—Shocter Theatre, Rice Theatre, and Zeidler Hall—plus a restaurant, bookshop, and classrooms. Erected on a constricted site bisected by a 30-foot-wide pedestrian right-of-way that serves as an enclosed mall, it combines a rust metal-and-glass greenhouse lobby with an angular, rust brick rear in which theaters and other facilities are stacked. Consultants: M. B. Engineering (structural); D. Panar & Assoc. (mechanical). Construction manager: Carlson Management Services.

See: *Progressive Architecture* 58 (July 1977): 68–71. *Process: Architecture*, no. 5 (1978): 108–13. *A + U: Architecture and Urbanism*, no. 98 (November 1978): 41–50. *Architectural Review* 164 (July 1978): 6–8.

MYERS & BENNETT

■ 290

East Bank Bookstore/Admissions and Records Facility (Williamson Hall), University of Minnesota; Minneapolis, MN; 1977.

All but 5 percent of this highly energy-

147

148

For original construction: Partner in charge: Perry B. Johanson. Project architect: Robert J. Pope; project designer: Donald A. Winkelmann. Engineers: Skilling, Helle, Christiansen, Robertson (structural); Valentine, Fisher & Tomlinson (mechanical/electrical). Consultant: Pietro Belluschi. Landscape architect: William Teufel. Contractor: Howard S. Wright Construction Co.

Honors: AISC Architectural Award of Excellence, 1969.

See: Architectural Record 147 (June 1970): 129–36. *Architettura* 16 (October 1970): 384–85.

Richard J. NEUTRA

Winner, AIA Gold Medal, 1977 (awarded posthumously).

■ 292

Eagle Rock Playground Club House; Los Angeles, CA; 1954.
A low rectangular clubhouse set in a public park, it offers open-air pavilion spaces on three sides. A raised rectangular platform at one end reaches out over a reflecting pool to a hillside slope to make the most of a natural amphitheater.
Collaborators: Dion Neutra and John Blanton.

Honors: AIA Merit Award, 1955.

See: Architectural Record 121 (March 1957): 213–16. *Arts + Architecture* 73 (April 1956): 14–15. *Interiors* 116 (November 1956): 84–85.

■ 293

Northwestern Mutual Fire Association Building; Los Angeles, CA; 1950.
A small office building with strong, simple lines, it is built of brick, steél, aluminum, and glass. Vertical louvers on the outside and "egg-crate" ceilings on the inside provide decoration while they lessen glare.
Contractor: C. W. Driver.

Honors: AIA Merit Award, 1952.

See: Architectural Forum 96 (February 1952): 111–13. *Architectural Review* 112 (October 1952): 227–34. *L'Architecture d'Aujourd'hui*, no. 40 (April 1952): 18–21.

Matthew NOWICKI

■ 294

Dorton Arena; Raleigh, NC; 1953.
Grandly sweeping lines and bold engineering characterize this stadium—officially known as the North Carolina State Fair Livestock Judging Pavilion, though more familiarly called the Cow Palace. Its dramatic outline is determined by two huge interlocking parabolic arches, which rise obliquely to a height of 90 feet above the ground; almost 10,000 people can be seated within it.
Architect for completion after Nowicki's death in 1950: William Henley Deitrick. Consulting engineers: Severud, Elstad & Krueger. General contractor: William Muirhead Construction Co.

Honors: AIA Honor Award, 1953.

See: Architectural Forum 97 (October 1952): 134–39; 98 (June 1953): 170–71; 100 (April 1954): 130–34.

A. G. O'DELL, Jr.

■ 295

Auditorium and Coliseum, Civic Center; Charlotte, NC; 1956 (see Illus. 149).
Sharing parking space and a plaza on a 23-acre site are a 2,500-seat auditorium for concerts and theatrical presentations and a round coliseum that seats 13,500 for sports events and other spectacles. Their construction is of concrete and steel, with the coliseum dome covered in aluminum.
Consulting engineers: Severud-Elstad-Krueger (structural); W. P. Wells (mechanical). Acoustical consultants: Bolt, Beranek & Newman. Landscape architect: John Lippard. General contractor: Thompson & Street.

See: Progressive Architecture 36 (June 1955): 134–35; 37 (September 1956): 112–21. *Techniques et Architecture* 15 (June 1955): 82–83.

149

ODELL ASSOCIATES

■ 296

Blue Cross and Blue Shield of North Carolina Service Center; Chapel Hill, NC; 1973.

The reflective glass walls of this regional headquarters slope sharply to give it a dynamic-looking rhomboid shape. One practical by-product: because these walls roughly parallel the rays of the sun, direct heat gain is considerably lower than it would be for a vertical, glass-enclosed building.

General contractor: Nello L. Teer Company.

Honors: AISC Architectural Award of Excellence, 1975.

See: Architectural Record 155 (May 1974): 133–40. *Architectural Review* 155 (April 1974): 242. *Deutsche Bauzeitung* 108 (November 1974): 993.

■ 297

Burlington Corporate Headquarters; Greensboro, NC; 1971 (see Illus. 150).

Sited on a lushly landscaped 34-acre former estate—complete with pool, high spouting fountain, and an intriguing sculpture—this corporate headquarters complex comprises two structures joined by bridges at three points. Its 6-story office structure is walled in reflecting glass and enclosed in a striking framework of exposed steel trusses. General contractor: Daniel Construction Company.

Honors: AISC Architectural Award of Excellence, 1971.

See: Architectural Record 151 (February 1972): 113–28. *Interiors* 132 (January 1973): 98–111. *Baumeister* 69 (November 1972): 1283–85.

Donald OLSEN see Joseph ESHERICK; Donald OLSEN; Vernon DEMARS

Douglas ORR and Louis I. KAHN (see also entry nos. 203–9. Subsequent name of Orr's firm: Douglas ORR WINDER & ASSOCIATES)

■ 298

Yale University Art Gallery and Design Center; New Haven, CT; 1953 (see Illus. 151).

This reinforced concrete building,

150

151

designed to provide virtually unbroken loft space to be partitioned at will for changing exhibits, has been widely praised for its candid yet beautifully detailed exposure of its structural elements. As one critic put it, "Here structure is so integral with architecture it has acquired the value of ornament." Engineers: Henry A. Pfisterer (structural); Meyer, Strong & Jones (mechanical). Landscape consultant: Christopher Tunnard. General contractor: George B. H. Macomber Co.

Honors: AIA Bicentennial List, two nominations; AIA Twenty-Five Year Award, 1979.

See: Progressive Architecture 35 (May 1954): 88–101, 130–31. *Perspecta,* no. 3 (1955): 46–59. David Guise, *Structure and Technology in Architecture* (New York: Wiley, 1985), 200–5.

John B. PARKIN *see also* Viljo REVELL; John B. PARKIN ASSOCIATES

■ **299**

Plant and offices for Thomas J. Lipton, Ltd.; Bramalea, Ontario; 1963?
Separate office, warehouse, and manufacturing spaces are provided in this 2-story, 155,000-square-foot corporate facility sheathed in white glazed brick flecked with black. A dozen prismatic skylights trimmed with black illuminate the office area, and the building's relatively few windows are accented by black frames and sashes.

Partner in charge of industrial structures: E. R. Wilbee; project designer: W. E. Sherriff; project architect: W. A. Flanagan. Structural engineer: J. Ozdowski; mechanical engineer: W. E. Emmerson. General contractor: Redfern Construction.

Honors: Massey Medal, 1964.

See: Architectural Record 140 (November 1966): 151–53. *Baumeister* 63 (October 1966): 1196–97. *Architectural Design* 34 (July 1964): 340–41. *RAIC Journal* 40 (September 1963): 71–74.

John B. PARKIN ASSOCIATES; BREGMAN & HAMANN (see also entry no. 342)

■ **300**

Toronto-Dominion Centre; Toronto, Ontario; 1969.
Designed by Mies van der Rohe but constructed after his death, this complex provides 3.1 million square feet of office space in two towers—the 56-story Toronto Dominion and the 46-story Royal Trust—plus a single-story, clear-span corner pavilion for a bank, all set among interlinked public plazas. Both the bank and the office slabs, reminiscent of the Seagram Building (see entry no. 258), have dark glass curtain walls. Parking and a shopping concourse are supplied underground.
Consultant architect; Mies van der Rohe;

executive architect: Sidney Bregman. Engineers: C. D. Carruthers and Wallace Consultants (structural); H. H. Angus & Assoc. (mechanical/ electrical).

See: Architectural Record 149 (March 1971): 105–14. *Architectural Review* 151 (January 1972): 48–57. *Interiors* 132 (September 1972): 116–23. *Canadian Architect* 12 (November 1967): 31–45.

PAYETTE ASSOCIATES see VENTURI RAUCH & SCOTT BROWN (exterior); PAYETTE ASSOCIATES (interior)

I. M. PEI

In 1968, I. M. Pei & Partners won the AIA's Architectural Firm Award. In 1979, I. M. Pei won the AIA Gold Medal; in 1983, he won the Pritzker Architecture Prize.

■ **301**

Denver Hilton Hotel; Denver, CO; 1960.
Sited on fashionable Zeckendorf Plaza, this 21-story, 884-room hotel features a geometrically patterned curtain wall of red granite aggregate and numerous spectacular interior spaces, including a block-long gold ceilinged lobby and a bridge, enclosed in arching plastic, that connects the lobby and a department store.
Partner in charge: Eason Leonard; in charge of design: Araldo Cossuta. Associated architects: Rogers & Butler. Consultant: William R. Tabler. Engineers: Weiskopf & Pickworth (structural); Jaros, Baum & Bolles (mechanical/electrical). General contractor: Webb & Knapp.

Honors: AIA Merit Award, 1961.

See: AIA Journal 35 (April 1961): 85. *Architectural Forum* 113 (August 1960): 94–99. *Interiors* 119 (October 1960): 109–17. *Western Architect and Engineer,* August 1960, 16–23.

■ **302**

Des Moines Art Center Addition; Des Moines, IA; 1968.
The original museum building was designed by Eliel Saarinen and completed in 1948. Pei's harmonious addition, a sculpture wing, encloses the fourth side of a central courtyard; its skylights and

expanses of deeply recessed windows serve to bathe the sculpture in natural light. A subsequent addition, designed by Richard Meier, is described in entry no. 247.

Architects in charge: Richards M. Mixon and Graeme A. Whitelaw. Engineers: Weiskopf & Pickworth (structural); Robson & Woese (mechanical/electrical). General contractor: The Weitz Co.

Honors: AIA Honor Award, 1969.

See: *AIA Journal* 51 (June 1969): 98. *Architectural Forum* 130 (June 1969): 54–67.

■ 303

East Building, National Gallery of Art; Washington, DC; 1978 (see Illus. 152).

This marble, glass, and concrete addition to a time-honored neoclassical gallery is confidently contemporary. Its lines are sleekly geometric; triangles recur in its plan and detailing; and exciting interior spaces abound.

Engineers: Weiskopf & Pickworth (structural); Syska & Hennessy (mechanical/electrical). Landscape architects: Kiley, Tyndall, Walker. Construction manager: Carl Morse, Morse/ Diesel, Inc. Builder: Charles H. Tomkins Co.

Honors: AIA Bicentennial List, one nomination.

See: *AIA Journal* 68 (mid-May 1979): 104–13. *Architectural Record* 164 (August 1978): 79–92 and cover. *Architecture* 73 (October 1984): 74–79. Paul Goldberger, *On the Rise* (New York: Times Books, 1983), 146–49.

■ 304

88 Pine Street (subsequently named

Wall Street Plaza); New York, NY; 1973.
This 33-story, Wall Street–area office building with a river view stands out thanks to startling white curtain walls made of aluminum with a baked-on enamel coating. Its elevator core is set off-center to provide large "bull pen" areas on one side, space for small private offices on the other.

Associate partner in charge: James Ingo Freed. Engineers: The Office of James Ruderman (structural); Cosentini Associates (mechanical/ electrical).

Honors: R. S. Reynolds Memorial Award, 1974; AIA Honor Award, 1975.

See: *AIA Journal* 63 (May 1975): 29. *Architectural Record* 157 (April 1975): 123–28. *Architecture Plus* 1 (March 1973): 36–37.

■ 305

Everson Museum of Art; Syracuse, NY; 1968.

This small museum built of concrete in an urban renewal area has coolly abstract lines inside and out. Its square-cut upper floors cantilever far out over a plaza; inside there's a sinuous spiral staircase and a two level, skylighted sculpture court.

Project associate: Kellogg Wong. Associate architects: Pederson, Hueber, Hares & Glavin. Engineers: R. R. Nicolet & Assoc. (structural); Robson & Woese Inc. (mechanical). General contractor: William C. Pahl Construction Co.

Honors: AIA Honor Award, 1969; AIA Bicentennial List, one nomination.

See: *AIA Journal* 51 (June 1969): 111. *Architectural Forum* 130 (June 1969): 54–67. *Architettura* 15 (February 1970): 678–79.

■ 306

Herbert F. Johnson Museum of Art, Cornell University; Ithaca, NY; 1973.

A concrete tower with assertive, abstract lines set on a promontory that overlooks a scenic lake and forms one end of a quadrangle otherwise bordered by quietly traditional low stone buildings. Two floors above grade, an open-air sculpture court occupies a multistory space that is lidded by a floor of galleries and lounges.

Architect in charge: John L. Sullivan III. Engineers: Nicolet Dressel Mercille, Ltd. (structural); Segner & Dalton (mechanical). Landscape architects: Dan Kiley & Partners. General contractor: William C. Pahl Construction Co.

Honors: AIA Honor Award, 1975.

See: *AIA Journal* 63 (May 1975): 40–41. *Architecture Plus* 1 (March 1973): 59; 2 (January/ February 1974): 52–59.

■ 307

Jacob K. Javits Convention Center (New York Expo and Convention Center); New York, NY; 1986.

The exterior of this mammoth, five-block-long building is an assemblage of rectilinear forms, all shaped by a framework of prefabricated steel modules fitted with clear glass. Inside, the structure is supported by tubular steel pillars that resemble chunky champagne glasses. At its south end there's a spectacular 150-foot-high lobby, dubbed the crystal palace. Also housed within the center's 1.8 million square feet: a 2,500-seat auditorium and acres of exhibition halls and meeting rooms.

Partner in charge of design: James Ingo Freed; partner in charge of management: Werner Wandelmaier. Associate architects: Lewis, Turner Partnership—Roger Lewis, partner in charge. Engineers: Weidlinger Associates—Matthys Levy, partner in charge; Salmon Associates (structural); Syska & Hennessy; Pierre A. Dillard (mechanical/electrical).

See: *Architectural Record* 174 (September 1986): 106–17 and cover. *L'Architecture d'Aujourd'hui,* no. 248 (December 1986): xlii–xliv. *Baumeister* 83 (November 1986): 56–60.

■ 308

John Fitzgerald Kennedy Library, Columbia Point on Dorchester Bay; Boston, MA; 1979 (see Illus. 153).

Not just a library, this—here visitors also can view JFK memorabilia and a film

152

152 East Building, National Gallery of Art; Washington, DC; 1978. *See* Entry 303. (Courtesy Information Office, National Gallery of Art; Washington, DC.)

153 John Fitzgerald Kennedy Library, Columbia Point on Dorchester Bay; Boston, MA; 1979. *See* Entry 308. (Courtesy John Fitzgerald Kennedy Library; Boston, MA.)

153

Cosentini Associates (mechanical/electrical). Contractor: Gilbane Building Company.

Honors: AIA Bicentennial List, two nominations; AIA Honor Award, 1977; AISC Architectural Award of Excellence, 1977.

See: AIA Journal 66 (May 1977): 37; 69 (December 1980): 18–25 and cover. *Architectural Record* 161 (June 1977): 117–26. *Interiors* 136 (May 1977): 108–21.

■ 310

Mile High Center; Denver, CO; 1955.

A 23-story office tower faced with an interweaving pattern of dark gray anodized aluminum and buff porcelain-enameled steel. There's a freestanding black steel entrance canopy and, behind the main lobby, a colonnade walk that looks out on two fountain pools.

about his era. Sited across the harbor from downtown Boston, it combines diverse geometric shapes, primarily a low white auditorium cylinder and a 110-foot-high dark-glass pavilion, roughly square—a vast space frame hung with a giant American flag—which meshes with a triangular white concrete tower that houses offices and the library proper. The main exhibition area is largely below grade.

Architect in charge: Theodore Musho; project architect: Robert Milburn; resident architect: Harry Barone. Engineers: Weiskopf & Pickworth (structural); Cosentini Assoc. (mechanical). Landscape architects: Kiley, Tyndall, Walker; Rachel Lambert Mellon. General contractor: Turner Construction.

See: AIA Journal 69 (mid-May 1980): 180–89. *Architectural Record* 167 (February 1980): 81–90. *A + U: Architecture and Urbanism,* no. 136 (January 1982): 44–49. *GA Document,* no. 1 (Summer 1980): 98–109.

■ 309

John Hancock Tower; Boston, MA; 1975 (see Illus. 154).

This 60-story office building, sheathed in reflective glass, has been roundly praised for fitting 2 million square feet of space into a small site while consorting agreeably with landmarks on a historic square. But when its glass panes—buffeted by high winds—started breaking by the dozens, lawsuits proliferated and a drastic program of reglazing had to be initiated.

Design partner: Harry N. Cobb. Engineers: The Office of James Ruderman (structural);

154 John Hancock Tower; Boston, MA; 1975. *See* Entry 309. (Courtesy John Hancock Mutual Life Insurance Co.; Boston, MA.)

154

Associated architects: Kahn & Jacobs;
G. Meredith Musick. Consulting engineers:
Jaros, Baum & Bolles; Severud-Elstad-Krueger.
General contractor: George A. Fuller Co.

Honors: AIA Merit Award, 1959.

See: *AIA Journal* 31 (June 1959): 92.
Architectural Forum 103 (November 1955):
128–37. *Progressive Architecture* 38 (June 1957):
170.

■ 311

**National Center for Atmospheric
Research; near Boulder, CO; 1967.**
This sharply angular and irregularly
shaped cluster of research facilities, set
against a background of rugged
mountains, was inspired by the cliff
dwellings of pre-Columbian Indians. Here
are towers, battlements, and parapets—all
modeled out of bush-hammered pinkish
concrete.
Associates in charge: James P. Morris, Richards
Mixon, Robert Lym. Engineers: Weiskopf &
Pickworth (structural); Jaros Baum & Bolles
(mechanical). Landscape architect: Dan Kiley.
General contractor: Martin K. Eby Construction
Co.

Honors: AIA Bicentennial List, one
nomination.

See: *AIA Journal* 68 (June 1979): 68–75 and
cover. *Architectural Forum* 127 (October 1967):
145–54. *Architectural Record* 142 (October
1967): 145–54. Y. Futagawa, ed., *I. M. Pei &
Partners: National Center for Atmospheric
Research*, text by W. Marlin, Global Architecture,
no. 41 (Tokyo: A. D. A. Edita, 1976).

■ 312

**Paul Mellon Center for the Arts,
Choate-Rosemary Hall; Wallingford,
CT; 1972.**
Shared by two prep schools and housing a
theater, studios, classrooms, and a lounge,
this concrete-and-steel, frankly
asymmetrical center boasts exciting
interior spaces and a strong sense of
interplay between indoors and outdoors.
Its two component structures are linked
by a square-cut bridge under which runs a
tile-paved pathway that links the two
schools.
Architect in charge: Ralph Heisel. Engineers:
Olaf Soot (structural); Campbell & Friedland
(mechanical). Theater consultants: George
Izenour Associates. Landscape architect: Joseph
R. Gangemi. General contractor: George B. H.
Macomber Co.

Honors: AIA Honor Award, 1974.

See: *AIA Journal* 61 (May 1974): 43.
Architectural Record 153 (January 1973): 111–
18. *Architecture Plus* 1 (March 1973): 58.

■ 313

**Society Hill Apartments;
Philadelphia, PA; town houses
completed 1963, Society Hill Towers
1964.**
Here's urban redevelopment with
understated good taste. Three-story brick
town houses, arranged around a
courtyard, share long continuous walls
broken only by windows and arched
private entrances; their companion
31-story apartment buildings are serenely
simple concrete and glass slabs.
Job captain for town houses: Owren J. Aftreth.
Associate architects for town houses: Wright,
Andrade & Amenta & Gane. General contractor
for town houses: Jack Feldman.

See: *Architectural Forum* 118 (April 1963): 90.
Progressive Architecture 45 (December 1964):
188–91. *Architectural Review* 134 (September
1963): 198–99.

■ 314

**University Plaza, Greenwich Village;
New York, NY; 1966 (see Illus. 155).**
Three almost identical 30-story apartment
slabs, arranged in pinwheel fashion on a
spacious landscaped site, and designed to
serve as housing for New York University
faculty and married graduate students.
Two-thirds of all apartments occupy
building corners and so enjoy double
exposure; an arresting Picasso sculpture
lends drama to the development's central
space.
Senior associate in charge: James Ingo Freed.
Engineers: Farkas & Barron (structural);
Caretsky Associates (mechanical). General
contractor: Tishman Construction Corporation.

Honors: AIA Honor Award, 1967; Bard Award,
1967.

See: *AIA Journal* 47 (June 1967): 63.
Architectural Forum 125 (December 1966): 21–
29. *Architecture Plus* 1 (March 1973): 72–73.

155 University Plaza,
Greenwich Village; New
York, NY; 1966. *See* Entry
314. (Photographer: Ashod
Kassabian; New York, NY.)

155

I. M. PEI; COSSUTA & PONTE

■ 315

**Christian Science Church Center;
Boston, MA; 1971/73.**
Incorporated into an already existing
complex on a 15-acre site are a high
Colonnade Building and a trim 3-story
Sunday school. Set among them are
formal gardens and a 670-foot-long
reflecting pool.
Associate in charge: Joseph V. Morog. Engineers:
Weiskopf & Pickworth (structural); Syska &
Hennessy (mechanical/electrical). Landscape
architects: Sasaki, Dawson, DeMay Associates.
General contractor: Aberthaw Construction Co.

Honors: AIA Bicentennial List, two
nominations; CRSI Design Award, 1974.

See: Architectural Forum 139 (September
1973): 24–39. *Progressive Architecture* 47 (June
1966): 154–57. *Architecture Plus* 1 (March 1973):
32–35.

I. M. PEI; HARPER & KEMP

■ 316

Dallas City Hall; Dallas, TX; 1978.
The strongly sloping, 560-foot-long front
facade of this monumental concrete
structure cantilevers 68 feet northward,
partly shading its 425-foot-deep plaza;

parts of its shorter east and west facades
also are cantilevered but step outward
floor by floor. Indoors there's a 100-foot-
high central court overhung
contrapuntally by balconies. The plaza
features a trio of giant flagpoles and a
round pool 180 feet in diameter;
concealed underneath is a 1,325-car
garage.
Team for I. M. Pei & Partners: I. M. Pei, Eason H.
Leonard, Theodore J. Musho, Theodore A.
Amberg, George Woo, Harry Barone.
Consultants: Terry-Rosenlund (structural);
Gaynor & Sirmen (mechanical). General
contractor: Robert E. McKee, Inc.

See: AIA Journal 67 (mid-May 1978): 112–17.
Progressive Architecture 60 (May 1979): 102–5.
GA Document, special issue, no. 1 (1980): 244–
47. *Architectural Review* 164 (November 1978):
300–301.

I. M. PEI; KING & KING

■ 317

**School of Journalism Building,
Syracuse University; Syracuse, NY;
1964.**
This concrete building with a neoclassical
air was designed to be the first of three in
the Samuel I. Newhouse Communications
Center. As the key structure in a projected
quadrangle, it was set on a raised plaza;
facilities that required no natural light and
might be shared by the other two
buildings were located centrally under the
plaza.

Architect in charge for I. M. Pei & Associates:
Kellogg Wong. Associated project architect for
King & King: Russell King. Engineers: Eckerlin &
Klepper (structural); Robson & Woese
(mechanical). General contractor: J. D. Taylor
Construction Co.

Honors: AIA First Honor Award, 1965.

See: AIA Journal 44 (July 1965): 23–46.
Progressive Architecture 45 (September 1964):
91–92; 46 (February 1965): 168–73.

PELLECHIA & MYERS (see entry no. 204)

Cesar PELLI (see also entry nos. 72 and 128–30)

Winner, AIA Architectural Firm Award,
1989.

■ 318

**Herring Hall, Rice University;
Houston, TX; 1984 (see Illus. 156).**
Home to the Jesse Jones Graduate School
of Administration, this contextual yet
postmodern building is bisected
lengthwise by an arcade that, midway,
looks out on a courtyard. Enthusiastically
ornamental brickwork in a range of
patterns animates its exterior. One of its
most intriguing interior spaces is a 2-story
library with much warm, traditional
detailing; its vaulted ceiling wears pale

156 Herring Hall, Rice
University; Houston, TX;
1984. *See* Entry 318. (Courtesy Cesar Pelli & Associates; New Haven, CT.
Photographer: © Paul Hes-
ter.)

156

wallpaper crisscrossed with dabs of turquoise and yellow.

Partners: Cesar Pelli, Diana Balmori, Frederick Clarke; design team leader: Kevin Hart. associated architects for contract administration: Brooks/Collier. Consultants: Walter P. Moore & Assoc. (structural); Ray S. Burns & Assoc. (mechanical). Construction manager: Mayan Construction Co.

Honors: AIA Honor Award, 1986.

See: Architecture 74 (May 1985): 174–81 and cover. *Progressive Architecture* 66 (April 1985): 86–97 and cover. *Arts + Architecture,* new series, 4 (July 1985): 78–83. *A + U: Architecture and Urbanism,* extra edition, no. 7 (July 1985): 120–43.

■ 319

Museum of Modern Art Residential Tower and Gallery Expansion; New York, NY; 1984 (see Illus. 157).

MoMA, often expanded and modified (see entry no. 187), this time has developed income property to help support its activities: a 53 story residential tower, designed to be "a background building," with a curtain wall that mistily mixes eleven tones of opaque glass. Meanwhile, the museum proper has doubled its gallery space and acquired a new auditorium and other amenities, most notably a greenhouselike Garden Hall that looks out on the Sculpture Garden.

Designers for Cesar Pelli & Associates: Fred Clarke, Diana Balmori, Thomas Morton. Edward Durell Stone Associates, P. C., for museum tower. Gruen Associates, early planning of gallery expansion and collaboration in earlier tower design. Engineers: Robert Rosenwasser Assoc. (structural); Cosentini Assoc. (mechanical). General contractor: Turner Construction.

See: Architectural Record 172 (October 1984): 164–77. *Architecture* 73 (October 1984): 87–95. *Architectural Design* 55, no. 1–2 (1985): 36–37. *GA Document,* no. 12 (January 1985): 42–49.

■ 320

World Financial Center, Battery Park City; New York, NY; in progress, anticipated completion date 1989 (see Illus. 158).

It's been called a latter-day Rockefeller Center, this riverfront office/commercial complex comprising two 10-story octagonal "gateway" buildings, four stocky office towers, a 50,000-square-foot Winter Garden with restaurants and palm trees,

157 Museum of Modern Art gallery expansion; New York, NY; 1984. *See* Entry 319. (Courtesy Cesar Pelli & Associates; New Haven, CT. Photographer: © Kenneth Champlin Photos.)

157

158 World Financial Center, Battery Park City; New York, NY; projected completion date: 1989. *See* Entry 320. (Courtesy Cesar Pelli & Associates; New Haven, CT. Photographer: Courtesy of Battery Park City Authority.)

158

and a 4-acre plaza. The ratio of granite to glass on the skins of the office towers decreases as they rise. They range in height from 34 to 51 stories; each has a different main entrance, silhouette, and geometric top.

Project principal: F. C. Clarke; project director: T. Morton; design team leader: J. Pickard; senior designer: M. Shoemaker. Adamson Associates and Haines, Lundberg & Waehler, architects of record. Consultants: M. Paul Friedberg & Partners, landscape; Lev Zetlin Assoc., M. S. Yolles & Partners, structural; Flack & Kurtz, mechanical. General contractor: Olympia & York Battery Park Co.

See: *Architecture* 75 (December 1986): 36–43. *Progressive Architecture* 66 (July 1985): 79–86 and cover. *Urban Land* 44 (September 1985): 22–26.

159

159 Beckman, Helipot Corporation plant; Newport Beach, CA; 1957/58. *See* Entry 321. (Courtesy Pereira Associates; Los Angeles, CA. Photographer: Julius Shulman.)

PEREIRA & LUCKMAN

■ 321

Beckman, Helipot Corporation plant; Newport Beach, CA; 1957/58 (see Illus. 159).
An industrial plant that resembles a resort hotel, it is geared to blend into a seaside town and attract high-caliber personnel. Designed for the manufacture of precision electronic components, it supplies high levels of light and close control of temperature, humidity, and dust.
Landscape architect: Fred Lang. Contractor: M. J. Brock & Sons.

Honors: AIA Merit Award, 1958.

See: *AIA Journal* 30 (July 1958): 40–41. *Arts + Architecture* 75 (May 1958): 10–11. *Architectural Record* 125 (January 1959): 147–70.

■ 322

CBS Television City; Los Angeles, CA; 1952 (see Illus. 160).
A complex of studios and related facilities for producing programs for TV. The studios are enormous: 130 by 110 feet by 42 feet high; hung from their ceilings are intricate systems of movable lights, cameras, and air-conditioning vents.
General contractor: William Simpson Construction Company.

Honors: AIA Merit Award, 1954.

See: *Architectural Forum* 96 (May 1952): 101–10; 98 (March 1953): 146–49. *Arts + Architecture* 70 (January 1953): 20–23.

PEREZ ASSOCIATES

■ 323

Louisiana World Exposition, 1984; New Orleans, LA; 1984 (see Illus. 161).
Built on 82 acres in a dock and warehouse district, this fair glowed with pastel colors, abounded in fanciful sculptures of giant alligators, mermaids, and the like, and featured a Wonderwall (permeable) 12 feet wide and half a mile long that simulated a parade of Mardi Gras floats. Fair buildings retained for use afterward include the Lousiana Convention Center and Riverwalk, a retail development to be managed by the Rouse Company.
Project director: Allen Eskew. Design team: Arthur Anderson, Leonard Salvato, Chuck

160

160 CBS Television City; Los Angeles, CA; 1952. *See* Entry 322. (Courtesy Pereira Associates; Los Angeles, CA. Photographer: Ronald Moore.)

161 Louisiana World Exposition; New Orleans, LA; 1984. *See* Entry 323. (Courtesy Perez Architects; New Orleans, LA.)

161

Sanders, Dennis Brady, Hank Liu. Design consultants: Charles Moore, William Turnbull, Herb Rosenthal Associates. Design consultant for amphitheater: Frank Gehry.

See: *Architectural Record* 172 (July 1984): 73–85. *Architecture* 73 (July 1984): 10–12. *Landscape Architecture* 74 (July–August 1984): 48–55. *Industrial Design* 31 (July–August 1984): 20–29.

August PEREZ; Charles MOORE

■ 324

Piazza d'Italia and St. Joseph's Fountain; New Orleans, LA; 1978 (see Illus. 162).

Splashed with bright colors, neon-lit at night, combining a tall outline of a campanile, allusions to the classical orders of architecture, and a fountain that pours water down an 80-foot-long map of Italy, this plaza has variously been called "spaghetti Disneyland" and "the richest expression yet of the historical revival in contemporary architecture."

Project designers: R. Allen Eskew and Malcolm Heard, Jr.; project coordinator: Robert Kleinpeter. Fountain design: Charles Moore. Consultants: Morphy, Makofsky & Masson (structural); Cary Gamble & Assoc. (mechanical/electrical). General contractor: Landis Construction.

162 Piazza d'Italia and St. Joseph's Fountain; New Orleans, LA; 1978. *See* Entry 324. (Courtesy Perez Architects; New Orleans, LA.)

162

See: *Progressive Architecture* 59 (November 1978): 81–87 and cover. *Architectural Design* 50, nos. 5–6 (1980): 20–25. *Architectural Review* 165 (May 1979): 255–56. Paul Goldberger, *On the Rise* (New York: Times Books, 1983), 134–36.

PERKINS & WILL

■ 325

Keokuk Senior High School and Community College; Keokuk, IA; 1953.

Spread out on a generous site in rolling grasslands, this school incorporates energy-efficient features such as sunshades and through ventilation. Along one long side of its 4-story classroom building, glass-walled corridors highlighted by red sun fins and yellow window frames give students inside beautiful views while presenting a lively and colorful facade.

Landscape architect: David Gill. General contractor: Lovejoy Construction Co.

Honors: AIA Merit Award, 1954.

See: Architectural Forum 101 (October 1954):

113–19. *Progressive Architecture* 32 (June 1951): 89–93; 35 (October 1954): 122–26.

PERRY, DEAN, STAHL & ROGERS

■ 326

Wellesley College Science Center; Wellesley, MA; 1977? (see Illus. 163).

Labs, office space, classrooms, and library facilities for eleven scientific disciplines are brought together in this high-tech reinforced concrete building. Virtually all mechanical and structural elements, often brightly color coded, are exposed; indeed, the roof bears a forest of exhaust stacks, and columns and beams seem oversized. Inside, there's a startling atrium: Sage Hall, a renovated neo-Gothic red brick building now connected to the center, supplies one of its walls.

Architect: Charles F. Roger II; job captain: Peter A. Ringenbach; structural consultant: John W. Nevins of Simpson, Gumpertz & Heger. Landscape architect: Mason & Frey. General contractor: George B. H. Macomber Co.

See: Progressive Architecture 59 (March 1978): 70–75. *Architettura* 24 (November 1977): 386–87; 24 (July 1978): 172–73. *Architectural Review*

162 (September 1977): 148–55. *L'Architecture d'Aujourd'hui,* no. 216 (September 1981): 78–81.

William Wesley PETERS see Frank Lloyd WRIGHT; William Wesley PETERS *and* TALIESIN ASSOCIATED ARCHITECTS

PETERSON & BRICKBAUER

■ 327

Maryland Blue Cross Inc.; Towson, MD; 1972.

At this jauntily imaginative headquarters in a suburban setting, offices are housed in a mirrored 134-foot cube, while mechanical services occupy a flame red, brick-faced 42-foot cube alongside.

Associate architects: Brown, Guenther, Battaglia, Galvin. Engineers: Sadler Associates (structural); Piccirillo & Brown (mechanical/electrical). General contractor: The Cogswell Construction Co.

See: Architectural Forum 135 (November 1971): 7. *Architecture Plus* 1 (April 1973): 16–21. G. E. Kidder Smith, *A Pictorial History of Architecture in America* (New York: American Heritage, 1976), 1: 243–45.

PIERCE & PIERCE see GOLEMAN & ROLFE; PIERCE & PIERCE

Warren PLATNER

■ 328

Windows on the World and The Club at the World Trade Center; New York, NY; 1976 (see Illus. 164).

Occupying the 1-acre 107th floor of the north tower of the World Trade Center (see entry no. 509), this has been called "the most spectacular restaurant in the world." Its whole periphery is devoted to dining spaces, frequently terraced, so up to 1,000 guests can enjoy magnificent harbor and city views. Separate areas, including banquet rooms and a bar, have their own distinctive flavors, thanks to a

163 Wellesley College Science Center; Wellesley, MA; 1977? *See* Entry 326. (Courtesy Perry Dean Rogers and Partners; Boston, MA. Photographer: © Edward Jacoby.)

163

164 Windows on the World and The Club at the World Trade Center; New York, NY; 1976. *See* Entry 328. (Courtesy Warren Platner Associates; New Haven, CT. Photographer: © Ezra Stoller.)

164

wealth of luxurious and imaginative architect designed details.

Associates of Warren Platner on this project: Robert Brauer, Harvey Kaufman (project architect, design); Jesse Lyons (project architect, construction). Consultants: Skilling Helle Christiansen Robertson (structural); Jaros Baum & Bolles (mechanical). Project management: Joseph Baum.

See: *Architectural Record* 161 (May 1977): 111–18. *Interiors* 136 (February 1977): 80–95. *Interior Design* 47 (December 1976): 102–27.

James Stewart POLSHEK

■ 329

500 Park Tower; New York, NY; 1984 (see Illus. 165).
This project renovated and greatly expanded the former Pepsi-Cola Building (see entry no. 420), an 11-story aluminum and glass masterpiece, while respectfully preserving and echoing its exterior. From a new 40-story granite tower, whose stonework blends in with nearby masonry facades, a narrow, 25-story aluminum and glass extension cantilevers harmoniously partway over the older building. The top floors contain residential condominiums; lower floors, old and new, supply office space.
Design partner: James Stewart Polshek, partner in charge: Paul S. Byard, design associate: James

165 500 Park Tower; New York, NY; 1984. *See* Entry 329. (Courtesy James Stewart Polshek and Partners; New York, NY. Photographer: Timothy Hursley.)

165

Garrison. Associated architects: Schuman-Lichtenstein-Claman-Efron. Engineers: Office of Irwin G. Cantor (structural); Cosentini Assoc. (mechanical). Construction manager: Turner Construction Company/Lehrer-McGovern Inc., A Joint Venture.

Honors: AIA Honor Award, 1986.

See: *Architectural Record* 172 (July 1984): 86–95. *Architecture* 75 (May 1986): 206–9. *Architettura* 30 (December 1984): 898–900.

■ 330

New York State Bar Center; Albany, NY; 1971 (see Illus. 166).
Three historic row houses were incorporated into the tasteful design of this bar association headquarters, which contains office space and a Great Hall used for large receptions and as a library/lounge. New structures are placed deferentially behind the old; large spaces, skylighted, are located underneath a modified courtyard.
Associate in charge: Howard M. Kaplan. Landscape architects: Johnson and Dee. Engineers: Aaron Garfinkel Associates (structural); Benjamin & Zicherman (mechanical/ electrical). General contractor: McManus, Longe, Brockwehl, Inc.

Honors: PA Design Award, 1969; AIA Honor Award, 1972.

See: *AIA Journal* 57 (May 1972): 33. *Architectural Record* 150 (December 1971): 94–99. *Baumeister* 69 (July 1972): 736–38.

166 New York State Bar Center; Albany, NY; 1971. *See* Entry 330. (Courtesy James Stewart Polshek and Partners; New York, NY. Photographer: George Cserna.)

166

POMERANCE & BREINES; M. Paul FRIEDBERG

■ 331

Amphitheater and Plaza, Jacob Riis Houses; New York, NY; 1966 (see Illus. 167).
Three acres of inviting—and virtually indestructible—facilities for outdoor recreation are set in the heart of a low-income housing development. Included in this mostly hard-paved space are a sculptural fountain, an amphitheater, a sequence of open-air "rooms," and lots of things to climb on.
Landscape architect: M. Paul Friedberg & Assoc. Engineers: Ames & Selnick (structural); I. M. Robbins & Assoc. (mechanical). General contractor: W. J. Barney.

Honors: AIA Honor Award, 1967; Bard Award, 1967.

See: *AIA Journal* 74 (December 1985): 48–53. *Architectural Forum* 125 (July–August 1966): 68–73. *Architectural Record* 140 (July 1966): 196–99; 140 (December 1966): 134–35. *Architecture* 74 (December 1985): 48–53.

167 Amphitheater and Plaza, Jacob Riis Houses; New York, NY; 1966. *See* Entry 331. (Courtesy Pomerance & Breines; New York, NY.)

167

John PORTMAN *see also* EDWARDS & PORTMAN

■ 332

Hyatt Regency San Francisco, Embarcadero Center; San Francisco, CA; 1972.
A breathtakingly huge and lovingly detailed prism-shaped interior space, 17 stories high and 300 feet long, is the focus of this 840-room hotel located in a gala downtown office/shopping/restaurant complex. Many of its rooms, poised on one sharply sloping facade, look out on a fountain designed by Lawrence Halprin. Mechanical engineers: Britt Alderman, Jr., & Assoc. General contractors: Jones-Allen-Dillingham, a joint venture of J. A. Jones Construction Co., J. B. Allen Co., and Dillingham Corp.

Honors: AIA Bicentennial List, two nominations.

See: *AIA Journal* 66 (October 1977): 36–43. *Architectural Forum* 140 (November 1973): 46–

55. *Interiors* 133 (October 1973): 78–93. Y. Futagawa, ed., *John Portman ... Hyatt Regency San Francisco,* text by Paul Goldberger, Global Architecture, no. 28 (Tokyo: A. D. A. Edita, 1974).

■ 333

Los Angeles Westin Bonaventure Hotel; Los Angeles, CA; 1976.

An eye-catcher for Tinseltown: a hotel in the shape of five glittering, mirrored cylinders, 30 to 37 stories high. It contains almost 1,500 rooms and suites plus a multitude of shops, and numerous restaurants including, at the top of its central cylinder, one with a revolving bar.
Consultants: Everett Conklin-West (landscape architects); John Blum & Assoc. (structural engineers); Britt Alderman Engineers (mechanical engineers). General contractors: C. L. Peck in joint venture with Henry C. Beck Co.

See: Progressive Architecture 59 (February 1978): 52–56. *Interior Design* 48 (December 1977)· 114–27. Y. Futagawa, ed., *John Portman & Associates ... Los Angeles Bonaventure Hotel ...,* text by Paul Goldberger, Global Architecture, no. 57 (Tokyo: A. D. A. Edita, 1981).

■ 334

Renaissance Center, Detroit, MI; 1977.

A 32-acre riverfront complex, nicknamed RenCen, it includes a shopping mall and convention facilities. At its center, the Detroit Plaza Hotel rises 73 stories, a shiny cylinder sheathed in reflective glass.

Symmetrically arranged around it are four octagonal office towers.
Consultants: John Grissim & Assoc. (landscape architects); Britt Alderman Associates (mechanical). General contractor: Tishman Construction Co.

See: AIA Journal 68 (September 1977): 28–31. *Progressive Architecture* 59 (February 1978): 57–61. Y. Futagawa, ed., *John Portman & Associates ... Los Angeles Bonaventure Hotel ... Renaissance Center,* text by Paul Goldberger, Global Architecture, no. 57 (Tokyo: A. D. A. Edita, 1981). Robert A. M. Stern, *Pride of Place* (Boston: Houghton Mifflin, 1986), 233–35.

Antoine PREDOCK

■ 335

La Luz; Albuquerque, NM; 1967–74 (see Illus. 168).

A hundred units of luxury cluster housing, desert style. Rows of adobe townhouses with 16-inch mud brick walls and many traditional—and environmentally sound —features are sited on high ground with a spectacular view of the Rio Grande valley and mountains below.
Structural consultant: James Innis.

See: Architectural Forum 131 (July–August 1969): 66–71. *Progressive Architecture* 55 (March 1974): 60–63. *Werk, Bauen + Wohnen* 71, no. 38[39] (March 1984): 66–68. *L'Architecture d'Aujourd'hui* 43 (August–September 1971): cxvii, 70–76.

QUINN & ODA

■ 336

Church of Our Divine Savior; Chico, CA; 1970.

An inviting small church, built on a tiny budget, to serve a neighborhood of trailer parks and modest homes. The sanctuary can seat as many as 370 or can be divided into two spaces; the altar is movable.

Honors: AIA Honor Award, 1971; Bartlett Award, 1971.

See: AIA Journal 55 (June 1971): 45–55. *Architectural Record* 154 (July 1973): 117–32. *Liturgical Arts* 38 (February 1970): 50–51.

George RANALLI

■ 337

First of August Store; New York, NY; 1977 (see Illus. 169).

This renovation took place when a dress shop in a brownstone expanded into the floor above and converted that small space (14 by 66 feet by 11 feet high) to use half for clothes and half for a beauty salon. At the sidewalk line a black grid, filled with clear glass, covers both floors while claiming additional space for the store. Inside, many needed roomettes are

168 La Luz; Albuquerque, NM; 1967–1974. *See* Entry 335. (Courtesy Antoine Predock Architect; Albuquerque, NM. Photographer: Goffe Photographic Associates.)

168

created with ingeniously detailed partitions enhanced by skillfully used light and color.

See: *Architectural Design* 47, nos. 7–8 (1977): 553–57. *Interior Design* 48 (March 1977): 120–25. *A + U: Architecture and Urbanism,* no. 84 (November 1977): 48–53.

Ralph RAPSON

■ 338

Cedar Square West; Minneapolis, MN; 1974 (see Illus. 170).
A 1,299-unit residential complex of eleven buildings ranging from 4 to 40 stories and designed to serve as the nucleus for a "new town in town" to be known as Cedar-Riverside. Curiously, although this development quickly found satisfied tenants, its expansion was fiercely opposed by community groups.
Engineers: Crosier, Greenberg & Partners (structural); Egan & Sons (mechanical).
Landscape architect: Sasaki, Walker Associates.
General contractor: Borson Construction Co.

Honors: AIA Honor Award, 1975; Bartlett Award, 1975; AIA Bicentennial List, one nomination.

See: *AIA Journal* 62 (December 1974): 33–35; 63 (May 1975): 28. *Architectural Record* 154 (December 1973): 102–3. Paul Goldberger, *On the Rise* (New York: Times Books, 1983), 206–9.

169 First of August Store; New York, NY; 1977. *See* Entry 337. (Courtesy George Ranalli, Architect; New York, NY. Photographer: George Cserna.)

169

170 Cedar Square West; Minneapolis, MN; 1974. *See* Entry 338. (Courtesy Ralph Rapson, FAIA, and Associates; Minneapolis, MN.)

170

Tyrone Guthrie Theater; Minneapolis, MN; 1963 (see Illus. 171).

This innovative theater has an asymmetrical open stage that can accommodate backdrops at the rear but is surrounded by seating on three sides. None of its 1,437 seats, also asymmetrically arranged, is more than fifteen rows from the stage.

Project coordinator: Gene Stuart Peterson. Engineers: Meyer & Borgman (structural); Oftedal, Locke & Broadston (mechanical). Acoustical consultant: Robert F. Lambert.

Honors: PA Design Citation, 1961.

See: *AIA Journal* 36 (August 1961): 84–85. *Progressive Architecture* 44 (December 1963): 98–105 and cover. *Arts + Architecture* 80 (August 1963): 16–17, 30.

171

171 Tyrone Guthrie Theater; Minneapolis, MN; 1963. *See* Entry 339. (Courtesy Ralph Rapson, FAIA, and Associates; Minneapolis, MN.)

John Lyon REID

Hillsdale High School; San Mateo, CA; 1955 (see Illus. 172).

An unusual school built around a giant courtyard that encompasses a small, simple stadium with two pools. Classrooms are located in two factorylike blocks of flexible loft space; many have no windows but are illuminated by skylights.

Partner in charge: Burton Rockwell. Structural engineers: Alexander G. Tarics. Landscape architects: Eckbo, Royston & Williams. General contractors: Rothschild, Raffin & Weirick and Northern Constructors.

Honors: AIA Honor Award, 1956.

172

REID, ROCKWELL, BANWELL & TARICS

Health Sciences Instruction and Research Towers, Unit 1, San Francisco Medical Center, University of California; San Francisco, CA; 1966/67 (see Illus. 173).

Twin 16-story towers built on a very constricted site provide column-free laboratory space 90 feet square, unhampered by a complex system of ducts positioned externally. Glass-walled perimeter corridors help to insulate the labs while making the most of attractive views.

Mechanical/electrical engineers: DeLeuw, Cather & Co. General contractor: Dinwiddie Construction Co.

Honors: PA Design Citation, 1961; AISC Architectural Award of Excellence, 1967; AIA Honor Award, 1968.

See: *AIA Journal* 49 (June 1968): 90. *Architectural Record* 143 (June 1968): 129–34. *Progressive Architecture* 42 (January 1961): 122–25.

Viljo REVELL; John B. PARKIN ASSOCIATES

Toronto City Hall; Toronto, Ontario; 1965 (see Illus. 174).

Built from a design that won over more than 500 others in an international competition, this remarkable City Hall looks like an eye from above: its two crescent office towers enfold a low, circular council chamber. Its spacious forecourt is marked by a sweeping ramp, an elevated walkway, and a pool designed to be used for skating in winter.

Engineers: Severud-Elstad-Kreuger Associates (structural); Jaros, Baum & Bolles (mechanical). Landscape architects: Sasaki Strong & Assoc. Acoustic consultant: Prof. V. L. Henderson. General contractor: Anglin-Norcross (Ontario) Limited.

See: *Architectural Forum* 123 (November 1965): 15–23. *Architectural Record* 138 (November 1965): 165–72. *Progressive Architecture* 46 (October 1965): 238–41. *Canadian Architect* 10 (October 1965): 44–57, 61–68.

172 Hillsdale High School; San Mateo, CA; 1955. *See* Entry 340. (Courtesy Reid & Tarics Associates; San Francisco, CA. Photographer: Rodger Sturtevant.)

173

174

REYNOLDS, SMITH & HILLS

■ 343

**Tampa International Airport; Tampa,
FL; 1971.**

This airport features an elevated transit
system that shuttles travelers between a
central "Landside" terminal building and
"Airside" boarding facilities arranged in a
semicircle around it.

Officer in charge: Ivan H. Smith. General
engineering consultant: J. E. Greiner Co.
General contractors: McDevitt & Street Co.; J. A.
Jones Construction Co.; C.A. Fielland, Inc.

See: Architectural Forum 135 (October 1971):
34–37. *Architectural Record* 152 (October
1972): 136–39. *Interiors* 133 (October 1973):
104–11.

RHONE & IREDALE (successor firm: THE IREDALE PARTNERSHIP)

■ 344

**Sedgewick Library, University of
British Columbia; Vancouver, British
Columbia; 1972 (see Illus. 175).**

To locate this terraced, largely
underground library centrally on campus
while preserving a distinctive row of eight

1973): 135–52. *Domus,* no. 542 (January 1975): 1–4. *Interior Design* 45 (August 1974): 122–27.

175

oak trees, a drum 30 feet in diameter was constructed around the roots of each tree and extended from mall level down through the building's lower floors. Interior study spaces were boldly varied and include "carpeted nooks and crannies suitable for very informal postures," as well as more formal areas enlivened by vivid graphics.

Partner in charge: Randle Iredale. Consultants: Canadian Environmental Science (structural/landscaping); D. W. Thomson & Co. (mechanical/electrical). General contractor: Cana Construction.

Honors: Canadian Architect Yearbook Award, 1970.

See: Canadian Architect 18 (April 1973): 40–45. *A+U: Architecture and Urbanism,* no. 50 (February 1975): 55–62. *Process: Architecture,* no. 5 (1978): 94–101.

RICHARDSON ASSOCIATES

■ **345**

Sea-Tac International Airport Expansion; near Seattle, WA; 1974.
For heightened convenience, facilities at this airport are interconnected by an automated transit system for passengers and an integrated baggage-handling system. A 4,300-car garage is located

within the chevron shape of the main terminal.

Project architect: Allen D. Moses. Engineering consultants: Victor O. Gray & Co., Andersen, Bjornstad & Kane (structural); Miskimen/Associates (mechanical). Landscape consultants: Sasaki, Walker & Associates. General contractor, passenger terminal: Morrison-Knudsen Company.

See: Architectural Record 154 (November

Kevin ROCHE John DINKELOO

Winner of the AIA's Architectural Firm Award for 1974. In 1982, Kevin Roche won the Pritzker Architecture Prize.

■ **346**

College Life Insurance Company of America; Indianapolis, IN; first phase, 1971 (see Illus. 176).
In this complex, three monolithic, 11-story office buildings, almost pyramidal in shape, are linked together by bridges and overlook a man-made lake. Windowless concrete walls predominate in their design, but two sloping sides of each building are sheathed in reflective glass. Engineers: Severud Associates (structural); Hubbard, Lawless & Osborne (mechanical/electrical). General contractor: Mid Republic Construction, Inc.

See: Architectural Forum 140 (March 1974): 26–31. *Domus,* no. 555 (February 1976): 26–28. Y. Futagawa, ed., *Kevin Roche John Dinkeloo . . . College Life Insurance Company Headquarters . . .,* text by William Marlin, Global Architecture, no. 29 (Tokyo: A. D. A. Edita, 1974).

175 Sedgewick Library, University of British Columbia; Vancouver, British Columbia; 1972. *See* Entry 344. (Courtesy The Iredale Partnership; Vancouver, BC, Canada. Photographer: John Roaf.)

176 College Life Insurance Company of America; Indianapolis, IN; 1971, first phase. *See* Entry 346. (Courtesy Kevin Roche, John Dinkeloo and Associates; Hamden, CT.)

176

■ **347**

Deere West, John Deere and Company Administrative Center; Moline, IL; 1978 (see Illus. 177).
A long steel-framed, glassed-in bridge connects this three-level addition of weathering steel to a seven-level corporate headquarters of similar construction that was designed by Eero Saarinen (see entry no. 375) and completed in 1964. Within Deere West there's a quarter-acre, glass-roofed, multilevel garden used in part for "outdoor" dining; an inviting cafeteria and other attractive eating areas are located nearby.
Mechanical engineers: AZCO Downey, Inc. Consultants: Tropical Plant Rental, Inc. (garden landscaping); Lankenau-Damgaard & Assoc. (exterior landscaping). General contractor: Turner Construction Co.

See: *AIA Journal* 68 (mid-May 1979): 138–45. *Architectural Record* 165 (February 1979): 85–92. *Interior Design* 50 (April 1979): 208–19.

■ **348**

Ford Foundation Building, New York, NY; 1967 (see Illus. 178).
Behind this prizewinner's serene granite and glass facade lies an elegantly wrought

177 Deere West, John Deere and Company Administrative Center; Moline, IL; 1978. *See* Entry 347. (Courtesy Kevin Roche, John Dinkeloo and Associates; Hamden, CT.)

178 Ford Foundation Building; New York, NY; 1967. *See* Entry 348. (Courtesy Kevin Roche, John Dinkeloo and Associates; Hamden, CT.)

and richly fitted 12-story office building with a one-third-acre garden within it, enclosed by walls of glass. Offices are grouped around this many-leveled courtyard to enhance the staff's sense of community.
Associates: Eugene Festa, Philip Kinsella. Engineers: Severud Associates (structural); Cosentini Associates (mechanical). Landscape architect: Dan Kiley. General contractor: Turner Construction Co.

177

Honors: Bard Award, 1968; AIA Bicentennial List, eleven nominations.

See: *Architectural Record* 143 (February 1968): 105–12 and cover. *Progressive Architecture* 49 (February 1968): 92–105. *Interiors* 127 (March 1968): 95–109. Y. Futagawa, ed., *Kevin Roche John Dinkeloo and Associates: The Ford Foundation Building . . . The Oakland Museum . . .*, text by William Marlin, Global Architecture, no. 4 (Tokyo: A. D. A. Edita, 1974). Y. Futagawa, ed., *Kevin Roche John Dinkeloo: The Ford Foundation Headquarters . . .*, text by Nobuo Hozumi, Global Architecture Detail, no. 4 (Tokyo: A. D. A. Edita, 1977).

■ **349**

General Foods Corporation Headquarters; Rye, NY; 1983 (see Illus. 179).
This 8-story building, which contains 560,000 square feet of office space and almost as much enclosed parking, resembles "a gleaming white . . . Beaux-Arts palace with two equal wings flanking a central rotunda." Clad in vinyl-coated aluminum siding, it's striped with relatively narrow strip windows for energy efficiency. Particularly striking is its 95-foot-high central atrium, which has a pitched, semicircular skylight and contains, among other things, a 480-seat employee cafeteria.
Architects: Kevin Roche, John Dinkeloo, Philip Kinsella, David Jacob. Engineers: Weiskopf & Pickworth (structural); Cosentini Assoc. (mechanical/electrical). Construction manager: Lehrer/McGovern.

178

Honors: R. S. Reynolds Memorial Award, 1985.

179 General Foods Corporation Headquarters; Rye, NY; 1983. *See* Entry 349. (Courtesy Kevin Roche, John Dinkeloo and Associates; Hamden, CT.)

179

See: Architectural Record 172 (September 1984): 104–19. *Architecture* 74 (February 1985): 60–69. *Landscape Architecture* 74 (May–June 1984): 48–53.

■ **350**

Knights of Columbus Headquarters; New Haven, CT; 1970 (see Illus. 180).

A 23-story office building primarily faced with glass shaded by massive overhangs of weathering steel, it has at its four corners tile-sheathed, circular concrete columns that contain lavatories and fire stairs and, in conjunction with the building's elevator core, support its structural girders. Steel overhangs are omitted from its more gently handled bottom three stories.
Project associates: David Powrie, Bruce Detmers. Engineers: Pfisterer, Tor & Associates (structural); Cosentini Associates (mechanical). General contractor: Koppers Company, Inc.

Honors: AISC Architectural Award of Excellence, 1970.

See: Architectural Record 148 (August 1970): 109–16. *Progressive Architecture* 51 (September 1970): 84–91. *Baumeister* 68 (March 1971): 241–43. David Guise, *Design and Technology in Architecture* (New York: Wiley, 1985).

■ **351**

Metropolitan Museum of Art Additions; New York, NY; in progress (see Illus. 181).

For over a decade, this museum has been changing and growing, gaining broad stairs and fountains along its Fifth Avenue

180 Knights of Columbus Headquarters; New Haven, CT; 1970. *See* Entry 350. (Courtesy Kevin Roche, John Dinkeloo and Associates; Hamden, CT.)

180

facade and a series of new wings of deliberately unobstrusive, abstract design, clad in limestone and glass. Notable additions include the Lehman Pavilion (1975), Egyptian Wings (1979), Douglas Dillon Galleries (1981), Michael Rockefeller Wing (1982), and the Wallace Galleries for Twentieth Century Art (1988). Ivy covers and softens many Central Park facades.

See: *AIA Journal* 70 (May 1981): 28–41; 71 (April 1982): 62–63. *Progressive Architecture* 56 (August 1975): 60–63; 60 (May 1979): 98–101. *Architectural Review* 161 (April 1977): 203–6.

■ 352

Oakland Museum; Oakland, CA; 1969 (see Illus. 182).

This wide-ranging complex—built on a four-block site and comprising art, cultural history, and natural science galleries on three separate levels—is elaborately terraced and ingratiatingly landscaped. Much of its exhibition space is underground, while plantings on its terraces and greenery on top endow it with many of the qualities of a botanical garden.

Associate on job: Philip Kinsella. Engineers: Severud Associates (structural); Alexander Boome (mechanical/electrical). Landscape architect: Dan Kiley. Contractor: B & R Construction Co.

Honors: AIA Bicentennial List, one nomination.

See: *AIA Journal* 66 (June 1977): 30–37. *Architectural Record* 147 (April 1970): 115–22. *Progressive Architecture* 50 (December 1969): 92–95. Y. Futagawa, ed., *Kevin Roche John Dinkeloo and Associates: The Ford Foundation Building . . . The Oakland Museum . . .* , text by William Marlin, Global Architecture, no. 4 (Tokyo: A. D. A. Edita, 1974).

■ 353

One United Nations Plaza; New York, NY; 1976 (see Illus. 183).

This 39-story tower, clad in reflective blue-green glass, contains both office space and the United Nations Plaza Hotel, which occupies the twenty-eighth to thirty-eighth floors. On its north facade, 45-degree slantbacks angle up from the twelfth and twenty-eighth floors. At its southeast corner near the twelfth floor, the facade parallels the lines of the northeast corner, slanting in and down, then continues downward, creating an additional wall. Near street level, a distinctive glass awning wraps around the building.

Engineers: Weiskopf & Pickworth (structural); Cosentini Assoc. (mechanical/electrical). Contractor: Turner Construction.

See: *Architectural Record* 160 (October 1976): 117–24. *Baumeister* 74 (May 1977): 429–31. *Architettura* 22 (April 1977): 712–13.

■ 354

Veterans Memorial Coliseum; New Haven, CT; 1972 (see Illus. 184).

This "big, brawny building," which can seat as many as 11,500 spectators, is situated in the heart of a downtown redevelopment area, adjacent to the Knights of Columbus Headquarters (see entry no. 350) designed by the same architectural firm. Spanning its arena is a four-level parking garage reached by two giant spiral ramps.

Engineers: Le Messurier Associates (structural); Hubbard, Lawless & Osborne (mechanical/electrical). Acoustical consultants: Bolt, Beranek & Newman. General contractor: Gilbane Building Co.

See: *Architectural Forum* 140 (March 1974): 36–41. *Architectural Review* 153 (April 1973): 216–32. *Domus,* no. 531 (February 1974): 2–5.

183

■ 355

Watts Towers; Los Angeles, CA; 1954.
One man's artistic fantasy is here given
substance: fanciful spires pieced together
over a period of thirty-three years from
steel reinforcing rods and wire mesh,
colorfully decorated with seashells and
fragments of broken dishes and bottles.

Honors: AIA Bicentennial List, one
nomination.

See: Architectural Forum 123 (September
1965): 19. *Architectural Review* 68 (July 1951):
23–25. *Arts + Architecture* 76 (September
1959): 27–28. *Process: Architecture,* no. 3
(December 1977): 224–25.

Richard ROGERS; KELBAUGH & LEE

In 1985, Richard Rogers received the
Royal Gold Medal for Architecture.

■ 356

**PA Technology Laboratory and
Corporate Facility ("Patscenter");
Hightstown, near Princeton, NJ; 1985.**
It looks like a factory, but in fact this
42,600-square-foot, 1-story building just
supplies office and lab space to an

international firm of technical consultants.
The roof is suspended from an **A**-frame of
nine 60-foot-high tubular steel masts hung
with cables, all finished in bright orange.
The crossbar of the **A** carries lots of
exposed, color-coded ducts and pipes, all
visible from below through an array of
bubble skylights.
For Richard Rogers & Partners: Ram Ahronov,
Gennaro Picardi, John McAslan. For Kelbaugh &
Lee: Sang Lee. Consultant architect: Pierre
Botschi. Consultants: Zion and Breen
(landscape); Ove Arup & Partners, and Robert
Silman Assoc. (structural); Ove Arup & Partners,
and Syska & Hennessy (mechanical). General
contractor: John W. Ryan Construction.

See: Progressive Architecture 66 (August 1985):
67–74 and cover. *Architectural Review* 178
(September 1985): 38–43. *Baumeister* 83
(November 1986): 40–43.

Emery ROTH AND SONS (see also entry
no. 509)

■ 357

**Helmsley Palace Hotel; New York, NY,
1980 (see Illus. 185).**
This 51-story 1,100-room hotel slab, clad
in bronzed glass, gains panache from the
landmark Villard Houses, which serve as
its entry wing. These "houses," a U-
shaped, five-level complex designed in
1882 by McKim, Mead & White, have been
lovingly restored to their original
grandeur. Many of their large, richly

183 One United Nations
Plaza; New York, NY; 1976.
See Entry 353. (Courtesy
Kevin Roche, John Dinke-
loo and Associates; Ham-
den, CT.)

184 Veterans Memorial
Coliseum; New Haven, CT;
1972. *See* Entry 354. (Courtesy Kevin Roche, John Dinkeloo and Associates;
Hamden, CT.)

184

185 Helmsley Palace Hotel; New York, NY 1980. *See* Entry 357. (Courtesy Emery Roth & Sons, P.C., Architects; New York, NY.)

electrical). General contractor: Diesel Construction Co.

See: Architectural Record 131 (May 1962): 195–200; 133 (May 1963): 151–58. *Progressive Architecture* 44 (April 1963): 59–62.

Bernard ROTHZEID (subsequent firm name: ROTHZEID KAISERMAN THOMSON & BEE)

■ 359

Turtle Bay Towers; New York, NY; 1977 (see Illus. 187).

Here's an imaginative renovation in which a 24-story factory loft building, badly damaged by a gas explosion, has been transformed into luxury housing. Greenhouse extensions tucked into the building's setbacks give attractive added space to its roomy, high-ceilinged apartments.

Partner in charge: Peter Thomson; project designers: Bernard Rothzeid, Carmi Bee. Engineers: Harwood & Gould (structural); George Langer (mechanical/electrical). General contractor: Rockrose Construction Corporation.

Honors: AIA Honor Award for Extended Use, 1978; Bard Award, 1979.

185

ornamented rooms are now public spaces within the hotel; others—in the north wing—constitute The Urban Center.

Partner in charge: Richard Roth, Jr.; project architect: John Secreti; designer: Vijay Kale; project architect for renovation and restoration of Villard House complex: James W. Rhodes.

See: Architectural Record 169 (mid-February 1981): 65–68. *Progressive Architecture* 62 (November 1981): 96–101. *Interior Design* 52 (February 1981): 206–21. *Technology & Conservation* 5 (Winter 1980): 32–46.

■ 358

Pan Am Building; New York, NY; 1963 (see Illus. 186).

A controversial, prism-shaped, giant office building—a 49-story tower on a 10-story base—it was erected just north of the stately old Grand Central Terminal and so visually obstructed Park Avenue. It was designed to accommodate 17,000 occupants and 250,000 visitors daily.

Design consultants: Walter Gropius, Pietro Belluschi. Engineers: James Ruderman (structural); Jaros, Baum & Bolles (mechanical/

186 Pan Am Building, New York, NY; 1963. *See* Entry 358. (Courtesy Emery Roth & Sons, P.C., Architects; New York, NY.)

186

See: *AIA Journal* 67 (mid-May 1978): 134–35.
Architectural Record 162 (September 1977):
111–26.

Paul RUDOLPH

■ 360

**Boston Government Service Center;
Boston, MA; 1971.**
A monumental megastructure shaped, in
plan, like a hollow wedge and built
around an elegantly contoured plaza. It
comprises the Division of Employment
Security Building (Shepley, Bulfinch,
Richardson & Abbott, architects), Mental
Health Building (Desmond & Lord,
architects), and Health, Welfare and
Education Building (M. A. Dyer and
Pedersen & Tilney, architects).
Coordinating architect, architectural designer
for the Mental Health and Health, Welfare and
Education buildings, and architect for the
garage and plaza: Paul Rudolph. Engineers:
Souza & True (structural); Greenleaf Associates
(mechanical/electrical).

See: *Architectural Record* 139 (June 1966):
140–41. *L'Architecture d'Aujourd'hui,* no. 157
(August 1971): 88–91. Y. Futagawa, ed., *Paul
Rudolph: Interdenominational Chapel,
Tuskegee . . . Boston Government Service
Center . . . ,* text by Carl Black, Jr., Global
Architecture, no. 20 (Tokyo: A. D. A. Edita,
1973).

■ 361

**Endo Laboratories Building; Garden
City, NY; 1964.**
A pharmaceutical manufacturing plant
designed to keep its skilled workers
happy while providing them with interior
spaces tailored for particular job
functions. Its cast-in-place concrete facade,
approached by a long, almost ceremonial
staircase, is marked by rows of fortresslike
turrets. For meals and breaks there's an
appealing roof garden topped off by a
spacious glass-enclosed pavilion.
Job captain: Bryant L. Conant. Structural
engineer: Henry A. Pfisterer. Mechanical
engineer and general contractor: Walter Kidde
Constructors, Inc. Landscape architects: Robert
Zion–Harold Breen.

See: *Progressive Architecture* 45 (November
1964): 168–73. *Architettura* 10 (April 1965):
816–17. *The Architecture of Paul Rudolph,*
introduction by Sibyl Moholy-Nagy (New York:
Praeger, 1970).

■ 362.

**Married Student Housing, Yale
University; New Haven, CT; 1961
(see Illus. 188).**
Five low-rise apartment units faced in
tweedy-textured brick are arranged
irregularly around a flight of steps that
almost bisects their steep site. This
unusual small housing development is
said to have been inspired by
Mediterranean hillside villages.
Engineers: Henry Pfisterer (structural), Van
Zelm, Heywood & Shadford (mechanical/
electrical). General contractor: George B. H.
Macomber Co.

See: *Architectural Forum* 116 (March 1962):
98–101. *Architectural Record* 129 (March 1961):
142–46. *Perspecta,* no. 7 (1961): 51–64.

187 Turtle Bay Towers;
New York, NY; 1977. *See*
Entry 359. (Courtesy Roth-
zeid, Kaiserman, Thomson
& Bee, P.C.; New York, NY.
Photographer: © Norman
McGrath.)

188 Married Student
Housing, Yale University;
New Haven, CT; 1961. *See*
Entry 362. (Courtesy Yale
University Office of Public
Information; New Haven,
CT.)

188

■ 363.

Mary Cooper Jewett Arts Center, Wellesley Collcgc; Wellesley, MA; 1959 (see Illus. 189).

A contemporary building whose lines, color, and scale fit in gracefully on a red brick and limestone Collegiate Gothic campus. Its three main elements are a 2-story music and drama unit that includes an auditorium, a taller and narrower visual arts unit set at right angles to it, and an exhibition gallery that seams together the art and music units while it serves as a foyer for the auditorium.

Associate architects: Anderson, Beckwith & Haible. Engineers: Goldberg, Le Messurier & Associates (structural); Stressenger, Adams, Maguire & Reidy (mechanical/electrical). Acoustical consultants: Bolt, Beranek & Newman. General contractor: George A. Fuller Co.

See: Architectural Forum 105 (December 1956): 100–106; 111 (July 1959): 88–95. *Architectural Record* 126 (July 1959); 175–86.

■ 364

Orange County Government Center; Goshen, NY; 1970.

Inside and out, this low, complex building displays geometric yet determinedly irregular lines. Constructed of exposed concrete and split-rib concrete block, it houses courtrooms of varying sizes—seating from 24 to 125 spectators—plus associated offices and other facilities. Project architects: William Bedford, James Brown. Engineers: Lev Zetlin Associates (structural); Caretsky & Assoc. (mechanical/electrical). General contractor: Corbeau Newman Construction Corporation.

See: Architectural Record 139 (June 1966): 137–39; 150 (August 1971): 83–92. *Architettura* 12 (January 1967): 597.

■ 365

Sarasota Senior High School; Sarasota, FL; 1959/60.

Well designed for a tropical climate, this school was sited on a hill, oriented north-south, and cleverly ventilated and provided with sunshades to make the most of prevailing breezes while shielding students from excessive glare and heat. Engineers: Sidney L. Barker (structural); Charles T. Healy (mechanical). Contractor: Coe Construction Co.

Honors: AIA Merit Award, 1962.

189

See: AIA Journal 37 (May 1962): 58–59. *Architectural Record* 125 (March 1959): 189–94; 127 (May 1960): 193–216.

■ 366

School of Art and Architecture, Yale University; New Haven, CT; 1963 (see Illus. 190).

This intricate, complex building's plan has been likened by its architect to that of a pinwheel. Constructed of rough-surfaced concrete inside and out, it boasts a wide variety of exciting interior spaces, some of them adorned by casts of works of art such as classic statues and Louis Sullivan friezes.

Engineers: Henry A. Pfisterer (structural); vanZelm, Heywood & Shadford (mechanical). General contractor: George B. H. Macomber Co.

Honors: AIA First Honor Award, 1964; AIA Bicentennial List, four nominations.

See: Progressive Architecture 45 (February 1964): 106–27. *Arts + Architecture* 81 (February 1964): 26–29. *Architectural Review* 135 (May 1964): 324–32.

190

189 Mary Cooper Jewett Arts Center, Wellesley College; Wellesley, MA; 1959. *See* Entry 363. (Courtesy Wellesley College Archives; Wellesley, MA. Photographer: Lawrence Lowry.)

190 School of Art and Architecture, Yale University; Ncw Haven, CT; 1963. *See* Entry 366. (Courtesy Yale University Office of Public Information; New Haven, CT.)

■ 367

Temple Street Parking Garage; New Haven, CT; 1962/63.
Two blocks long, five levels high, spare yet with a look of formidable authority, here is a car park with a difference. Modeled out of cast-in-place concrete, its levels—rounded shelves without walls—rise on a series of gracefully molded pillars.
Engineers: Henry Pfisterer (structural); Jerome Mueller (mechanical). General contractor: Fusco-Amatruda Co.

Honors: AIA Merit Award, 1964.

See: Architectural Forum 118 (February 1963): 104–9. *Architectural Record* 133 (February 1963): 145–50. *L'Architecture d'Aujourd'hui,* no. 110 (October–November 1963): 34–37.

Paul RUDOLPH; DESMOND & LORD

■ 368

Southeastern Massachusetts University (formerly Southeastern Massachusetts Technological Institute); North Dartmouth, MA; master plan and first stage, 1966.
This campus's configuration resembles Venice's Piazza San Marco and includes a central tower like the piazza's Campanile. Buildings are constructed of concrete and are tidily ornamented inside and out with ribbed concrete block; they spiral around the tower down the hillside and look out through trees to a nearby lake.
Job captain: Grattan Gill. Structural engineers: Congdon, Gurney & Towle. Structural consultant: Sepp Firnkas. General contractor: Franchi Construction Co.

See: Architectural Record 140 (October 1966): 145–60; 157 (January 1975): 123–40. *L'Architecture d'Aujourd'hui,* no. 128 (October–November 1966): 2–5.

Paul RUDOLPH; FRY & WELCH

■ 369

Chapel, Tuskegee University; Tuskegee, AL; 1969.
Central to the campus of a historic black college, this church was erected to replace one that had burned down a dozen years before. Its sharply angled, almost windowless exterior conceals a high lofting asymmetrical sanctuary, which has been called "one of the most dramatic and powerful spaces to be built in this century."
Architects and planners: Fry & Welch. Associate architect (design phase): Paul Rudolph. Engineers: Donald J. Neubauer (structural); A. Dee Counts (mechanical). Acoustical consultants: Bolt, Beranek & Newman. Contractors: George B. H. Macomber Co.; F. N. Thompson, Inc.

See: Architectural Record 146 (November 1969): 117–26. *Architettura* 15 (March 1970): 741–43. Y. Futagawa, ed., *Paul Rudolph: Interdenominational Chapel, Tuskegee . . . ,* text by Carl Black, Jr., Global Architecture, no. 20 (Tokyo: A. D. A. Edita, 1973).

George Vernon RUSSELL

■ 370

Republic Supply Company Offices and Plant; San Leandro, CA; 1952.
A multipurpose industrial building constructed on a modest budget yet attractive to employees and customers. Graciously landscaped, it features a large patio—bounded by two wings of offices—that can be used as a lounge, for meetings, and for outdoor dining.
Landscape architect: Lawrence Halprin. Contractor: Swinerton & Walberg Co.

Honors: AIA Merit Award, 1953.

See: Architectural Forum 99 (August 1953): 107–9. *Arts + Architecture* 71 (July 1954): 28–29. *L'Architecture d'Aujourd'hui,* nos. 67–68 (October 1956): 74–77.

Eero SAARINEN

Winner, AIA Gold Medal, 1962.

■ 371

Bell Telephone Laboratories Research Center; Holmdel, NJ; 1966.
Sited on 456 rural acres, this is an immense office and laboratory facility: 700 feet long, 350 feet wide, and 6 stories high, with a 700-by-100-foot central covered garden. Though it was one of the first buildings to be completely sheathed in reflective glass, none of its labs or offices have windows; continuous corridors around its perimeter lessen problems of climate control.
Landscape architects: Sasaki-Dawson-DeMay Associates. Engineers: Severud Associates (structural); Jaros, Baum & Bolles (mechanical/electrical).

See: Architectural Forum 117 (October 1962): 88–97; 126 (April 1967): 33–41. Y. Futagawa, ed., *Eero Saarinen: Bell Telephone Corporation Research Laboratories . . . ,* text by Cesar Pelli and Diana Pelli, Global Architecture, no. 6 (Tokyo: A. D. A. Edita, 1971).

■ 372

CBS Building; New York, NY; 1965.
A 38-story, rectangular office tower of determined simplicity, it is set off from its neighbors by a sunken plaza. On all four of its sides, closely spaced triangular pillars faced with dark gray granite run without interruption from ground level to roof.
Engineers: Paul Weidlinger (structural); Cosentini Associates (mechanical). General contractor: George A. Fuller Co.

Honors: AIA Honor Award, 1966; AIA Bicentennial List, two nominations.

See: Architectural Forum 124 (April 1966): 20–37. *Architectural Record* 138 (July 1965): 111–18. *Progressive Architecture* 46 (July 1965): 187–92. David Guise, *Design and Technology in Architecture* (New York: Wiley, 1985), 164–74.

■ 373

Concordia Senior College; Fort Wayne, IN; 1958.
In designing this wholly new campus for a college with 450 Lutheran preministerial students, Saarinen's goal was to create a kind of tranquil, self-sufficient village. All its buildings have pitched, dark gray tile roofs and are constructed of reinforced concrete plus nonbearing whitewashed brick. The simple chapel is particularly noteworthy.
Engineers: Severud-Elstad-Krueger (structural); Samuel R. Lewis & Assoc. (mechanical). Landscape architect: Dan Kiley. General contractors: Wermuth, Inc.; Hagerman Construction Corp.; Grewe Contractors, Inc.

Honors: PA Design Award, 1956; AIA Honor Award, 1959.

See: AIA Journal 31 (June 1959): 80.

Progressive Architecture 39 (December 1958): 88–101. *Baumeister* 57 (August 1960): 536–41.

■ 374

David S. Ingalls Hockey Rink, Yale University; New Haven, CT; 1958.

This remarkable building—whose shape has been compared to that of a Viking warship or a giant dinosaur—is a study in dramatic curves and adventurous engineering. It seats 2,900 for hockey matches, as many as 5,000 for lectures and commencement exercises, and it has excellent acoustics.

Associate architect: Douglas W. Orr. Engineers: Severud-Elstad-Krueger Associates (structural); Jaros, Baum & Bolles (mechanical/electrical). General contractor: George B. H. Macomber C

Honors: AIA Bicentennial List, one nomination.

See: *Architectural Forum* 109 (December 1958): 106–11. *Architectural Record* 124 (October 1958): 151–58. *Bauen + [und] Wohnen* 14 (August 1959): 270–71.

■ 375

Deere & Company Administrative Center; Moline, IL; 1964.

This headquarters for a farm equipment manufacturer pioneered in the use of weathering steel—high-tensile steel that, if left unpainted, forms its own cinnamon brown protective coating. Set on a wooded site with two man-made lakes, its three original facilities were an auditorium, an office building, and a display building, the latter two connected by a bridge across a ravine. Their strong yet artfully detailed lines bear a curious resemblance to Japanese temple architecture. See also Deere West (entry no. 347), designed by Kevin Roche John Dinkeloo, successor firm to Eero Saarinen & Assoc.

Engineers: Ammann & Whitney (structural); Burns & McDonnell Engineering Co. (mechanical/electrical). Landscape architects: Sasaki, Walker & Assoc. General contractor: Huber, Hunt & Nichols.

Honors: AIA Honor Award, 1965; AIA Bicentennial List, three nominations.

See: *Architectural Forum* 121 (July 1964): 76–85. *Architectural Record* 136 (July 1964): 135–42. Y. Futagawa, ed., *Eero Saarinen: Bell Telephone Corporation Research Laboratories . . . Deere & Company Headquarters . . .*, text by Cesar Pelli and Diana Pelli, Global Architecture, no. 6 (Tokyo: A. D. A. Edita, 1971).

■ 376

Dulles International Airport Terminal Building; Chantilly, VA; 1962.

Set on a huge (10,000-acre), flat site, this is a highly distinctive building with colonnades of tipped and tapered columns on its two long facades, a gracefully curving roof hung between them, and a pagodalike control tower nearby. Mobile lounges are used to carry passengers from the terminal to their planes.

Engineers: Ammann & Whitney (structural); Burns & McDonnell Engineering Co. (mechanical/electrical). Landscape architect: Dan Kiley. Contractors: Humphreys & Harding; Corbetta Construction Co.

Honors: AIA Honor Award, 1966; AIA Bicentennial List, seventeen nominations.

See: *AIA Journal* 69 (November 1980): 46–51 and cover. *Architectural Record* 134 (July 1963): 101–10. *Progressive Architecture* 44 (August 1963): 86–101. Y. Futagawa, ed., *Eero Saarinen: TWA Terminal Building . . . Dulles International Airport . . .*, text by Nobuo Hozumi, Global Architecture, no. 26 (Tokyo: A. D. A. Edita, 1973).

■ 377

Gateway Arch; St. Louis, MO; 1965–68.

Part of the Jefferson National Expansion Memorial, this remarkable, tapered arch symbolizes the role of St. Louis as gateway to the West. It is 630 feet high, measures 630 feet across at its base, and is constructed of a steel double wall filled with concrete at its lower levels and stiffened with steel farther up where it is narrower. Its exterior is clad in polished stainless steel.

Landscape architect: Dan Kiley.

Honors: AISC Architectural Award of Excellence, 1967; AIA Bicentennial List, nine nominations.

See: *AIA Journal* 67 (November 1978): 57, 63. *Architectural Forum* 128 (June 1968): 32–37. George McCue, *The Building Art in St. Louis: Two Centuries* (St. Louis: American Institute of Architects, 1964). Joel Meyerowitz, *St. Louis and the Arch.* (Boston: N.Y. Graphic Society, 1980).

■ 378

Kresge Auditorium, Massachusetts Institute of Technology; Cambridge, MA; 1955 (see Illus. 191).

This "festival hall on the banks of the Charles River" contains a little theater, a concert hall, and rehearsal rooms. It is noted for its graceful white dome: one-eighth of a sphere anchored on hidden abutments at three points. On the three faces between, glass walls arch upward to meet its thin concrete shell.

Associate architects: Anderson & Beckwith. Engineers: Ammann & Whitney (structural); Hyde & Bobbio (mechanical/electrical); Bolt, Beranek & Newman (acoustical). General contractor: George A. Fuller Co.

See: *Architectural Forum* 103 (July 1955): 128–

191 Kresge Auditorium, Massachusetts Institute of Technology; Cambridge, MA; 1955. *See* Entry 378. (Courtesy News Office, Massachusetts Institute of Technology; Cambridge, MA. Photographer: Calvin Campbell.)

29. *Architectural Record* 118 (July 1955): 131–37. *Progressive Architecture* 35 (June 1954): 120–25.

■ 379

Kresge Chapel, Massachusetts Institute of Technology; Cambridge, MA; 1955 (see Illus. 192).

This interdenominational chapel built on a small hemmed-in site masterfully achieves an atmosphere conducive to meditation. Reached by a glassed-in walkway that crosses a tiny moat, on the outside it's a windowless, brick-faced cylinder; inside, its brick walls undulate gently and natural light comes in indirectly from the sides and above.

Associate architects: Anderson & Beckwith. Engineers: Ammann & Whitney (structural); Hyde & Bobbio (mechanical/electrical); Bolt, Beranek & Newman (acoustical). General contractor: George A. Fuller Co.

Honors: AIA Bicentennial List, one nomination.

See: *Architectural Forum* 104 (January 1956): 116–21. *Architectural Record* 119 (January 1956): 154–57. *Progressive Architecture* 37 (January 1956): 65–67.

■ 380

Milwaukee County War Memorial; Milwaukee, WI; 1957.

Shaped like a hollow cross, this unusual community center contains meeting rooms, an auditorium, and an art gallery; the memorial courtyard at its center overlooks Lake Michigan through the building's supporting pylons. When first built, its engineering was considered daring because its two upper floors cantilever out over 29 feet.

Associated architects: Maynard W. Meyer & Assoc. Engineers: Ammann & Whitney (structural); Samuel R. Lewis & Assoc. (mechanical). General contractor: James McHugh Construction Co.

Honors: PA Award Citation, 1955.

See: *Architectural Forum* 107 (December 1957): 90–95, 144. *Zodiac,* no. 4 (1959): 38–45.

■ 381

Samuel F. B. Morse and Ezra Stiles Colleges, Yale University; New Haven, CT; 1962.

Because Yale students preferred Gothic rooms to Georgian on campus, the architect set out to design these residence

192 Kresge Chapel, Massachusetts Institute of Technology; Cambridge, MA; 1955. *See* Entry 379. (Courtesy Massachusetts Institute of Technology; Cambridge, MA.)

192

halls—which contain dining halls, lounges, and small libraries as well as bedrooms—as "citadels of earthy monolithic masonry." Medium-rise buildings set in rambling fashion around courtyards, their concrete construction is relieved by decorative sculpture and by interior detailing in stone and oak.

Engineers: Henry A. Pfisterer (structural); Van Zelm, Heywood & Shadford (mechanical). Landscape architect: Dan Kiley. General contractor: E & F Construction Co.

Honors: AIA Honor Award, 1963.

See: *Architectural Forum* 117 (December 1962): 105–11. *Architectural Record* 132 (December 1962): 93–100. *Progressive Architecture* 43 (November 1962): 57–60.

■ 382

TWA Terminal, Kennedy (formerly Idlewild) International Airport; New York, NY; 1962.

This is surely one of the world's most dramatic airline terminals. Few straight lines here: approached head on, its curving contours uncannily suggest a bird in flight. Inside, the main lobby's soaring, swooping walls, its carefully modeled staircases, seating areas, and many other features are a blend of graceful sculptural forms selected "to suggest the excitement of the trip."

Engineers: Ammann & Whitney (structural);

Jaros, Baum & Bolles (mechanical). Contractor: Grove, Shepherd, Wilson & Kruger.

Honors: AIA Merit Award, 1963; AIA Bicentennial List, three nominations.

See: *AIA Journal* 70 (November 1981): 36–51 and cover. *Architectural Forum* 117 (July 1962): 72–75. *Architectural Record* 130 (September 1961): 162–64. *Progressive Architecture* 43 (October 1962): 158–65. Y. Futagawa, ed., *Eero Saarinen: TWA Terminal Building Kennedy Airport . . .*, text by Nobuo Hozumi, Global Architecture, no. 26 (Tokyo: A. D. A. Edita, 1973).

Eero SAARINEN; SKIDMORE, OWINGS & MERRILL

■ 383

Vivian Beaumont Theater, Lincoln Center; New York, NY; 1965; interior remodeled, 1981/82.

A highly flexible, mechanized theater, it was originally designed to serve as home for a repertory company, its huge (10,000-square-foot) stage can be used in either proscenium or open-apron form. It is housed on lower levels of the same building that contains the Lincoln Center Library and Museum of the Performing Arts.

Collaborating designer for the theater: Jo Mielziner. Consultants: Ammann & Whitney (structural); Syska & Hennessy (mechanical). General contractor: Turner Construction Co.

See: *Progressive Architecture* 46 (November 1965): 189–94. 47 (April 1966): 176–83. *Interiors* 125 (December 1965): 84–91.

Eero SAARINEN; SMITH, HINCHMAN & GRYLLS

■ 384

General Motors Technical Center; Warren, MI; 1956.
Situated on a square mile of lightly wooded countryside, this extraordinary assemblage of twenty buildings, a sizable man-made lake complete with fountains, and a handsomely modeled stainless steel–sheathed water tower has been called "a coordinated research town" and "an industrial Versailles." Particularly noteworthy is the use of walls and panels of vivid colors as enlivening accents inside and out.
Engineers: Smith, Hinchman & Grylls. Landscape architect: Thomas D. Church; Associate landscape architect: Edward A. Eichstedt. General contractor: Bryant & Detwiler Co.

Honors: AIA Honor Award, 1953; AIA Honor Award, 1955, for Central Restaurant Building; AIA Bicentennial List, three nominations; AIA Twenty-Five Year Award, 1985.

See: *Architectural Forum* 101 (November 1954): 100–19; 104 (May 1956): 122–29; 134 (June 1971): 21–28.

SAARINEN, SAARINEN

Eliel Saarinen won the AIA Gold Medal in 1947 and the Royal Gold Medal in 1950; in 1962 his son, Eero Saarinen, also won the AIA Gold Medal.

■ 385

Christ Church; Minneapolis, MN; 1948/49.
Spare yet not severe, asymmetrical in plan yet serenely proportioned and balanced, here is a modest brick Lutheran church of lasting architectural value. In its sanctuary, natural light from a tall window masked from the congregation floods the altar. One long wall includes splayed panels of open jointed brick, which add texture while they help absorb sound. Structural, acoustical, and mechanical elements are "integrated into the form with no compromise."
Associate architects: Hills, Gilbertson & Hayes. Acoustics: Bolt, Beranek & Newman. General contractor: Kraus-Anderson Inc.

Honors: AIA Bicentennial List, one nomination; AIA Twenty-five Year Award, 1977.

See: *AIA Journal* 66 (May 1977): 28–29. *Architectural Forum* 91 (December 1949): 60; 93 (July 1950): 80–85.

SAARINEN, SWANSON & SAARINEN

■ 386

Opera Shed, Berkshire Music Center; Stockbridge, MA; 1947.
This concert hall for audiences of up to 1,200, constructed inexpensively, primarily of wood, owes its fine acoustics to the loving care and attention to detail with which it was built. Its most striking structural feature is a series of laminated arches exposed above its roof; these arches link with supporting trusses.
Acoustical consultant: Charles C. Potwin.

See: *Progressive Architecture* 28 (March 1947): 53–58. *Architectural Review* 101 (May 1947): 163–64. Henry-Russell Hitchcock and Arthur Drexler, eds., *Built in USA: Post-War Architecture* (New York: Museum of Modern Art, 1952), 98–99.

Moshe SAFDIE; DAVID, BAROTT, BOULVA

■ 387

Habitat; Montreal, Quebec; 1967 (see Illus. 193).
This extraordinary housing development comprising 158 units of from one to four bedrooms, with many small gardens and decks, was planned as a prototype for a system that would streamline the building process and cut costs. It was assembled from 354 reinforced-concrete building modules, ingeniously stacked so as to give privacy and views to each unit. Unfortunately, construction costs proved to be prohibitive.
Structural consultant: Dr. A. E. Komendant. Structural engineers: Monti, Lefebvre, Lavoie, Nadon. Mechanical and electrical engineers: Huza-Thibault, and Nicholas Fodor & Assoc. General contractor: Anglin-Norcross Quebec Ltd.

Honors: Massey Medal, 1967.

See: *Progressive Architecture* 47 (October 1966): 226–37; 49 (March 1968): 138–47. *Canadian Architect* 12 (October 1967): 31–49. *Architectural Design* 37 (March 1967): 111–19. Leon Whiteson, *Modern Canadian Architecture* (Edmonton: Hurtig, 1983), 218–21.

193 Habitat; Montreal, Quebec; 1967. *See* Entry 387. (Courtesy Moshe Safdie and Associates; Somerville, MA. Photographer: Taal Safdie.)

193

Joseph SALERNO

■ 388

United Church House of Worship; Rowayton, CT; 1962.
A small church with an extraordinary roof that spirals skyward like an upended mollusk shell. Douglas fir was used to build a frame of intricately curved, laminated arch ribs that join in a spoked wheel at the back where the roof wraps around itself, leaving room for a curved clerestory window.
Structural engineer: Wayman C. Wing.

Honors: AIA Honor Award, 1963.

See: *Architectural Forum* 117 (December 1962): 80–83. *Architectural Record* 131 (June 1962): 184–87. *L'Architecture d'Aujourd'hui,* no. 108 (June–July 1963): 19–21.

Louis SAUER ASSOCIATES

■ 389

The Glass Palace, NewMarket; Philadelphia, PA; 1975.
A prizewinner when originally designed as a commercial/retail/apartment complex to be known as Head House East, it was then enlarged, stripped of apartments, officially dubbed NewMarket, and popularly nicknamed The Glass Palace. Located in a neighborhood of eighteenth- and nineteenth-century town houses, it presents a lively contrast: a collection of steel-framed, glass-walled cubes that face onto a "water plaza."
Consultants: Design Associates (landscape); Joseph L. Hoffman & Assoc. (structural); M. Michael Garber & Assoc. (mechanical).

Honors: PA Design Citation, 1969.

See: *Architectural Record* 158 (December 1975): 107. *Progressive Architecture* 57 (April 1976): 76–79. *Design & Environment* 6 (Summer 1975): 18–19.

SCHAFER, FLYNN, VAN DIJK (subsequent name of firm: VAN DIJK, JOHNSON & PARTNERS)

■ 390

Blossom Music Center; Peninsula, OH; 1968 (see Illus. 194).
Acoustical considerations dictated this pavilion's unusual design, in which a giant steel arch tilted 16 degrees from the horizontal serves as "backbone for an intricate lacework of wall and roof trusses." Some 15,000 concertgoers can be accommodated; 4,500 within the pavilion, the rest on the sloping lawn around it.
Associate in charge of design: Ronald A. Straka. Consulting architect: Pietro Belluschi. Engineers: R. M. Gensert Associates (structural); Byers, Urban, Klug & Pittenger (mechanical/electrical). Acoustical consultants: Heinrich Keilholz, Christopher Jaffee. General contractor: Turner Construction Co.

Honors: AISC Architectural Award of Excellence, 1969.

See: *AIA Journal* 52 (August 1969): 67–68. *Architectural Forum* 129 (December 1968): 67. *Architectural Record* 145 (June 1969): 191–96. G. E. Kidder Smith, *A Pictorial History of Architecture in America* (New York: American Heritage, 1976), 2: 510.

SCHIPPOREIT-HEINRICH ASSOCIATES

■ 391

Lake Point Tower; Chicago, IL; 1968.
This stunning instant landmark, the first skyscraper ever entirely faced with undulating glass walls, when first completed was—with its 65 stories and 900 units—the tallest apartment house in the world. Its design was suggested by sketches and models made in 1921 by Mies van der Rohe.
Associated architects: Graham, Anderson, Probst & White. Engineers: William Schmidt & Assoc. (structural); William Goodman (mechanical/electrical). Landscape architect: Alfred Caldwell. General contractor: Crane Construction Co.

Honors: AIA Honor Award, 1970; AIA Bicentennial List, one nomination.

See: *AIA Journal* 53 (June 1970): 80. *Architectural Record* 146 (October 1969): 123–30 and cover. *Architettura* 15 (April 1970): 818–19.

194 Blossom Music Center, Peninsula, OH; 1968. *See* Entry 390. (Courtesy van Dijk, Johnson & Partners; Cleveland, OH. Photographer: Jack Sterling Architectural & Editorial Photography.)

SERT, JACKSON

Winner of the AIA's Architectural Firm Award, 1977. In 1981, Jose Luis Sert won the AIA Gold Medal.

■ 392

Eastwood, Roosevelt Island; New York, NY; 1976.
This housing development in a new town comprises 1,003 apartments, two minischools, a day-care center, and commercial space on lower floors. Buildings range from 6 to 22 stories and define three courtyards with considerable sunlight and river views. Those situated along the main shopping street overhang the sidewalk to create a protected arcade 1,000 feet long.
Principal in charge: Jose Luis Sert; project manager: William Lindemulder. Engineers: Weidlinger Assoc. (structural); Cosentini Assoc. (mechanical). General contractor: Building Systems Housing Corp., Turner Construction, and Sovereign Construction.

Honors: AIA Honor Award.

See: AIA Journal 70 (mid-May 1981): 256–58. *Architectural Record* 160 (August 1976): 101–7. *Process: Architecture,* no. 34 (December 1982): 146–'53. *L'Architecture d'Aujourd'hui,* no. 186 (August–September 1976): 22–27.

■ 393

Holyoke Center, Harvard University; Cambridge, MA; 1966.
One block square, this megastructure has many wings of varying heights, a 22-foot-high arcade running through its center, and offbeat fenestration: occupants can decide whether their windows are to be paned with clear glass or filled with translucent panels. Shops and a bank take up most street-level space; offices and a health center occupy most of the remainder of the building's 360,000 square feet.
Associate: J. Zalewski. Associate and job captain: P. Krueger. Landscape architects: Sasaki, Dawson, DeMay Associates. Engineers: Cleverson, Varney & Pike. Contractors: George A. Fuller Co.

Honors: AIA Bicentennial List, two nominations.

See: AIA Journal 68 (January 1979): 48–51. *Architectural Forum* 126 (January–February

1967): 64–77. *Architectural Record* 131 (May 1962): 134–37.

■ 394

Undergraduate Science Center and Chilled Water Plant, Harvard University; Cambridge, MA; 1973.
This strongly rectilinear, multilevel megastructure, which takes up a full city block, contains almost 300,000 square feet devoted to labs, classrooms, administrative offices, four large lecture theaters, three libraries, and a glass-enclosed cafe. Also included is a chilled water plant, which occupies another 58,000 square feet.
Principals in charge: Paul H. Krueger, Joseph Zalewski. Engineers: Lev Zetlin Associates (structural); Syska & Hennessy (mechanical); Bolt, Beranek & Newman (acoustical). General contractor: Turner Construction Co.

Honors: AIA Honor Award, 1979.

See: AIA Journal 68 (mid-May 1979): 170–71; 74 (April 1985): 88–93. *Architectural Record* 155 (March 1974): 111–18 and cover. *A+U: Architecture and Urbanism,* no. 54 (June 1975): 97–106.

SERT, JACKSON & GOURLEY

■ 395

Francis Greenwood Peabody Terrace (Married Student Housing), Harvard

University; Cambridge, MA; 1964 (see Illus. 195).
In this unusual development, one structural unit—three bays wide and three stories high with a stair in its central bay—is repeated and used in contrasting combinations to create a lively mix of low-, mid- and high-rise buildings with varied facades. Its 499 apartments range in size from efficiencies to three bedrooms.
Associate: Joseph Zalewski. Landscape architects: Sasaki, Walker & Assoc. Engineers: Nichols, Norton & Zaldastani (structural); Sidney J. Greenleaf & Associates (mechanical/electrical). General contractor: Vappi & Company.

Honors: AIA Honor Award, 1965; AIA Bicentennial List, four nominations.

See: AIA Journal 66 (June 1977): 30–37. *Progressive Architecture* 45 (December 1964): 122–33. *Kenchiku Bunka* 20 (November 1965): 101–8.

SERT JACKSON & GOURLEY; HOYLE, DORAN & BERRY

■ 396

Additions to campus, Boston University; Boston, MA; 1965.
Given a sliver of riverfront for additions to an existing campus, the architects chose to build relatively high-rise buildings and so preserve space for plazas and terraces. Tallest is the 19-story Law and Education Tower, which is connected by a bridge to

195 Francis Greenwood Peabody Terrace (Married Student Housing), Harvard University; Cambridge, MA; 1964. *See* Entry 395. (Courtesy Harvard News Office; Cambridge, MA. Photographer: Laura Wulf.)

the Pappas Law Library; another added building is the Student Union. All have vigorous facades alive with rhythmically repeating yet varied projections.

See: Architectural Forum 120 (June 1964): 122–23. *Architectural Record* 135 (May 1964): 161–92. *Architectural Design* 35 (August 1965): 383–88.

SITE PROJECTS, INC.

■ **397**

Best Products showrooms; various locations; 1970s– (see Illus. 196).
In a series of whimsical projects for a mail-order chain, SITE, an artists' group, has imposed startling images of structural chaos and collapse on otherwise mundane stores. These include a peeling brick facade in Richmond, Virginia; a crumbling facade in Houston; a displaced, sliding corner in Baltimore and again in Sacramento; a facade apparently rent apart by giant oaks in Henrico, Virginia, and an ostensibly half-dismembered facade (Inside/Outside Building) in Milwaukee.
Project directors include: James Wines, Cynthia Eardley and Emilio Sousa.

See: Architectural Record 172 (March 1984): 144–45; 173 (May 1985): 140–45. *Architectural Review* 163 (March 1978): 132–35. *A +U:*

Architecture and Urbanism, no. 84 (November 1977): 58–59.

SKIDMORE, OWINGS & MERRILL

In 1957, Louis Skidmore won the AIA Gold Medal; in 1962, Skidmore, Owings & Merrill won the AIA's Architectural Firm Award; in 1983, Nathaniel A. Owings won the AIA Gold Medal. (See also entry nos. 171, 383, and 504.)

■ **398**

Air Force Academy Chapel; Colorado Springs, CO; 1963.
The focal point of a prizewinning campus is this spectacular and colorful building which bears, like sleek yet spiky trappings, 100 tetrahedrons clad with aluminum sheeting and rising to 17 spires. Inside are separate chapels for Catholics, Protestants, and Jews.
Partner in charge and designer: Walter A. Netsch, Jr. Acoustical consultant: Bolt, Beranek & Newman. General contractor: Robert E. McKee, Inc.

Honors: R. S. Reynolds Memorial Award, 1964; AIA Bicentennial List, two nominations (for whole campus).

See: AIA Journal 41 (June 1964): 27–29. *Architectural Record* 132 (December 1962): 85–92. *L'Architecture d'Aujourd'hui* 34, no. 108 (June–July 1963): 10–16.

■ **399**

Albright-Knox Art Gallery Addition; Buffalo, NY; 1962.
The original museum, a fine example of neoclassical architecture, was designed by Edward B. Green in 1905. The added wing, though modern in its simple lines, blends in with it artfully. Faced primarily with matching white marble, it comprises two long galleries and a garden restaurant, which bound a central sculpture court, plus a third large gallery topped by a contrasting black cube, which contains an auditorium.
Partner in charge of design: Gordon Bunshaft. Design assistant: Sherwood A. Smith. Consulting engineers: Paul Weidlinger (structural); Jaros, Baum & Bolles (mechanical/electrical). General contractor: The John W. Cowper Co.

Honors: AIA Honor Award, 1963.

See: AIA Journal 39 (May 1963): 32–33. *Architectural Forum* 116 (March 1962): 118–21. *Bauen + [und] Wohnen* 18 (February 1963): 78–81.

■ **400**

Allied Bank Plaza; Houston, TX; 1983.
A pleasing mix of planes and gentle curves, formed by two linked yet offset quarter cylinders, shapes this immense office tower—71 stories and 985 feet tall, with 1.8 million square feet of floor space. Clad almost entirely in reflective green glass except for polished black granite at street level, it rises straight up, like "an

196 Best Products showroom: Forest Building; Henrico, VA; 1980. *See* Entry 397. (Courtesy SITE Projects, Inc.; New York, NY.)

196

abstract sculptural object" from a landscaped plaza. Its sleekly formal lobby features a grandly curving staircase, which leads to the bank one floor up.
Design partner; Richard Keating; project manager: Louis Skidmore. Engineers: SOM (Robert Halvorson, engineering partner), structural; I. A. Naman + Assoc., mechanical.

Honors: AISC Architectural Award of Excellence, 1983.

See: Architecture 73 (April 1984): 38–47. *A + U: Architecture and Urbanism,* no. 177 (June 1985): 43–48. *GA Document,* no. 12 (January 1985): 96–99. Albert Bush-Brown, *Skidmore, Owings & Merrill, Architecture and Urbanism: 1973–1983* (New York: Van Nostrand Reinhold, 1984), 204–7.

■ 401

American Republic Insurance Company National Headquarters; Des Moines, IA; 1965.

This unusual 8-story office building, which has an inviting entrance court topped by a glassed-in terrace floor with dining and lounge facilities, has been called "a load-bearing Lever House." A large and distinguished collection of modern art embellishes it throughout.
Partner in charge: William S. Brown; partner in charge of design: Gordon Bunshaft. Engineering consultants: Paul Weidlinger (structural); Syska & Hennessy (mechanical). General contractor: Arthur H. Neumann & Brothers.

Honors: AIA Honor Award, 1967; AIA Bicentennial List, one nomination.

See: Progressive Architecture 47 (February 1966): 144–51. *L'Architecture d'Aujourd'hui,* no. 122 (September–November 1965): 22–23. *Skidmore, Owings & Merrill,* introduction and

notes by Christopher Woodward (New York: Simon & Schuster, 1970), 77–82.

■ 402

BMA Tower (Business Men's Assurance Company Building); Kansas City, MO; 1964.

This 19-story office tower's gray glass window walls are recessed 6 feet back from a severely elegant white grid made of structural steel sheathed in gleaming marble. It is set in an expansive plaza paved in a distinctive purple brick that continues into the lobby area.
Partner in charge: Bruce J. Graham. Engineers: Skidmore, Owings & Merrill (structural); Black & Veatch (mechanical/electrical). General contractor: Winn-Senter Construction Co.

Honors: AIA Honor Award, 1964; AISC Architectural Award of Excellence, 1964.

See: AIA Journal 42 (July 1964): 28–29. *Architectural Forum* 121 (July 1964): 86–91. G. E. Kidder Smith, *A Pictorial History of Architecture in America* (New York: American Heritage, 1976), 2: 696–97.

■ 403

Beinecke Rare Book and Manuscript Library, Yale University; New Haven, CT; 1963 (see Illus. 197).

In this stately treasure chest of a building, designed to house 800,000 volumes and over a million manuscripts, white marble is used in extraordinary fashion: in steel-framed slabs just 1¼ inches in thickness, thin enough to be translucent. During the day, light flows through the walls and accentuates the marble's veining; by night the library glows from within.
Partner in charge of design: Gordon Bunshaft; partner in charge of coordination: David H.

Hughes. Consultants: Paul Weidlinger (structural); Jaros, Baum & Bolles (mechanical). Contractor: George A. Fuller Co.

Honors: AIA Honor Award, 1967; AIA Bicentennial List, one nomination.

See: AIA Journal 47 (June 1967): 59. *Architectural Record* 134 (November 1963): 12–14. *Progressive Architecture* 45 (February 1964): 130–33.

■ 404

Carmel Valley Manor; Carmel Valley, CA; 1963 (see Illus. 198).

A retirement community of 170 residential units set on 23 acres of beautiful rolling country. Its gable-roofed, white stuccoed houses and casually landscaped grounds recall a Mediterranean village—comfortably "human scale."
Landscape architects: Sasaki, Walker & Associates. General contractor: Williams & Burrows.

Honors: AIA Merit Award, 1964.

See: Progressive Architecture 45 (April 1964): 136–53. *House and Home* (November 1964): 74–75. *Architecture of Skidmore, Owings & Merrill, 1963–1973,* introduction by Arthur Drexler (New York: Architectural Book Publishing, 1974): 264–67.

■ 405

Central Facilities Building, Baxter Corporate Headquarters; Deerfield, IL; 1975.

The focal point of a corporate complex set in a landscaped park is this building, the roof of which is dramatically suspended by cables hung from two giant masts that

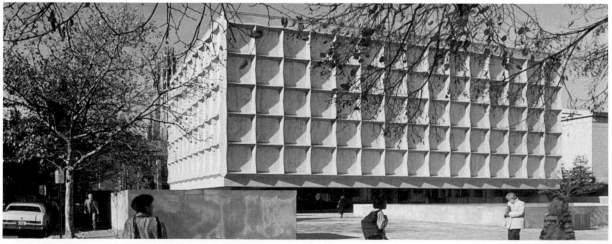

197 Beinecke Rare Book and Manuscript Library, Yale University; New Haven, CT; 1963. *See* Entry 403. (Courtesy Yale University Office of Public Information; New Haven, CT. Photographer: T. Charles Erickson.)

198

rise 35 feet above the roof proper. The "central facilities" contained inside include a spectacular cafeteria—which among other things contains good-sized trees—an auditorium, a sales training center, and an executive dining room. Design partner: Bruce J. Graham; partner in charge: John K. Turley; senior architect: Brigitta Peterhans. Structural partner: Fazlur Khan.

Honors: AISC Architectural Award of Excellence, 1975. Chicago AIA Distinguished Building Award, 1976.

See: Architectural Review 162 (October 1977): 231–36. *Architettura* 23 (December 1977): 442–47, 454-55.

■ **406**

Central Staff Office Building, Ford Motor Company; Dearborn, MI; 1957.
Set on 90 landscaped acres, this huge and handsome administrative building designed to house some 3,100 employees comprises about a million square feet of flexible office space plus parking for 2,600 cars, a 500-seat conference room, a 625-seat cafeteria, lounges, a sandwich shop, and an executive penthouse with private dining rooms and a roof garden. Most of its office space is contained in a 12-story structure 537 feet long.
Partner in charge: J. Walter Severinghaus; project designer: Charles E. Hughes; project manager: Robert K. Posey.

See: Architectural Record 121 (March 1957): 242. *Progressive Architecture* 38 (June 1957): 181–91; 40 (May 1959): 148–49.

■ **407**

Circle Campus, University of Illinois; Chicago, IL; phase 1, 1965.
Unusual features of this urban campus on 106 acres include elevated walks, designed to serve as "pedestrian expressways," which come together at a central plaza that also serves as the roof for a lecture center underneath. This elevated plaza has been called "one of the great spaces in college architectural planning."
Partner in charge: Walter A. Netsch, Jr. Consultants: Sasaki, Dawson, DeMay Associates (landscape); Bolt, Beranek & Newman (acoustics). General contractor: Gust K Newberg Construction Co.

Honors: AIA Bicentennial List, one nomination.

See: AIA Journal 66 (January 1977): 24–31 and cover. *Architectural Forum* 123 (September 1965): 21–45. *Progressive Architecture* 46 (October 1965): 222–31.

■ **408**

Connecticut General Life Insurance Company; Bloomfield, CT; 1957.
An insurance company's stylish low-rise office complex sited on 280 acres of amiable countryside. Glass walled, with few fixed partitions and with a main area that contains 400,000 square feet of floor space unbroken by structural columns, it boasts such amenities as a swan pond, Noguchi sculptures, and elegant courtyards and terraces.
Engineers: Weiskopf & Pickworth (structural); Syska & Hennessy (mechanical/electrical). General contractor: Turner Construction Co.

Honors: PA Award Citation, 1955; AIA First Honor Award, 1958.

See: AIA Journal 30 (July 1958): 33. *Architectural Forum* 107 (September 1957): 112–27. *Casabella,* no. 309 (September 1966): 30–34. *Architecture of Skidmore, Owings & Merrill, 1950–1962,* introduction by Henry-Russell Hitchcock (New York: Praeger, 1963): 62–73.

■ **409**

Headquarters building, Emhart Manufacturing Company; Bloomfield, CT; 1963.
This strongly horizontal steel-and-concrete building caps a commanding suburban ridge. Its single-story office portion—a modified hollow square—is raised on striking treelike pillars above ground level; cars park beneath while, within the square, lab facilities are housed in a separate 2-story structure.
Partner in charge: Gordon Bunshaft; project manager: Allan Labie; design assistant: Natalie DeBlois. Engineers: Paul Weidlinger and Weiskopf & Pickworth (structural); Syska & Hennessy (mechanical). General contractor: George A. Fuller Co.

Honors: AIA Honor Award, 1964.

See: Architectural Forum 119 (July 1963): 88–95. *L'Architecture d'Aujourd'hui,* no. 119 (March 1965): 9. *Architecture of Skidmore, Owings & Merrill, 1963–1973,* introduction by Arthur Drexler (New York: Architectural Book Publishing, 1974), 74–79.

■ **410**

Inland Steel Building; Chicago IL; 1958.
All the structural columns of this unusual 19-story office building are located outside its glass and steel curtain wall. Its service core—elevators, air-conditioning ducts, rest rooms, stairs, etc.—is confined to a windowless 25-story stainless steel tower set off at one corner of the total structure.
General contractor: Turner Construction Co.

Honors: AIA Bicentennial List, one nomination.

See: Architectural Forum 108 (April 1958): 88–93. *Architectural Record* 123 (April 1958): 169–78. *Architecture of Skidmore, Owings & Merrill*

198 Carmel Valley Manor; Carmel Valley, CA; 1963. *See* Entry 404. (Courtesy Skidmore, Owings & Merrill; San Francisco, CA. Photographer: Morley Baer.)

1950–1962, introduction by Henry-Russell Hitchcock (New York: Praeger, 1963), 74–81.

■411

John Hancock Building; New Orleans, LA; 1961.

Windows are recessed behind a sun-shading, precast-concrete frame in this tasteful building, which provides office space on the ground floor for the Hancock Insurance Company, plus six stories of rental space above. It looks out on a raised, triangular plaza adorned by a sculpture fountain by Isamu Noguchi. Partner in charge: William S. Brown; partner in charge of design: Gordon Bunshaft. Associate architects: Nolan, Norman & Nolan. Engineers: Paul Weidlinger (structural); Syska & Hennessy (mechanical). General contractor: R. P. Farnsworth & Co.

Honors: AIA Merit Award, 1963.

See: Progressive Architecture 44 (September 1963): 126–35. *L'Architecture d'Aujourd'hui,* no. 111 (December 1963–January 1964): 11. *Architecture of Skidmore, Owings & Merrill, 1950–1962,* introduction by Henry-Russell Hitchcock (New York: Praeger, 1963), 182–85.

■412

John Hancock Center; Chicago, IL; 1970.

This "blunt, black obelisk" is 1,100 feet and 100 stories high. Geared for multiple uses, it contains 700 apartment units, over 800,000 square feet of office space, and such amenities as restaurants, health clubs, a swimming pool, and an ice-skating rink.

Honors: Partner in charge of design: Bruce Graham; associate partner in charge of design: Robert Diamant. Chief structural engineer: Fazlur Khan; project structural engineer: H. Srinivasa Iyengar. Structural consultants: Paul Weidlinger; Ammann & Whitney. General contractor: Tishman Construction Co.

Honors: AISC Architectural Award of Excellence, 1971; AIA Bicentennial List, six nominations.

See: AIA Journal 69 (October 1980): 68–73. *Architectural Forum* 133 (July–August 1970): 36–45. *Architectural Review* 151 (April 1972): 202–10.

■413

Joseph H. Hirshhorn Museum and

Sculpture Garden; Washington, DC; 1974.

This controversial circular museum, designed during the uproar of the 1960s, has been compared to both a doughnut and a military bunker. Raised on 14-foot-high piers above ground level, its facade is windowless except for one glazed horizontal slit. In its hollow center there's a circular courtyard, a fountain, and windows for its 3 stories of galleries. The sunken sculpture garden was originally reached by a tunnel under a nearby road. Partner in charge: Gordon Bunshaft. Consultants: Weidlinger Associates (structural); Jaros, Baum & Bolles (mechanical/electrical). General contractor: Piracci Construction Co.

Honors: AIA Bicentennial List, one nomination.

See: Progressive Architecture 56 (March 1975):

42–47 and cover. *Architectural Review* 157 (February 1975): 119–20.

■414

Lever House; New York, NY; 1952 (see Illus. 199).

A trend-setting triumph of an office building, this 24-story beauty faced with blue-green glass and stainless steel takes up just a fraction of its ample site; only its second story, supported on trim columns, describes an irregular hollow square over the bulk of its space. At ground level underneath are pedestrian walkways, which hospitably invite passersby to enjoy the building's garden court. In 1983 it was declared a landmark to save it from being demolished and replaced by a larger building.

Partner for coordination: William S. Brown; partner for design: Gordon Bunshaft. Engineers:

199 Lever House: New York, NY; 1952. *See* Entry 414. (Courtesy Lever Brothers Company; New York, NY.)

199

Weiskopf & Pickworth (structural); Jaros, Baum & Bolles (mechanical). General contractor: George A. Fuller Co.

Honors: AIA Honor Award, 1952; AIA Bicentennial List, eleven nominations; AIA Twenty-Five Year Award, 1980.

See: *Architectural Forum* 96 (June 1952): 101–11. *Architectural Record* 111 (June 1952): 130–35. *Werk* 41 (February 1954): 49–54. Paul Goldberger, *On the Rise* (New York: Times Books, 1983), 252–56.

■ **415**

Manufacturers Trust Company Bank; New York, NY; 1954.
A remarkable 5-story bank on Fifth Avenue whose glass walls and glowing interior attracted the passerby's attention to its prominently displayed giant vault, as artfully designed and finished as a piece of decorative sculpture.
Partner for coordination: William S. Brown; partner for design: Gordon Bunshaft. Engineers: Weiskopf & Pickworth (structural); Syska & Hennessy (mechanical/electrical). Interior consultant: Eleanor Le Maire. Builders: George A. Fuller Construction Co.

Honors: PA Award Citation, 1954; AIA Honor Award, 1954; AIA Bicentennial List, one nomination.

See: *Architectural Forum* 101 (December 1954): 104–11. *Architectural Record* 116 (November 1954): 149–56 *Bauen +[und] Wohnen* 11 (February 1956): 49–52.

■ **416**

Marine Midland Building (140 Broadway); New York, NY; 1968.
Here's a sleek, dark office tower, 52 stories high, built in the shape of a trapezoid to make the most efficient use of its oddly shaped site, and surrounded by a plaza that is enlivened by a vivid red, tipsy cube of a sculpture by Noguchi.
Partner in charge of design: Gordon Bunshaft; partner in charge of administration: Edward J. Matthews. Engineers: Office of James Ruderman (structural); Jaros, Baum & Bolles (mechanical). General contractor: Diesel Construction.

See: *Architectural Forum* 128 (April 1968): 36–45. *Interiors* 127 (June 1968): 90–97. *Architettura* 14 (October 1968): 462–63.

■ **417**

Mauna Kea Beach Hotel; Kamuela, HI; 1965.
Tropical vegetation, painstakingly planted in a previously barren area, lends drama to this hotel's interior courtyards and reception areas and softens the tailored look of its neatly terraced facade. Construction is of sand-colored concrete set off by retaining walls of dark local lava.
Partner in charge: John R. Weese; partner in charge of design: Marc E. Goldstein. Landscape architects: Eckbo, Dean, Austin & Williams. General contractor: Haas & Haynie.

Honors: AIA Honor Award, 1967.

See: *AIA Journal* 71 (March 1982): 72–77. *Architectural Forum* 124 (May 1966): 80–87. *Interiors* 125 (March 1966): 118–24. *Architettura* 12 (January 1967): 606–7.

■ **418**

One Chase Manhattan Plaza; New York, NY; 1962.
Two city blocks were combined into one to permit this massive 60-story office building to be built straight up, without setbacks, while creating welcome open space around it in the crowded Wall Street area. An executive lounge and dining room on the top floor enjoy spectacular harbor views.
Partner in charge: J. Walter Severinghaus; partner in charge of design: Gordon Bunshaft. Consulting engineers: Weiskopf & Pickworth (structural); Jaros, Baum & Bolles (mechanical). General contractor: Turner Construction Co.

See: *Architectural Record* 130 (July 1961): 141–50. *Bauen +[und] Wohnen* 17 (January 1962): 9–21. *Interiors* 120 (September 1961): 112–17.

■ **419**

One Shell Plaza; Houston, TX; 1971.
When first completed, this 715-foot-high, 50-story office tower set on a landscaped podium one block square was the tallest building west of the Mississippi. Sheathed with 27 tons of travertine marble, it contains over 1,500,000 square feet of rentable space.
Partner in charge: Bruce J. Graham. Associate architects: Wilson Morris Crain & Anderson. Landscape architects: Sasaki, Dawson & DeMay Associates. Mechanical/electrical engineers: Chenault & Brady. General contractor: Bellows Construction Co.

See: *Architectural Forum* 136 (April 1972): 24–

39. *Architectural Design* 42 (January 1972): 22–23. *Architettura* 18 (September 1972): 324–25. David Guise, *Design and Technology in Architecture.* (New York: Wiley, 1985), 176–83.

■ **420**

Pepsi-Cola World Headquarters; New York, NY; 1960 (see Illus. 200).
As originally built, this was a gleaming glass-and-aluminum, 11-story office building that nestled with great self-possession on a Park Avenue corner. Generously set back from its legal building line and with its lobby areas further recessed, it boasted its own small plaza and sophisticated detailing inside and out. Subsequently known as the Olivetti Building, it is now part of 500 Park Tower (see entry no. 329), designed by James Stewart Polshek.
For original building, partner in charge: Robert W. Cutler; project manager: Albert Kennerly. Engineers: Severud-Elstad-Krueger Associates (structural); Slocum & Fuller (mechanical/electrical). General contractor: George A. Fuller Co.

Honors: AIA Honor Award, 1961; Bard Award, 1964.

See: *AIA Journal* 35 (April 1961): 80–81. *Architectural Forum* 112 (March 1960): 102–8. *Architectural Design* 32 (February 1962): 79–82.

■ **421**

Portland Center; Portland, OR; first phase, 1968 (see Illus. 201).
In this delightfully "splashy" development, three rather severe apartment towers, several rows of town houses, a shopping mall, and related facilities share a midtown site with a spectacular fountain/plaza contoured in concrete to suggest a mountain setting alive with bubbling, rushing water.
Partner in charge: David A. Pugh. General contractor: Portland Center Building Co. For parks and malls, landscape architects and urban designers: Lawrence Halprin & Assoc.; partner in charge: Satoru Nishita; resident landscape architect: David Thompson. Architectural consultants: Moore & Turnbull. Engineers: Gilbert, Forsberg, Deikman & Schmidt (structural); Yanow & Bauer (mechanical). General contractor: Shrader Construction Co.

See: *Architectural Forum* 125 (July–August 1966): 74–79. *Progressive Architecture* 49 (May 1968): 163–65. *Bauen + [und] Wohnen* 21 (April 1967): 134–37. *Process: Architecture,* no. 4 (February 1978): 159–84.

200 Pepsi-Cola World Headquarters; New York, NY; 1960. *See* Entry 420. (Photographer: © Ashod Kassabian.)

200

201 Portland Center; Portland, OR; 1968, first phase. *See* Entry 421. (Courtesy Skidmore, Owings & Merrill; Portland, OR. Photographer: Morley Baer.)

201

■ **422**

Rapid Transit Stations; Chicago, IL; 1971.

In designing seventeen stations—their boarding platforms, fare collection areas, and areas in which to wait for connecting buses—the architects stressed exposed steel construction and painted the steel off-white throughout. Many station platforms have curved, glazed canopies that cantilever as much as 18 feet from both sides of a single row of columns. Partner in charge of design: Myron Goldsmith; project designer: Pao-Chi Chang. Coordinating engineers: DeLeuw Cather & Company. General contractors: J. M. Corbett Co.; Paschen Construction, Inc.; W. E. O'Neil Construction Co.

Honors: AISC Architectural Award of Excellence, 1971.

See: Architectural Record 150 (November 1971): 129–32. *Architectural Review* 154 (July 1973): 51. *Industrial Design* 15 (October 1968): 46–49.

■ **423**

The Republic; Columbus, IN; 1972.

Home for a century-old daily newspaper, this is a long, low industrial building with considerable style in the Miesian tradition. Presses housed within are floated on a special pad to cut down noise and vibration; detailing is crisp and careful; and tempered glass walls put brightly painted equipment and architect-designed furnishings confidently on display. Partner in charge: Myron Goldsmith; project manager: George Hays; senior designer: Jin H. Kim; interior design: George Larson. Contractor: Dunlap Construction.

Honors: AIA Honor Award, 1975.

See: AIA Journal 63 (May 1975): 26–43. *Architectural Record* 151 (May 1972): 114–28. *Architectural Review* 154 (July 1973): 50.

■ **424**

Reynolds Metals Company General Office Building; Richmond, VA; 1958.

A finely tooled corporate showplace set on 38 suburban acres and designed—from exterior column covers and sun louvers to ceilings and doorknobs—to display the many uses of aluminum. Its offices, dining facilities, reception areas, and an auditorium occupy a trim, low-rise building constructed in a hollow square around a formal, brick-paved courtyard. Facilities planning/engineering/construction management: Ebasco Services, Inc. Acoustical consultants: Bolt, Beranek & Newman. Landscape consultant: Charles F. Gillette. General contractor: George A. Fuller Co.

See: *AIA Journal* 30 (December 1958): 42–46. *Architectural Forum* 109 (September 1958): 90–97. *Architecture of Skidmore, Owings & Merrill, 1950–1962,* introduction by Henry-Russell Hitchcock (New York: Praeger, 1963), 82–89.

■ 425

Robert R. McMath Solar Telescope; Kitt Peak, AZ; 1962.

When built on its mountaintop site, this extraordinary structure—in effect, "a camera with a 300-foot focal length"—was by far the largest solar telescope in the world. It consists of a 500-foot-long shaft, three-fifths underground, which is inclined 32 degrees to the horizontal and points to the north celestial pole. The portion aboveground is supported and stabilized by a 100-foot-tall concrete tower.

Partner in charge: William E. Dunlap; senior designer: Myron Goldsmith. Chief structural engineer: Alfred Picardi; chief mechanical engineer: Sam Sachs. Contractor: Western Knapp Engineering Co.

Honors: AISC Architectural Award of Excellence, 1963.

See: *Architectural Forum* 127 (October 1967): 44–49. *Inland Architect* 17 (May 1973): 9–13 and cover. *Architecture of Skidmore, Owings & Merrill, 1963–1973,* introduction by Arthur Drexler (New York: Architectural Book Publishing, 1974), 244–47.

■ 426

Sears Tower; Chicago, IL; 1974 (see Illus. 202).

The tallest building in the world when completed, this 110-story office tower, which tops out at 1,450 feet—the limit set by the Federal Aviation Administration for Chicago—is remarkable also for its innovative engineering. Its structural strength in a notoriously windy city follows from construction as a cluster of "bundled structural tubes": nine interconnected skyscrapers with ample cross bracing.

Partner in charge of design: Bruce Graham; chief structural engineer: Fazlur Khan. Electrical and mechanical engineers: Jaros, Baum & Bolles. Contractor: Diesel Construction.

Honors: AISC Architectural Award of

202 Sears Tower; Chicago, IL; 1974. *See* Entry 426. (Courtesy Sears, Roebuck and Co.; Chicago, IL. Photographer: Hedrich-Blessing.)

202

Excellence, 1975. AIA Bicentennial List, three nominations.

See: *Architectural Forum* 140 (January–February 1974): 24–31. *Architecture Plus* 1 (August 1973): 56–59. *Interior Design* 45 (December 1974): 116–17, 120–27.

■ 427

Tenneco Building (formerly the Tennessee Building); Houston, TX; 1963 (see Illus. 203).

The glass walls of this handsome 33-story office tower are recessed five feet back from a structural framework that supplies shade against the Southwestern sun. Its first two floors—very high ceilinged and occupied by a bank—are set back still farther from massive exterior columns to create a 50-foot-high entrance portico and arcade.

Consulting engineers: Bolt, Beranek & Newman (acoustics); Engineers Testing Laboratory (foundation/materials); Bramlett McClelland, Inc. (foundation design). General contractor: W. S. Bellows Construction Corp.

Honors: AIA Honor Award, 1969; Bartlett

Award, 1969; AIA Bicentennial List, one nomination.

See: *AIA Journal* 51 (June 1969): 106. *Architectural Forum* 119 (September 1963): 124–31. *Architecture of Skidmore, Owings & Merrill, 1963–1973,* introduction by Arthur Drexler (New York: Architectural Book Publishing, 1974), 124–27.

■ 428

270 Park Avenue (formerly Union Carbide Building); New York, NY; 1960.

Construction of this imposing, 52-story office tower, clad in stainless steel, was complicated by the fact that three-quarters of its two-block site lay directly over two levels of heavily used railroad tracks! At street level it is surrounded by a generous amount of open space and bisected by a 60-foot-wide pedestrian arcade.

Partner in charge: William S. Brown; partner in charge of design: Gordon Bunshaft; project designer: Natalie deBlois. Engineers: Weiskopf & Pickworth (structural); Syska & Hennessy (mechanical/electrical). General contractor: George A. Fuller Co.

203 Tenneco Building (formerly the Tennessee Building); Houston, TX; 1963. *See* Entry 427. (Courtesy Skidmore, Owings & Merrill; San Francisco, CA.)

203

See: *Architectural Forum* 113 (November 1960): 114–21. *L'Architecture d'Aujourd'hui,* no. 100 (February–March 1962): 12–17. *Architecture of Skidmore, Owings & Merrill, 1950–1962,* introduction by Henry-Russell Hitchcock (New York: Praeger, 1963), 142–51.

■ **429**

U.S Naval Postgraduate School of Engineering; Monterey, CA; 1954 (see Illus. 204).
An unpretentious yet attractive campus built on a budget. To cut costs while providing laboratories and classroom buildings with sharp, clean lines and tasteful detailing, prefabricated modular wood-and-glass window wall units were used between framing concrete columns. Associate partner in charge of design: Walter A. Netsch. Engineers: Isadore Thompson (structural); Keller & Gannon (mechanical).

204 U.S. Naval Postgraduate School of Engineering; Monterey, CA; 1954. *See* Entry 429. (Courtesy Skidmore, Owings & Merrill; San Francisco, CA.)

Honors: AIA Merit Award, 1955.

See: *Architectural Record* 115 (June 1954): 150–57; 117 (April 1955): 159–71. *L'Architecture d'Aujourd'hui,* no. 67–68 (October 1956): 36–41.

■ **430**

Wells Fargo Bank–American Trust Company branch bank; San Francisco, CA; 1959 (see Illus. 205).
Here's a dainty confection of a 1-story bank: circular, glass walled, with a fanciful, wavy-edged roof that looks from above like a pleated doily and is garnished at its center with a blossom-shaped skylight. It's located on the plaza of SOM's Crown Zellerbach building (see entry no. 171). General contractor: Haas &Haynie.

Honors: AISC Award of Excellence, 1960.

See: *Architectural Record* 129 (January 1961): 112–14. *Japan Architect* 36 (April 1961): 70–72. *Western Building* 40 (February 1961): 12.

■ **431**

Weyerhaeuser Headquarters; Tacoma, WA; 1971.
Hailed as "a building that makes its own landscape," this immense corporate headquarters, a quarter-mile long, spans a valley and dams a natural creek into a lake. Its five levels are intricately terraced and planted to wed it visually with its woodland site.

204

Landscape architect: Sasaki, Walker Associates.
Landscaping contractor: Landscaping, Inc.
General contractor: Swinerton & Walberg.

Honors: AIA Honor Award, 1972; Bartlett
Award, 1972; AIA Bicentennial List, two
nominations.

See: Architectural Forum 136 (March 1972):
20–27. *Interiors* 131 (March 1972): 76–91.
Industrial Design 19 (March 1972): 38–43.

■ **432**

**Wyeth Laboratories, Inc. office and
laboratory complex; Radnor, PA;
1956.**
Here laboratory, office, and auxiliary
facilities share 26 acres of rolling country.
Sister low-rise buildings, connected by a
glass-walled, single-story reception lobby
and enclosing an appealing landscaped
court, supply office space on one side, lab
space on the other. Both are faced with
blue-green glass and porcelain-enameled
panels of a deeper blue-green.
Partner in charge: Robert W. Cutler; associate
partner in charge of design: Roy O. Allen.
Engineers: Seelye, Stevenson, Value & Knecht.
General contractors: George A. Fuller Co.

Honors: PA Award Citation, 1954: AIA Merit
Award, 1957.

See: Architectural Record 121 (April 1957):
195–200. *Progressive Architecture* 35 (January
1954): 109.

SKIDMORE OWINGS & MERRILL;
BROOKS, BARR, GRAEBER & WHITE

■ **433**

**Lyndon Baines Johnson Library,
University of Texas; Austin, TX; 1971.**
This monumental library—200 by 90 feet
by 65 feet high with just a few narrow
strips of windows and with an
emphatically cantilevered top story—has
vast, travertine-walled interior spaces and
is set on a raised and formal plaza.
Adjoining it is a long, low companion
building that houses related collections
and the LBJ School of Public Affairs.
Partner for design: Gordon Bunshaft. Engineers:
Paul Weidlinger–W. Clark Craig & Associates
(structural); Gregorson, Gaynor & Sirmen, Inc.
(mechanical/electrical). General contractor: T. C.
Bateson Construction Co.

See: Architectural Record 150 (November
1971): 113–20. *Architectural Design* 43
(February 1972): 87–90. *Architettura* 18 (July
1972): 188–89.

Eberle M. SMITH ASSOCIATES

■ **434**

**Greenfield Elementary School;
Birmingham, MI; 1957.**
To make the most of a cramped,
characterless site for two kindergartens
and classrooms to be grouped in threes,
elementary classrooms in this long
rectangular school face onto appealing
courtyards and are divided into grade
units by an imaginary line down the
center. The two kindergarten rooms
occupy a contrasting hexagonal building
set off to one side and reached by a
covered walkway.

Honors: PA Design Award, 1957.

See: Architectural Record 123 (February 1958):
217–19. *Progressive Architecture* 38 (July 1957):
101–4; 41 (March 1960): 131–37.

HAMILTON SMITH *see* MARCEL
BREUER *and* HAMILTON SMITH

SMITH & WILLIAMS

■ **435**

**Union Service Center, Local 887,
UAW-CIO; Los Angeles, CA; 1957? (see
Illus. 206).**
Though largely glass walled and located in
a busy, distracting neighborhood, this
inexpensively built, 2-story center gains
privacy and shade from "an architectural
buffer zone" created by a strip of
plantings alongside the building, further
enclosed by a long, enameled metal
screen. Inside, structural elements—50-
foot open-web steel trusses on steel
columns—are left exposed while stained-
glass insets brighten a stairwell.
Landscape architect: Eckbo, Roystan & Williams.
Engineers: Kolesoff & Kariotis (structural); J. F.
Reardon (mechanical). General contractor:
Roulac Company.

Honors: AIA Merit Award, 1958.

See: AIA Journal 30 (July 1958): 50–51. *Bauen-
Wohnen* 15 (February 1960): 55–57. *Arts +
Architecture* 76 (May 1959): 16–17, 32.

205 Wells Fargo Bank-
American Trust Company
branch bank; San Francisco,
CA; 1959. *See* Entry 430.
(Courtesy Skidmore, Ow-
ings & Merrill; San Fran-
cisco, CA.)

206

is housed in a renovated 5-story tenement supplemented by a small concrete block structure with strong, attractive lines, which was built economically for the program and is surrounded by hard-landscaped recreation areas.
Engineers: William Atlas (structural); Wald & Zigas (mechanical). General contractor: Graphic Construction Co.

Honors: AIA Honor Award, 1969; Bard Award, 1969.

See: *AIA Journal* 51 (June 1969): 107. *Architectural Forum* 129 (October 1968): 62–65. *Baumeister* 67 (September 1970): 1034–37.

Paoli SOLERI

■ 438

Arcosanti; near Dugas, AZ; 1971– (see Illus. 208).
A utopian community in the desert created by one of architecture's leading visionaries with the help of paying—not paid—apprentices. Fanciful structures sand-cast from concrete, rich with texture and color, replete with arcs, circles, and other geometric motifs, and hung with bells made on the premises crowd together in a complex that one day, it is hoped, will house 3,000 people. Included are foundries, studios, and a crafts/visitors center.

See: *Progressive Architecture* 54 (April 1973):

SMITH, HINCHMAN & GRYLLS (see also entry no. 384)

■ 436

First Federal Building; Detroit, MI; 1965.
Located on a roughly triangular site, this 23-story office building has a tripartite structure with services consolidated in a central, windowless tower from which two glass-and-granite-faced towers extend. The latter two towers are completely free of interior columns and together offer six corner office spaces per floor. This unusual design leaves space at ground level for a small plaza.
Partner in charge: Bernard L. Miller; partner in charge of design: Sigmund F. Blum. General contractor: George A. Fuller Co.

Honors: AISC Architectural Award of Excellence, 1966; AIA Honor Award, 1967.

See: *Architectural Record* 138 (December 1965): 140–43. *Baumeister* 65 (May 1968): 512–14. Thomas J. Holleman and James P. Gallagher, *Smith, Hinchman & Grylls; 125 Years of Architecture & Engineering* (Detroit: Wayne State University Press, 1978).

SMOTRICH & PLATT

■ 437

Exodus House, East Harlem; New York, NY; 1969 (see Illus. 207).
This rehabilitation center for drug addicts

207

208 Arcosanti; near Dugas, AZ; 1971–. *See* Entry 438. (Courtesy Cosanti Foundation; Scottsdale, AZ. Photographer: Tomiaki Tamura.)

208

76–81. *L'Architecture d'Aujourd'hui,* no. 167 (May–June 1973): 84–87. *Kenchiku Bunka* 31 (December 1976): 31–58.

J. E. STANTON *see* Welton BECKET *and* J. E. STANTON

Robert A. M. STERN

■ 439

Point West Place; Framingham, MA; 1984 (see Illus. 209).

It's been called a "turnpike palazzo"—this 5-story, roadside office building that simulates Renaissance elements with contemporary materials and means. Horizontal strips of rose and gray glass suggest traditional stone coursing; an elaborately detailed porch and a "balcony of appearances" at the rear, both rendered in pink granite veneer, are shallower than they seem; and false perspectives in the mahogany-paneled lobby make it seem larger than it is.
For Robert A. M. Stern Architects, associate in charge: John Ike. Associated architects: Drummey Rosane Anderson, Owen Beenhouwer, principal in charge; Maurice King, project manager. Engineers: Weidlinger Assoc. (structural); R. G. Vanderweil (mechanical/electrical). General contractor: Vappi and Co.

See: Architectural Record 174 (February 1986): 128–35 and cover. *Architectural Design* 55, no. 1/2 (1985): 38–43. *A + U: Architecture and Urbanism,* no. 179 (August 1985): 75–114.

209

209 Point West Place; Framingham, MA; 1984. *See* Entry 439. (Courtesy Robert A.M. Stern Architects. Photographer: Timothy Hursley, The Arkansas Office.)

STEVENS & WILKINSON

■ 440

Georgia Center for Continuing Education, University of Georgia; Athens, GA; 1957 (see Illus. 210).

This conference center contains such unusual facilities as its own closed-circuit TV station, an exhibit lounge, studio bedrooms, and dining areas, as well as meeting rooms and an auditorium. A 5-story red brick building with trim contemporary lines, it's built around a graciously landscaped courtyard. As of 1988, a substantial expansion of the center by the original architects was under way.
For original project, consulting architect: Louis Sarvis. Landscape architects: Thomas D. Church & Assoc.; Edward L. Daugherty. Structural engineers: Morris, Beohmig & Tindel. General contractor: de Give Dunham & O'Neill.

Honors: PA Award Citation, 1955.

See: Architectural Forum 108 (January 1958): 100–105. *Interiors* 117 (February 1958): 72–77.

STICKNEY & HULL

■ 441

Los Gatos Civic Center; Los Gatos, CA; 1966.

Designed for a small but growing community, here are what appear to be three separate, quietly handsome

210 Georgia Center for Continuing Education, University of Georgia; Athens, GA; 1957. *See* Entry 440. (Courtesy Stevens & Wilkinson, Inc.; Atlanta, GA.)

210

concrete-and-brick buildings—a library plus quarters for city administration and police—placed at the corners of a multilevel plaza. Under the plaza lies a council chamber, which connects with all three surrounding structures, thus linking the whole complex into a single building. Engineers: McClure & Messinger (structural); Chamberlain & Painter (mechanical/electrical). Landscape architects: Sasaki, Walker, Lackey Associates. General contractor: E. A. Hathaway & Co.

Honors: AIA Honor Award, 1967.

See: Architectural Record 141 (April 1967): 159–64. *Lotus* 5 (1968): 130–34. *L'Architecture d'Aujourd'hui,* no. 135 (December 1967–January 1968): 40–41.

James STIRLING, Michael WILFORD

In 1980, Stirling won the Royal Gold Medal for Architecture; in 1981, he won the Pritzker Architecture Prize.

■ 442

Anderson Hall expansion, School of Architecture, Rice University; Houston, TX; 1981.
In this surprisingly conservative project by an avant-garde British architect, an L-shaped, 16,500-square-foot addition interlocks with a renovated 2-story building to form an open courtyard. Its intricately patterned brick and limestone

211 Arthur M. Sackler Museum, Harvard University; Cambridge, MA; 1985. *See* Entry 443. (Courtesy Harvard News Office; Cambridge, MA. Photographer: Laura Wulf.)

exterior and tile roof echo existing campus motifs. A few nontraditional touches stand out, for example, two shuttlecocklike conical skylights that mark entries to a central gallery and a pass-through for pedestrian traffic, and an off-center oculus in a gabled end wall.
Assistants: Alexis Pontvik, Paul Keogh. Associated architects: Ambrose & McEnany. Consultants: Walter P. Moore & Assoc. (structural); Cook & Holle (mechanical). General contractor: Miner-Dederick Construction.

See: Progressive Architecture 62 (December 1981): 53–61. *Arts + Architecture,* new series, 1 (Winter 1981): 47–49. *GA Document,* no. 5 (1982): 50–71. *Architectural Review* 171 (February 1982): 50–57.

■ 443

Arthur M. Sackler Museum, Harvard University; Cambridge, MA; 1985 (see Illus. 211).
This L-shaped museum, largely faced in stripes of orange and gray brick, has three stories of tall galleries on its inner side; along its outer side, floors of offices and other spaces—half the height of the galleries—wrap around. A striking staircase, glass roofed and walled with stripes, rises in a straight line between. An elaborate entrance is flanked by two giant columns. Bolts atop them, and a huge window over the entry, testify to a bridge—planned but not built—to connect to the Fogg Museum across the street.
Associated architects: Perry, Dean, Rogers. Consultants: Syska & Hennessy (mechanical); LeMessurier/SCI (structural). General contractor: Turner Construction.

See: Architecture 75 (January 1986): 46–51. *Progressive Architecture* 66 (October 1985): 27–28. *Interiors* 145 (April 1986): 172–77. *Architectural Review* 180 (July 1986): 26–33.

Edward Durell STONE

■ 444

Community Hospital of the Monterey Peninsula; Carmel, CA; 1962, expansion 1972.
In this tastefully appointed hospital, all patients have private rooms and there are attractive garden courts, balconies, and a 72-foot-square central courtyard with a

211

pool and fountains. However, construction costs were not exorbitant. Resident architect: John C. Hill. Engineers: Pregnoff & Matheu (structural); G. M. Simonson (mechanical/electrical). Landscape architect: Georg Hoy. General contractor: Daniels & House.

Honors: AIA Merit Award, 1963.

See: *AIA Journal* 39 (May 1963): 44–45. *Architectural Forum* 117 (October 1962): 108–11. *Architectural Record* 152 (September 1972): 137–44.

■ 445

John F. Kennedy Center for the Performing Arts; Washington, DC; 1971 (see Illus. 212).

Planning for this building began in 1958 when Congress appropriated a 17-acre site on the banks of the Potomac for a national cultural center. Monumental and marble clad, it is 100 feet high, 630 feet long, and 300 feet wide and contains an opera house, a concert hall, and a theater. Engineers: Severud-Perrone-Fisher-Sturm-Conlin-Bandel Associates (structural); Syska & Hennessy (mechanical/electrical). Stage consultant: Donald Oenslager. Acoustics: Cyril Harris.

See: *AIA Journal* 56 (October 1971): 8; 70 (August 1981): 24–31. *Interior Design* 42

212

(October 1971): 102. *Theatre Design and Technology,* no. 12 (February 1968): 16–27.

■ 446

Museo de Arte de Ponce; Ponce, PR; 1965 (see Illus. 213).

This museum, which makes the most of its tropical setting, comprises a small open-air theater, gardens, and an expansive sculpture terrace as well as indoor exhibit space. On its second floor are a row of seven hexagonal galleries topped by skylights, set into a space-frame structure of recessed triangles. Thanks to a system

of open grilles, the galleries enjoy natural cross ventilation.

Architect for construction supervision: Carlos Sanz. Engineers: Paul Weidlinger (structural); Cosentini Associates (mechanical/electrical). General contractor: Edward J. Gerrits de Puerto Rico, Inc.

Honors: AIA Honor Award, 1967.

See: *AIA Journal* 47 (June 1967): 47. *Architectural Forum* 124 (January–February 1966): 77. *Architectural Record* 139 (April 1966): 195–206.

213

■447

Stuart Company plant and office building; Pasadena, CA; 1958 (see Illus. 214).

Sited on a downslope, this 1- and 2-story building and its adjacent recreation area, complete with pool, are veiled from view by a 400-foot-long "Persian facade," a lacy-looking grille made of open-worked concrete blocks. Inside there's a dramatic atrium with a striking, geometrically coffered ceiling and lush plantings. Landscape architect: Thomas D. Church & Assoc. Engineers: Hall, Pregnoff & Matheu (structural); Stockly & Bamford (mechanical). Contractors: Myers Bros.; Brummet & Demblon.

Honors: AIA Honor Award, 1958.

See: *AIA Journal* 30 (July 1958): 32. *Architectural Forum* 108 (April 1958): 124–28. *Architectural Record* 123 (April 1958): 161–68.

214 Stuart Company plant and office building; Pasadena, CA; 1958. *See* Entry 447. (Courtesy Edward Durell Stone Associates, P.C.; New York, NY.)

214

Edward Durell STONE; HARALSON & MOTT

■448

Fine Arts Center, University of Arkansas; Fayetteville, AR; 1951 (see Illus. 215).

This peacefully rambling complex provides a unified environment for a concert hall, a library, and a 3-story classroom block, as well as for indoor and outdoor theaters, workshops, and exhibit space. Detailing and embellishment throughout are artful yet unpretentious and were designed by Stone—a native of Fayetteville—to be built inexpensively. Associate: Karl J. Holzinger, Jr. Theater consultant: Edward Cole. Landscape architect: Christopher Tunnard. Sculptors: Alexander Calder; Gwen Lux. General contractor: Harmon Construction Co.

See: *Architectural Forum* 95 (September 1951): 164–69. *Progressive Architecture* 33 (September 1952): 126–27. *Arts + Architecture* 68 (November 1951): 35–37. *Architectural Review* 112 (September 1952): 156–59.

215 Fine Arts Center, University of Arkansas; Fayetteville, AR; 1951. *See* Entry 448. (Courtesy Edward Durell Stone Associates, P.C.; New York, NY.)

215

Hugh STUBBINS

In 1967, Hugh Stubbins & Associates won the AIA's Architectural Firm Award.

■ 449

Citicorp Center; New York, NY; 1978 (see Illus. 216).
Here's a towering office building that stands out not only because of its diagonal roofline—slanted as if for a solar collector but not bearing one—but also because of the popular appeal of The Market, its 7-story atrium entered at street level and designed for leisurely shopping, eating,

216

and browsing. Built on the site of St. Peter's Lutheran Church, Citicorp shares its space with that congregation's new quarters, also designed by Stubbins. Project architect: W. Easley Hammer. Associated architects: Emery Roth & Sons. Consultants: LeMessurier Associates/SCI, Office of James Ruderman (structural and foundations); Joseph R. Loring & Assoc. (mechanical/electrical); Sasaki Associates (landscape). Construction manager: HRH Construction Corporation.

Honors: AIA Honor Award, 1979; AISC Architectural Award of Excellence, 1978; Bard Award, 1978.

See: *Architectural Record* 163 (June 1978): 107–16. *Progressive Architecture* 59 (December 1978): 49–69. *Building* 234 (May 5, 1978): 64–

67. *Process: Architecture,* no. 10 (1979): 24–41. David Guise, *Design and Technology in Architecture* (New York: Wiley, 1985), 156–63.

■ 450

Federal Reserve Bank of Boston; Boston, MA; 1978 (see Illus. 217).
Banking operations requiring tight security are housed in a U-shaped structure with three basement levels and four aboveground. Its upper floors also accommodate an auditorium, museum, and cafeteria. Astride this structure and attached to it stands a 602-foot-tall office tower with a span of 143 feet between its supports at either end; its first full floor is 35 feet above the smaller structure's roof. Aluminum spandrels overhanging tower windows supply sunshade and lessen problems with wind. Interiors throughout are unusually attractive.
Principal in charge: Hugh A. Stubbins, Jr.; project managers: Eugene Racek and Emmett Glynn; project designer: Peter McLaughlin. Consultants: LeMessurier/SCI (structural); Golder, Gass (foundations); Jaros, Baum and Bolles (mechanical/electrical). General contractor: Perini Corp.

See: *Architectural Record* 164 (September 1978): 109–18. *Interiors* 138 (December 1978): 66–71. *Process: Architecture,* no. 10 (1979): 42–51.

■ 451

Francis A. Countway Library of Medicine, Harvard University Medical School; Boston, MA; 1965 (see Illus. 218).
This medical research center, shared by several institutions, provides temperature and humidity-controlled quarters for up to 750,000 volumes and a variety of small, comfortable reading areas for scholars. A bold and massive square building with a large central court, it is six stories high with two more levels below ground level, and has reinforced concrete framing and buff limestone walls.
Collaborator in design: Peter Woytuk; site planner: S. T. Lo. Consulting engineers: LeMessurier Associates (structural); Greenleaf Associates (mechanical). General contractor: George A. Fuller Co.

Honors: AIA Merit Award, 1966.

See: *Progressive Architecture* 46 (November 1965): 166–77. *Arts + Architecture* 83 (April 1966): 20–23. *Process: Architecture,* no. 10 (1979): 120–25.

216 Citicorp Center; New York, NY; 1978. *See* Entry 449. (Courtesy The Stubbins Associates, Inc.; Cambridge, MA. Photographer: Edward Jacoby/APG.)

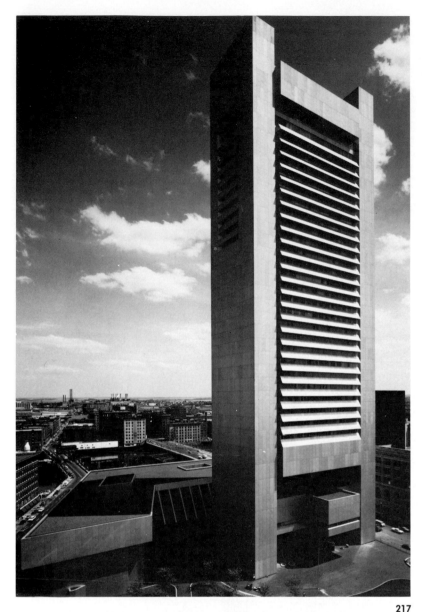

217 Federal Reserve Bank of Boston; Boston, MA; 1978. *See* Entry 450. (Courtesy The Stubbins Associates, Inc.; Cambridge, MA. Photographer: Edward Jacoby/APG.)

217

218 Francis A. Countway Library of Medicine, Harvard University Medical School. *See* Entry 451. (Courtesy The Stubbins Associates, Inc.; Cambridge, MA. Photographer: Edward Jacoby/APG.

218

■ 452

Loeb Drama Center, Harvard University; Cambridge MA, 1960 (see Illus. 219).

An early example of a theater designed for use in any of three modes: proscenium, arena, and in the round. Housed in an elegant concrete and brick structure ornamented with travertine and an intricate sunscreen, this highly flexible and mechanized auditorium can seat up to 600 people.

Job captain: Gordon Anderson. Landscape consultant: John Wacker. Engineers: Goldberg, LeMessurier & Assoc. (structural); Delbrook Engineering (mechanical); Bolt, Beranek & Newman (acoustical). Theatrical consultant: George C. Izenour. Contractor: George A. Fuller Co.

See: Architectural Forum 113 (October 1960): 90–97. *Architectural Record* 128 (September 1960): 151–60. *Process: Architecture,* no. 10 (1979): 130–35.

Hugh STUBBINS; ASHLEY, MYER

■ 453

Warren Gardens; Roxbury, MA; 1970.

This 228-unit development, which makes the most of a hilly, rocky site, provides low-income housing in the form of attractive row houses, many of which have entries on two different levels. Its construction—of clapboard and concrete block—fits comfortably into its New England setting.

Engineers: Souza & True (structural); Samuel Lesburg Associates (mechanical). Landscape architect: John Lee Wacker. Contractor: Starrett Brothers & Eken.

Honors: AIA Design Award for Nonprofit-Sponsored Low and Moderate Income Housing.

See: Architectural Record 149 (mid-May 1971): 86–87. *House & Home* 42 (July 1972): 80–83. *Process: Architecture,* no. 10 (1979): 92–105.

William B. TABLER

■ 454

San Francisco Hilton Hotel; San Francisco, CA; 1964/65 (see Illus. 220).

This 18-story, 1,200-room downtown hotel

219 Loeb Drama Center, Harvard University; Cambridge, MA; 1960. *See* Entry 452. (Courtesy The Stubbins Associates, Inc.; Cambridge, MA. Photographer: Warren Jagger.)

219

220

includes seven levels of parking space enclosed within a rectangle of rooms and surmounted by an outdoor pool. Its windows are arranged in a checkerboard pattern to permit earthquake-resistant diagonal reinforcement of its poured concrete walls.

Associate in charge: Eugene R. Branning. Engineers: Wayman C. Wing (structural); Jaros, Baum & Bolles (mechanical/electrical). General contractor: Cahill Brothers.

See: *Architectural Record* 138 (July 1965): 143–50. *Interior Design* 36 (April 1965): 160–63. *Kenchiku Bunka* 21 (February 1966): 71–77.

TAC *see* The ARCHITECTS COLLABORATIVE

TAFT ARCHITECTS

■ 455

Grove Court; Houston, TX; 1981 (see Illus. 221).

A system of low walls, their tops playfully curved and stepped, give this six-unit townhouse cluster a look all its own; more decorative symbols than barriers, they demarcate a private entry court for each apartment. All units enjoy courtyards at either end and through ventilation.

220 San Francisco Hilton Hotel; San Francisco, CA; 1964/1965. *See* Entry 454. (Courtesy William B. Tabler Architects; New York, NY. Photographer: Karl H. Riek.)

221 Grove Court; Houston, TX; 1981. *See* Entry 455. (Courtesy Taft Architects; Houston, TX.)

221

Handsome old trees on the site were saved.

Partners: John J. Casbarian, Danny Samuels, Robert H. Timme. Engineers: Cunningham Assoc. (structural). Contractor: Frank Lawther Co.

Honors: AR Record Apartments, 1981.

See: *Architectural Record* 169 (July 1981): 80–83. *A + U: Architecture and Urbanism,* no. 139 (April 1982): 88–91. *GA Houses,* no. 9 (1981): 142–47. *Architectural Design* 53, no. 7/8 (1983): 88–91.

■ **456**

222 Hendley Building renovation and addition; Galveston, TX; 1980. *See* Entry 456. (Courtesy Taft Architects; Houston, TX.)

Hendley Building renovation and addition; Galveston, TX; renovation completed 1980 (original building completed 1859) (see Illus. 222).

To disrupt a Victorian commercial building as little as possible while renovating it for use by a local historical foundation, architects extended a sagging facade five feet. This allowed them to add steel buttressing, a new staircase and exit, and updated services such as heating and plumbing. The new wall itself—part tile, part open grid—adds a sprightly touch; it lets passersby glimpse the stairs and a door within.

Partners: John J. Casbarian, Danny Samuels, Robert H. Timme. Consultants: George Cunningham Assoc. (structural); Arthur Rice Assoc. (mechanical). General contractor: Trentham Corp.

222

Honors: AIA Honor Award, 1981.

See: *AIA Journal* 70 (mid-May 1981): 254–55. *Progressive Architecture* 62 (February 1981): 94–95. *A + U: Architecture and Urbanism,* no. 133 (October 1981): 84–87.

■ **457**

River Crest Country Club; Fort Worth, TX; 1984 (see Illus. 223).

Elements of traditional architecture—columns, arches, a porte cochere, a grand staircase—come together in this 51,000-square-foot, 3-story clubhouse in a

decidedly postmodern way. It's faced with meticulously detailed red brick, green terra cotta tile, and rusticated concrete, and topped by hipped roofs and four oversized chimneys.

Partners: John J. Casbarian, Danny Samuels, Robert H. Timme. Associate architects: Geren Architectural Division/CRS Sirrine, Charles W. Nixon, project director. General contractor: JBM Builders.

See: *Architectural Record* 172 (October 1984): 178–87 and cover. *Architecture* 74 (May 1985): 210–15. *A + U: Architecture and Urbanism,* no. 172 (January 1985): 107–12.

223

■ 458

YWCA Downtown (Masterson) Branch and Metropolitan Office Building; Houston, TX; 1982 (see Illus. 224).

Two low buildings and an outdoor play area are screened by a decorative 350-foot-long front wall in which large terra cotta tiles, cream and gray stucco scored with a grid, and rows of small blue tiles combine to form intriguing geometric patterns and enhance entrances. Indoors, geometric ornamentation is achieved by imaginative use of vividly colored moldings, acoustic panels, and air grilles.

Also of interest: an undulating ramp that leads to a gym and a pool.
Partners: John J. Casbarian, Danny Samuels, Robert H. Timme. Project assistants: Marc Boucher, Jeffrey Averill. Consultants: Karl Krause Engineers (structural); MNM Engineering Assoc. (mechanical).

Honors: PA Citation for Architectural Design, 1980; AIA Honor Award, 1983.

See: *AIA Journal* 72 (May 1983): 254–56. *Progressive Architecture* 63 (June 1982): 65–71. *Architectural Design* 53, no. 7/8 (1983): 92–95. *Werk, Bauen & Wohnen* 37 (October 1982): 20–28.

TALIESIN ASSOCIATED ARCHITECTS
see Frank Lloyd WRIGHT; William Wesley PETERS *and* TALIESIN ASSOCIATED ARCHITECTS

Paul THIRY, principal architect

■ 459

Seattle World's Fair; Seattle, WA; 1962.
This ingratiating world's fair located on 74

224

downtown acres was successfully designed to remain an asset to the city after its official close. High spots include Thiry's Coliseum; John Graham's Space Needle (see entry no. 120); Yamasaki's Federal Science Pavilion; the International Fountain, designed by Matsushita & Shimizu; and the main complex, designed by Naramore, Bain, Brady & Johanson.

See: *Architectural Forum* 116 (June 1962): 94–103. *Architectural Record* 131 (June 1962): 141–48. *Progressive Architecture* 43 (June 1962): 49–56.

R. J. THOM PARTNERSHIP; CLIFFORD & LAWRIE; CRANG & BOAKE

■ 460

Metropolitan Toronto Zoo; Toronto, Ontario; 1974.
Hailed as "the first major ecological animal park in the world," this zoo shows species in pavilions that simulate their native environments. Two of these, the African and Indo-Malayan, are vaguely tentlike hyperbolic paraboloids with supporting buttresses. Hypar shells—steel pipes screwed together—are filled with alternating stretches of wood and glass. Their peaks allow tall trees to grow indoors.
Project director: David H. Scott; project manager: Alan Chapple. Consultants: M. S. Yolles & Assoc. (structural); H. H. Angus & Assoc. (mechanical); Johnson Sustronk Weinstein (landscape). Contractor: Milne & Nicholls.

See: *Process: Architecture,* no. 5 (1978): 50–57. *Baumeister* 74 (April 1977): 341–44. *Canadian Architect* 19 (October 1974): 41–53. Leon Whiteson, *Modern Canadian Architecture* (Edmonton: Hurtig, 1983), 180–83.

Benjamin THOMPSON

■ 461

Design Research Building; Cambridge, MA; 1969.
A retail store with a difference: a glittering, many-faceted showcase for home furnishings and clothes, with added space upstairs for offices. Its glass walls float on concrete slabs that jut out at odd angles, cantilevered boldly from supporting concrete columns. Inside are many blunt yet stylish touches: clean-lined open staircases with black pipe railings; floors of brick, concrete, or wood.
Associate in charge: Thomas Green. Engineers: LeMessurier Associates (structural); Reardon & Turner (mechanical/electrical). Contractor: Canter Construction Co.

Honors: AIA Honor Award, 1971.

See: *Architectural Record* 147 (May 1970): 105–12. *Interiors* 129 (May 1970): 108–17. *Architectural Review* 151 (January 1972): 28–34.

■ 462

Harborplace; Baltimore, MD; 1980.
Sited within Baltimore's Inner Harbor (master plan by Wallace, McHarg, Roberts & Todd), this lively market and recreational area is created by two 2-story pavilions, exuberantly decorated, set at right angles to each other and fronting on a plaza. The shedlike buildings—skylighted, with mezzanine balconies around greenery-filled atriums—contain 145,000 square feet of space for shops, restaurants, and browsing. Another 100,000 square feet outdoors complete the marketplace.
Partner in charge: Bruno D'Agostino; project architect: Charles Izzo; interior architect: Wendy Tinker. Engineers: Gilum-Colaco (structural); Robert G. Balter Co. (soils); Joseph R. Loring & Assoc. (mechanical/electrical). Landscape architects: Wallace, McHarg, Roberts & Todd. General contractor: Whiting-Turner Contracting.

Honors: AISC Architectural Award of Excellence, 1981.

See: *AIA Journal* 70 (June 1981): 32–41 and cover. *Architectural Record* 168 (October 1980): 100–5. *Interiors* 140 (September 1980): 100–3.

■ 463

Mt. Anthony Union High School; Bennington, VT; 1967.
This U-shaped, three-level, "inward looking" school has few windows on its outer margins; built around a courtyard, it has generously glazed corridors around the court's perimeter, and most of its classrooms have windows that face onto those corridors. Exposed waffle slab construction adds interest to ceilings, colorful accent walls and vivid graphics further enliven the interior, and a spacious, skylighted library is the school's central focus.
Associate in charge: Thomas Green. Landscape architect: Carol R. Johnson. Engineers:

LeMessurier Associates (structural); Shooshanian Engineering Co. (mechanical). Contractor: George A. Fuller & Co.

Honors: PA Design Award, 1965; Award of Merit, Library Buildings Award Program, 1968.

See: *Architectural Record* 143 (January 1968): 120–24. *Progressive Architecture* 49 (February 1968): 128–35. *Interiors* 127 (February 1968): 84–90.

Benjamin THOMPSON, for The ROUSE COMPANY

■ 464

Faneuil Hall Marketplace and Quincy Market Restoration; Boston, MA; first phase, 1976; second phase, 1977.
Here a once-rundown but historic area has been transformed into a vibrant complex of restaurants and shops with office space inconspicuously provided upstairs in renovated landmarks. Well-chosen graphics and hardy landscaping brighten pedestrian spaces; aisles alongside the complex's long buildings are glassed over to extend market space all year-round.
Principals: Benjamin Thompson, Thomas Green. Engineers: Zaldastani Associates (structural); J. C. Higgins Co. (mechanical). General contractor: George H. B. Macomber.

Honors: PA Design Citation, 1975; AIA Honor Award (Extended Use), 1978; Bartlett Award, 1978; AISC Architectural Award of Excellence, 1978; AIA Bicentennial List, two nominations.

See: *AIA Journal* 67 (mid-May 1978): 118–43; 70 (June 1981): 24–31. *Architectural Record* 162 (December 1977): 116–27. *Interiors* 138 (January 1979): 66–71.

THOMPSON, VENTULETT, STAINBACK

■ 465

CNN Center (formerly Omni International); Atlanta, GA; 1976 (see Illus. 225).
This spectacular steel, glass, and limestone megastructure covers 5½ acres and contains two office buildings, a hotel, and an indoor family amusement center, as well as many shops and restaurants. Flamboyant touches here include a 205-

foot escalator that soars through a huge central space, a laser beam sculpture, and 700 prisms positioned to split sunshine that comes through skylights into splashes of colored light.
Associate in charge: Marvin Housworth. Consultants: Jimmy H. Kluttz & Assoc. (landscape); Lazenby & Assoc. (mechanical engineers); Prybylowski & Gravino (structural engineers); One + One (design). General contractor: Ira H. Hardin Co.

Honors: AISC Architectural Award of Excellence.

See: *Progressive Architecture* 57 (May 1976): 51–69. *Interior Design* 45 (January 1974): 110–11. *A + U: Architecture and Urbanism,* no. 94 (July 1978): 87–94.

Stanley TIGERMAN

■ 466

Arby's Restaurant; Chicago, IL; 1977 (see Illus. 226).
Here's a stylish renovation of a small commercial building, 20 feet wide and 4 stories high, to suit a fast-food restaurant. The facade sleekly combines curves and planes, glass and stucco, and eye-catching signage. In the vividly decorated interior, ducts are exposed and color coded.
Engineers: Raymond Beebe (structural); Wallace & Migdal (mechanical). Contractor: Pepper Construction.

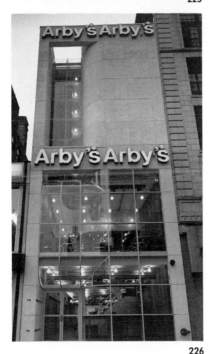

226

See: *Architectural Record* 163 (January 1978): 90–91. *A + U: Architecture and Urbanism,* no. 84 (November 1977): 54–57. *Contract Interiors* 137 (April 1978): 74–75. *Baumeister* 76 (February 1979): 152–53.

Stanley TIGERMAN; Joseph W. CASSERLY (City Architect of Chicago)

■ 467

Illinois Regional Library for the

Blind and Physically Handicapped; Chicago, IL; 1978 (see Illus. 227).
This triangular library—2 stories high with 3 stories of stacks—has many features considerate of the handicapped: a "tactile service counter" that signals staff locations to the blind, soft corners, and built-in furniture whose location can be memorized. Much of its exterior gleams with red metal panels accented by yellow and blue. The hypotenuse wall, concrete painted gray, is pierced by an extraordinary, 165-foot-long window, its upper margin a whimsically wavy line.
Engineers: Ray Beebe (structural); Wallace & Migdal (mechanical/electrical). General contractor: Walsh Construction.

Honors: AIA Honor Award, 1982.

See: *AIA Journal* 71 (mid-May 1982): 222–24. *Progressive Architecture* 59 (April 1978): 76–81 and cover. *Design Quarterly,* no. 105 (1978): 17–32. *Architecture Intérieure Crée,* (May–June 1979): 108–12.

TIPPETTS-ABBETT-McCARTHY-STRATTON (subsequent name of firm: TAMS Consultants)

■ 468

Pan American World Airways Passenger Terminal, Kennedy International Airport; New York, NY; phase 1, 1960; phase 2, 1976 (see Illus. 228).
As originally built, this terminal was "revolutionary in style"; its oval, 4-acre parasol of a roof was cantilevered from a glassed-in central core so planes could pull up under the roof for convenient boarding. When expansion became necessary, a much larger, fan-shaped terminal was added to it; together they accommodate today's larger planes and utilize a modified drive-to-the-gate system to load and unload passengers.
Associate architects, phase 1: Ives, Turano & Gardner. Consulting architect, phase 2: Philip Ives. Contractors: Turner Construction Co. (phase 1); Corbetta, Humphreys & Harding (phase 2).

Honors: AISC Architectural Award of Excellence, 1961.

See: *Architectural Record* 160 (October 1976): 125–40. *Progressive Architecture* 42 (November 1961): 140–45. *Bauwelt* 63 (April 1972): 566–68. *Edilizia Moderna,* no. 75 (April 1962): 25–32.

225 CNN Center (formerly Omni International); Atlanta, GA; 1976. *See* Entry 465. (Courtesy Thompson, Ventulett, Stainback & Associates; Atlanta, GA. Photographer: E. Alan McGee Photography.)

226 Arby's Restaurant; Chicago, IL; 1977. *See* Entry 466. (Courtesy Tigerman, Fugman, McCurry; Chicago, IL.)

227

227 Illinois Regional Library for the Blind and Physically Handicapped; Chicago, IL; 1978. *See* Entry 467. (Courtesy Tigerman, Fugman, McCurry; Chicago, IL.)

228 Pan American World Airways Passenger Terminal, Kennedy International Airport; New York, NY; phase 1, 1960; phase 2, 1976. *See* Entry 468. (Courtesy TAMS Consultants, Inc.; New York, NY.)

229 Vehicle Assembly Building, John F. Kennedy Space Center; Cape Canaveral, FL; 1966. *See* Entry 469. (Courtesy Office of Max O. Urbahn; Mystic, CT.)

228

an opening 500 feet high and 70 feet wide.

Engineers: Roberts & Schaefer Co. (structural); Seelye, Stevenson, Value & Knecht (mechanical/electrical/civil); Moran, Proctor, Mueser & Rutledge (foundation).

Honors: AIA Bicentennial List, two nominations.

See: Architectural Forum 126 (January–February 1967): 50–59. *Perspecta,* no. 11 (1967): 218. *L'Architecture d'Aujourd'hui,* no. 133 (September 1967): 98–103.

VAN DER RYN CALTHORPE

■ 470

Gregory Bateson Building (Site 1 State Office Building); Sacramento, CA; 1981.

Combining good looks with energy efficiency in a sunny, dry, often hot climate, this 4-story, 267,000-square-foot office building is built around a huge enclosed atrium whose roof contains both skylights and operable louvers. Its concrete structure, which stores nighttime coolness, and a watered, 660-ton rock bed are used for temperature control. When first opened, defective ventilation briefly caused problems.

California state architect; Sim Van der Ryn; deputy state architect: Barry Wasserman; designers: Peter Calthorpe, Bruce Corson, and Scott Matthews.

Honors: PA Citation for Architectural Design, 1979.

See: AIA Journal 70 (January 1981): 58–60; 71 (September 1982): 18, 22. *A + U: Architecture and Urbanism,* no. 140 (May 1982): 57–64. *Interiors* 139 (May 1980): 128–29, 154–56.

Max URBAHN

■ 469

Vehicle Assembly Building, John F. Kennedy Space Center; Cape Canaveral, FL; 1966 (see Illus. 229).

A colossus among buildings, this gigantic workshop is visible 14 miles away and contains 130 million cubic feet of space. Designed as a "garage" for space vehicles, its entry doors slide vertically to provide

229

VENTURI & RAUCH

■ 471

Allen Memorial Art Museum addition, Oberlin College; Oberlin, OH; 1977 (original museum designed in 1917 by Cass Gilbert) (see Illus. 230).

Two sections make up this addition to a Renaissance-style museum: a 3,750-square-foot double-height gallery in the form of a "decorated shed," clad in a checkerboard pattern of pink and red stone, and a much larger, 3-story "loft" building, clad in buff brick striped with bands of windows and housing a library, studios, workshops, and art storage. One memorable touch: a structural steel pier sheathed with wood slats to look like an oversized Ionic column.

Project manager: Jeff Ryan. Consultants: Keast & Hood (structural); Vinokur-Pace (mechanical/ electrical). General contractor: J&R Construction.

See: Progressive Architecture 58 (October 1977): 50–55 and cover. *L'Architecture d'Aujourd'hui,* no. 197 (June 1978): 58–63. *Harvard Architecture Review* 1 (Spring 1980): 197–201. *Architectural Design* 48, no. 1 (1978): 38–40.

■ 472

Dixwell Fire Station; New Haven, Ct; 1974 (see Illus. 231).

Practicality, whimsy, and sly references to the commonplaces of vernacular architecture coexist in this fire station with a difference. An almost square building set diagonally—for reasons of mobility—on its site, it is built of intensely red brick, is tidily detailed, and features a projecting banner of a wall, which bears in giant letters the names of local firefighting units.

Engineers: The Keast and Hood Company (structural); Vinokur-Pace Engineering Services (mechanical/electrical). Contractor: J. H. Hogan.

See: Architectural Record 159 (June 1976):

111–16. *A + U: Architecture and Urbanism,* no. 87 (January 1978): 3–80. *Venturi and Rauch: The Public Buildings,* Architectural Monographs, no. 1 (London: Academy Editions, 1978).

■ 473

Franklin Court; Philadelphia, PA; 1976 (see Illus. 232).

To memorialize Benjamin Franklin on the site of his home and print shop—now impossible to replicate for lack of historic data—a large courtyard was landscaped to resemble an eighteenth-century garden; in it, "ghost" frameworks of steel recall the lost buildings, and remains of old foundations can be viewed through glass. Underneath, there's a large museum and theater. Five eighteenth-century houses nearby, restored on the outside and renovated inside, house additional exhibits.

Project architect: David M. Vaughn. Consultants: National Heritage Corp., reconstruction design for Market Street houses; Synterra Ltd, landscape architects. Engineers: Keast and Hood (structural); Vinokur-Pace (mechanical).

232

Honors: AIA Honor Award for Extended Use, 1977.

See: AIA Journal 66 (May 1977): 35. *Progressive Architecture* 57 (April 1976): 69–76. *A + U: Architecture and Urbanism,* no. 87 (January 1978): 53–62. *Domus,* no. 568 (March 1977): 53.

■ **474**

Guild House, Friends' Housing for the Elderly; Philadelphia, PA; 1963–65 (see Illus. 233).

This 6-story brick apartment house contains ninety-one units designed for low-income elderly tenants. Its distinctive appearance stems from an oversized arched window above its entry and other facade details modeled after a Renaissance chateau at Anêt, as well as from subtle variations of size in its other windows, in its bricks, and in the spacing of fence supports.

Associated architects: Cope & Lippincott. Consultants: Keast & Hood (structural); Pennel & Wiltberger (mechanical/electrical).

See: AIA Journal 69 (February 1980): 38–41. *Progressive Architecture* 48 (May 1967): 124–48. *Lotus* 4 (1967/68): 98–105. *Venturi and Rauch: The Public Buildings,* Architectural Monographs, no. 1 (London: Academy Editions, 1978).

233

■ **475**

Gordon Wu Hall, Butler College, Princeton University; Princeton, NJ; 1983 (see Illus. 234).

This 3-story student center connected to a preexistent building (Wilcox Hall) contains dining facilities, a lounge, offices, and a small library. Clad in orange brick with limestone trim, it bears over its entrance two arresting gray and white panels of abstract shapes derived from heraldic forms that decorated Elizabethan manor houses. Also reminiscent of Elizabethan architecture: 2-story bay windows at either end and a broad oak staircase within.

Partner in charge: Robert Venturi; project team: Arthur Jones, Missy Maxwell. Engineers: Keast & Hood (structural); Vinokur-Pace (mechanical). General contractor: Scozzari Construction.

Honors: AIA Honor Award, 1984.

See: Architectural Record 171 (September 1983): part II, 86–97 and cover. *Architecture* 73 (May 1984): 200–203. *A + U: Architecture and Urbanism,* no. 160 (January 1984): 73–86. *GA Document,* no. 10 (May 1984): 76–81.

■ **476**

Knoll Center showroom; New York, NY; 1979.

Clever design transformed two floors of an unremarkable, low-ceilinged office building into this dramatic setting for furniture and fabrics. A pouffy, 2-story cascade of velvets dominates the lobby. Sliding panels of long wood slats, irregular in width and wavy in profile, hide distracting outside views. Fat, quasi-Egyptian columns with gracefully spreading capitals mask all but the uppermost inches of structural piers; uplighting is concealed within the capitals. Partner in charge: Robert Venturi; project managers: Stanford Hughes, John Chase. Consultants: George Izenour (lighting); Flack & Kurtz (mechanical); Leichtman & Lincer (structural).

Honors: Interiors Award for Retail/Showroom Design, 1980.

See: Architectural Record 167 (March 1980):

234

97–102. *Interior Design* 51 (March 1980): 226–35. *L'Architecture d'Aujourd'hui,* no. 210 (September 1980): 56–57.

VENTURI, RAUCH & SCOTT BROWN (exterior); PAYETTE ASSOCIATES (interior)

■ 477

Lewis Thomas Laboratory, Princeton University; Princeton, NJ; building 1985, landscaping 1986 (see Illus. 235).
Bands of ornamental brickwork, predominantly rose and brown, in several patterns stand out against a limestone background on the exterior of this 110,000-square-foot molecular biology laboratory. Three floors of labs are topped, for part of their area, by an 18-foot-high fourth floor devoted to mechanicals and clad on much of its facade with oversize checkerboard patterns. Interiors, not high tech, sport lots of red oak; exposed ducts are painted an inconspicuous white.
For Payette Associates, David Rowan, principal in charge; James Collins, Jr., project architect. For Venturi, Rauch and Scott Brown, Robert Venturi, principal in charge; Ronald McCoy and David Schaaf, project architects. Engineers: R. G. Vanderweil Engineers (mechanical/electrical/plumbing); Simpson, Gumpertz & Heger (structural). General contractor: Barr & Barr.

Honors: AIA Honor Award.

See: Architectural Record 174 (August 1986): 104–13 and cover. *Architecture* 76 (May 1987): 174–76. *Casabella* 50 (September 1986): 4–13.

WALLACE, McHARG, ROBERTS & TODD (see also entry no. 462)

■ 478

Amelia Island Plantation; Amelia Island, FL; master plan 1971, development (phase 1) opened 1974.
A resort/residence community of one-family homes and mid-rise apartment houses, it was originally located in a series of "neighborhoods" on 450 acres and later doubled in size; it now also boasts two championship golf courses. Sensitive design protects the area's animal and plant ecology—particularly its fragile oceanfront sand dunes—from destructive incursions.

Honors: PA Design Award, 1973; Honor Award, ASLA Professional Competition, 1973.

See: Landscape Architecture 63 (April 1973): 239–50. *House & Home* 46 (November 1974): 59–71. *Urban Land Institute Project Reference File* 10 (October–December 1980), no. 16.

John Carl WARNECKE (see also entry no. 36)

■ 479

Asilomar Housing, Asilomar Beach State Park; near Monterey, CA; phase 1, 1959, gradually expanded thereafter (see Illus. 236).
The original buildings at this conference center, located in a region of great natural beauty, were designed by Julia Morgan around 1920. The tasteful and unassuming housing and lounge-conference facilities that Warnecke added are built of redwood, cedar, and local stone; they maintain the site's serenity and harmonize well with the original buildings.
Structural engineers: William B. Gilbert & Associates.

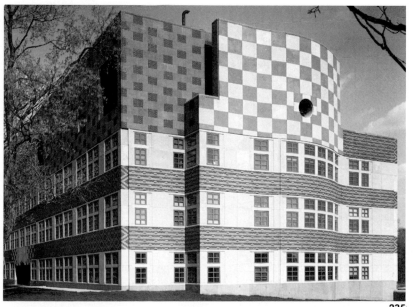

235

234 Gordon Wu Hall, Butler College, Princeton University; Princeton, NJ; 1983. *See* Entry 475. (Courtesy Venturi, Rauch and Scott Brown; Philadelphia, PA. Photographer: Tom Bernard.)

235 Lewis Thomas Laboratory, Princeton University; Princeton, NJ; 1985. *See* Entry 477. (Courtesy Venturi, Rauch and Scott Brown; Philadelphia, PA. Photographer: Matt Wargo.)

236

Honors: AIA Merit Award, 1960.

See: *Architectural Record* 127 (March 1960): 145–60; 140 (August 1966): 123–38. *Interiors* 126 (October 1966): 130–33.

■ 480

Hennepin County Government Center; Minneapolis, MN; 1976 (see Illus. 237).

This centerpiece to a new civic center was designed to combine "informality with monumentality." It comprises twin towers, 24 stories high—one intended for county offices, the other for district and municipal courts. Between the two towers is a 350-foot-high glassed-in atrium boldly bordered by exposed steel diagonal bracing.

Associated architects: Peterson, Clarke & Associates. Engineers: Ketchum, Konkel, Barrett, Nickel & Austin (structural); Donald Bentley & Associates (mechanical/electrical/plumbing). General contractor: Knutson Construction Company.

Honors: AISC Architectural Award of Excellence, 1977.

See: *Architectural Record* 161 (March 1977): 101–6. *Architettura* 23 (November 1977): 388–89. *Contract Interiors* 137 (August 1977): 86–89.

237

WARNECKE & WARNECKE (see also entry nos. 36 and 122)

■ 481

Residence halls, University of California; Berkeley, CA; 1959/60 (see Illus. 238).

This attractive complex is appealingly landscaped with ample open space, including several sunken courtyards. It takes up almost all of three consecutive city blocks and combines eight reinforced concrete, 9-story dormitories, brightened on some facades by colored metal panels, with four 2-story dining/recreation buildings with gracefully curving roofs. Exteriors of both kinds of buildings are enhanced by decorative cast stone grilles.
Engineers: Isadore Thompson (structural); Dudley Deane & Associates (mechanical). Landscape architect: Lawrence Halprin. General contractor: Dinwiddie Construction Company.

Honors: PA Award Citation, 1959.

See: Architectural Record 127 (March 1960): 154–60. *Progressive Architecture* 40 (January 1959): 150–51. *Arts + Architecture* 73 (October 1956): 20–21.

WARNER BURNS TOAN LUNDE

■ 482

Hofstra University Library; Hempstead, NY; 1967.

An unusual covered pedestrian bridge that spans a turnpike ensures accessibility for this concrete and glass library while calling attention to it. The 2-story pavilion that contains the library's basic public services is surmounted by an 8-story tower. Space is provided for a collection of 400,000 volumes.
Partner in charge: Danforth W. Toan; associate/design: Yung Wang. Engineers: Severud, Perrone, Fischer, Sturm, Conlin & Bandel (structural); Stinard, Piccirillo & Brown (electrical/mechanical). Landscape architect: M. Paul Friedberg & Assoc.

Honors: Award of Merit, Library Buildings Award Program, 1968.

See: Architectural Forum 126 (January–February 1967): 78–79. *Architectural Record* 143 (March 1968): 149–64. *Interiors* 128 (December 1968): 120–26.

238 Residence halls, University of California; Berkeley, CA; 1959/60. *See* Entry 481. (Courtesy John Carl Warnecke & Associates; San Francisco, CA. Photographer: Joshua Freiwald.)

Harry WEESE

In 1978, Harry Weese & Associates won the AIA's Architectural Firm Award.

■ 483

First Baptist Church and Chapel; Columbus, IN; 1965.

In this extraordinary church building, the sternly geometric lines of the section that contains the sanctuary are echoed by those of an attached school-and-chapel wing. Built around an enclosed court, both the sanctuary and the chapel wings have steeply pitched roofs, covered in slate, while several exterior walls are rounded, recalling medieval architecture.
Engineers: The Engineers Collaborative (structural); Samuel R. Lewis & Associates (mechanical). Landscape architect: Dan Kiley. General contractor: Repp & Mundt Construction Service.

See: Architectural Record 138 (December 1965): 113–17. *Process: Architecture,* no. 11 (1979): 32–35. *L'Architecture d'Aujourd'hui,* no. 125 (April–May 1966): 72–73.

■ 484

Metro subway stations; Washington, DC; first phase, 1977.

Although built of simple materials— primarily concrete with touches of tile, granite, and bronze—these have been called "the most noble series of underground halls and simple and elegant ground level stations." Grandly vaulted, coffered ceilings lend drama to the underground spaces.

Honors: CRSI Design Award, 1985, for Huntington Station, a suburban station built in a later phase of Metro expansion.

See: AIA Journal 64 (December 1975): 38–43. *Architectural Review* 163 (February 1978): 99–102. *Process: Architecture,* no. 11 (1979): 134–39.

■ 485

Milwaukee Center for the Performing Arts; Milwaukee, WI; 1969.

Built on the banks of the Milwaukee River, this handsome travertine-sheathed center contains three auditoriums: a 2,327-seat concert hall, a 526-seat theater with a thrust stage, and a multipurpose 482-seat recital hall. Acoustical elements in the concert space, Uihlein Hall, are not concealed; instead they have been "designed into the room."
Theater consultants: George C. Izenour Associates. Acoustical consultants: Bolt, Beranek & Newman; Dr. Lothar Cremer. Engineers: The Engineers Collaborative (structural); S. R. Lewis & Associates (mechanical/electrical). Landscape architect: Office of Dan Kiley. Contractor: Klug & Smith Co.

Honors: AIA Honor Award, 1970; AISC Architectural Award of Excellence, 1970.

See: *AIA Journal* 53 (June 1970): 88. *Architectural Record* 146 (November 1969): 147–64. *Process: Architecture,* no. 11 (1979): 56–67.

■ 486

William J. Campbell Courthouse Annex; Chicago, IL; 1975.
This wedge-shaped, 27-story jail on Chicago's Loop has a facade that looks like an IBM card; its irregularly placed slit windows are 7½ feet long but only 5 inches wide—the maximum width allowed without bars by the Bureau of Prisons. Each prisoner has a private room and other amenities.
Engineers: Severud-Perrone-Sturm-Bandel (structural); H. S. Nachman & Associates (mechanical/electrical). Landscape architects: Joe Karr & Associates. General contractor: Turner Construction Co.

Honors: AIA Honor Award, 1977; Chicago AIA 22d Annual Distinguished Buildings Award.

See: *AIA Journal* 66 (May 1977): 28–49. *Inland Architect* 19 (July 1975): 7–13. *A+U: Architecture and Urbanism,* no. 94 (July 1978): 79–86.

WHITTLESEY, CONKLIN & ROSSANT

■ 487

Lake Anne Center; Reston, VA; 1966 (see Illus. 239).
This lakeside pedestrian plaza, central to one of seven villages in a noted planned community, is surrounded by low buildings, uniform in style, that contain shops, cafes, offices, and apartments. Even such details as its storefronts and signs have been designed by architects.

Honors: AIA Bicentennial List, one nomination.

See: *Progressive Architecture* 47 (May 1966): 194–201. *Werk* 54 (March 1967): 170–72. G. E. Kidder Smith, *A Pictorial History of Architecture in America* (New York: American Heritage, 1976), 1: 392–93.

WOLF ASSOCIATES

■ 488

Beatties Ford Road and Park Road branches, North Carolina National Bank; Charlotte, NC; Beatties Ford Road branch 1971, Park Road branch 1973.
Both of these single-story, sleekly white branch banks are strongly geometric in plan: Beatties Ford Road is triangular; Park Road, a drive-in bank, is shaped like a parallelogram. Both are designed for ready accessibility to the handicapped.
Engineers: Ray V. Wasdell Assoc. (structural); Mechanical Engineers, Inc. (mechanical).

Honors: AIA Honor Awards, 1971 and 1974; Bartlett Awards, 1971 and 1974.

See: *AIA Journal* 55 (June 1971): 45–55; 61 (May 1974): 41–49. *Architectural Record* 153 (June 1973): 111–20.

■ 489

Mecklenburg County Courthouse; Charlotte, NC; 1978.
This dignified, oblong, 3-story courthouse links diverse elements—an office building, garage, elevated walkway, and park—in a city/county government center while helping to define a central plaza. One long side has a glass and aluminum curtain wall; public corridors adjacent look into the plaza and lead to courtrooms. On the opposite side there's a formal limestone facade with few windows; judges' chambers and jury rooms are reached by secluded corridors alongside.
Engineers: King-Hudson (structural); James A. Story & Assoc. (mechanical). General contractor: Parke Construction.

Honors: AIA Honor Award, 1983; Honor Award, North Carolina Chapter, AIA, 1978; CRSI Design Award, 1979; Building Stone Institute Tucker Award, 1979.

See: *AIA Journal* 72 (May 1983): 257–59. *Architectural Record* 165 (May 1979): 109–16. *A+U: Architecture and Urbanism,* no. 178 (July 1985): 97–100.

Frank Lloyd WRIGHT

Winner, Royal Gold Medal, 1941; AIA Gold Medal, 1949.

■ 490

Annunciation Greek Orthodox Church; Wauwatosa, WI; 1961.
An extraordinary and colorful church inspired by, but not imitative of, the

239 Lake Anne Center; Reston, VA; 1966. *See* Entry 487. (Courtesy Conklin Rossant; New York, NY. Photographer: J. Alexander.)

Byzantine tradition. Its shallow dome, about 100 feet in diameter, is covered with blue ceramic tile; lively patterns of arcs and circles recur inside and out.

See: *Architectural Forum* 115 (December 1961): 82–87. Ralph W. Hammett, *Architecture in the United States* (New York: Wiley, 1976), 225–27.

■ 491

China and gift shop for V. C. Morris, Maiden Lane; San Francisco, CA; 1949.
This remarkable store has no display windows; its blank facade of golden yellow brick is broken only by a fastidiously crafted, asymmetrical archway through which just a glimpse of the interior can be seen. Light filters from above through a decorative screen that incorporates plastic disks and half bubbles. Instead of stairs, there's a spiraling ramp that prefigures the more famous one in Wright's Guggenheim Museum (see entry no. 496).

See: *Architectural Forum* 92 (February 1950): 79–85. *Architect's Journal* 110 (November 10, 1959). 512, 516. Henry-Russell Hitchcock and Arthur Drexler, eds., *Built in USA: Post-War Architecture* (New York: Museum of Modern Art, 1952), 118–19.

■ 492

Johnson Wax Company Research and Development Tower; Racine, WI; 1950.
This innovative, 153-foot-high research tower—when completed, the tallest building ever erected without foundations under its side walls—was designed, said its architect, to provide "clear light and space all around every floor"; he called it "the Helio-lab." Its floors are cantilevered out from a central core; 40 feet square but with rounded corners, it is glazed with 2-inch-wide glass tubing laid horizontally and sealed horizontally with plastic.
Resident architect: John Halama. General contractor: Wiltscheck & Nelson, Inc.

Honors: AIA Bicentennial List, eleven nominations.

See: *Architectural Forum* 94 (January 1951): 75–81. *Architect and Engineer* 183 (December 1950): 20–24. Y. Futagawa, ed., *Frank Lloyd Wright: Johnson & Son Administrative Building and Research Tower . . . ,* text by Arata Isozaki, Global Architecture, no. 1 (Tokyo: A. D. A. Edita, 1970).

■ 493

Kalita Humphreys Theater; Dallas, TX; 1959.
Housed in a controversial concrete building with oddly layered masses, this theater originally was designed to be used in the round, but to correct technical problems it was modified to create an apron stage arrangement. A 32-foot section of its 40-foot circular stage revolves; many other facilities are highly mechanized.
Supervising architect: W. Kelly Oliver. Lighting and mechanical consultant for stage: George C. Izenour. Mechanical engineers: Herman Blum Engineers. Contractor: Henry C. Beck Co.

See: *Architectural Forum* 112 (March 1960): 130–35. *Architectural Record* 127 (March 1960): 161–66. G. E. Kidder Smith, *A Pictorial History of Architecture in America* (New York: American Heritage, 1976), 598–99.

■ 494

Meetinghouse, First Unitarian Society; Madison, WI; 1951.
The auditorium/chapel of this wood and stone building has a triangular, upthrusting roof that resembles a prow. Outside it forms a 40-foot spire; seen from inside, it frames a simple stone pulpit flanked by ample windows that open the room to views of trees and sky. Wright was a member of this congregation and his fellow parishioners, along with members of the Taliesin Fellowship, contributed labor to the construction of this meetinghouse.

See: *Architectural Forum* 97 (December 1952): 85–92. *Perspecta,* no. 1 (Summer 1952): 16–17.

■ 495

Price Tower; Bartlesville, OK; 1955.
Both office space and apartments are contained in this 186-foot-high reinforced-concrete tower with gently angular lines and considerable cantilevering of its upper floors. Its facade is adorned by copper louvers and other copper facings, geometrically marked and preoxidized to a greenish cast.
Mechanical engineer: Collins & Gould. General contractor: Haskell Culwell Construction Co.

Honors: AIA Bicentennial List, one nomination; AIA Twenty-Five Year Award, 1983.

See: *Architectural Forum* 98 (May 1953): 98–105; 104 (February 1956): 106–13. *Architectural Record* 119 (February 1956): 153–60.

■ 496

Solomon R. Guggenheim Museum; New York, NY; 1959.
A remarkable art museum—New York's only permanent building by Wright—its main gallery area is built in the form of one continuous, irregularly spiraling ramp around a great central well. Display walls slant outward, easel-fashion. As of early 1988, expansion was being contemplated along lines originally planned by Wright.

Honors: AIA Bicentennial List, six nominations; AIA Twenty-Five Year Award, 1986.

See: *Architectural Forum* 111 (December 1959): 86–93. *Architectural Record* 123 (May 1958): 182–90. Y. Futagawa, ed., *Frank Lloyd Wright: Solomon R. Guggenheim Museum . . . ,* text by B. B. Pfeiffer, Global Architecture, no. 36 (Tokyo: A. D. A. Edita, 1975).

■ 497

Taliesin East; Spring Green, WI; 1959.
Wright's own Eastern studio and home, sited on a hillside in the district of his "roots," was begun in 1911 and repeatedly modified and enlarged over the years. Along with Taliesin West (see entry no. 498), it was workshop and home also to generations of architect-apprentices of the Taliesin Fellowship. (Taliesin is a Welsh word meaning "shining brow.")

See: *Architectural Forum* 68 (January 1938): 2–23; 110 (June 1959): 132–37. *Inland Architect* 13 (July 1969): 22–25. Y. Futagawa, ed., *Frank Lloyd Wright: Taliesin East . . . Taliesin West . . . ,* text by Masami Tanigawa, Global Architecture, no. 15 (Tokyo: A. D. A. Edita, 1972).

■ 498

Taliesin West; near Scottsdale, AZ; 1959.
Wright's desert studio and home, begun in 1934 and, like Taliesin East (see entry no. 497), repeatedly enlarged and modified by the architect-apprentices of the Taliesin Fellowship working under Wright's supervision.

Honors: AIA Twenty-five Year Award, 1972.

See: *Architectural Forum* 88 (January 1948): 87–88; 110 (June 1959): 132–37. *House Beautiful* 83 (December 1946): 186–95, 235. *House and Home* 15 (June 1959): 88–98. Y. Futagawa, ed., *Frank Lloyd Wright: Taliesin East . . . Taliesin West . . . ,* text by Masami Tanigawa, Global Architecture, no. 15 (Tokyo: A. D. A. Edita, 1972).

■ **499**

Marin County Civic Center; San Rafael, CA; 1972.
An immensely long megastructure, richly and colorfully decorated, and roughly boomerang shaped in plan. It was designed to comprise twelve different elements, including an administration building, post office, and separate museums for natural history and art. Its Hall of Justice alone boasts a 600-foot-long gallery, from which adjacent courtrooms look out on scenic bay and hillside views.

See: *AIA Journal* 69 (April 1980): 46–57 and cover. *Architectural Forum* 117 (November 1962): 122–29; 133 (December 1970): 54–59. Y. Futagawa, ed., *Frank Lloyd Wright: Solomon R. Guggenheim Museum . . . Marin County Civic Center,* text by Bruce Brooks Pfeiffer, Global Architecture, no. 36 (Tokyo: A. D. A. Edita, 1975).

Lloyd WRIGHT (the son of Frank Lloyd Wright)

■ **500**

Wayfarers Chapel; Palos Verdes, CA; 1951.
Designed to be sheltered by a grove of redwoods, this Protestant chapel that overlooks the Pacific has shoulder-high walls of native stone, topped by plantings and heavily bermed outside. Above these low walls, on up through its arching roof, it is built almost entirely of glass, sectioned off into geometric patterns by a framework of redwood.

Honors: AIA Bicentennial List, two nominations.

See: *Architectural Forum* 95 (August 1951): 153–55. *Arts + Architecture* 83 (October 1966): 22–26. G. E. Kidder Smith, *A Pictorial History of Architecture in America* (New York: American Heritage, 1976), 2: 774–75.

WURSTER, BERNARDI & EMMONS

Winner of the AIA's Architectural Firm Award, 1965. In 1969, William Wilson Wurster won the AIA Gold Medal.

■ **501**

Center for Advanced Study in the Behavioral Sciences; Palo Alto, CA; 1954.
One-story redwood and glass buildings on a graciously landscaped site provide quarters for scholars doing research on human behavior. A cross-shaped central building houses administrative and group facilities; rows of separate study rooms, affording ample comfort and privacy, are located in long, narrow units distributed around the grounds.
Mechanical engineer: Buonaccorsi, Murray & Lewis. Landscape architect: Thomas D. Church. General contractor: Swinerton & Walberg.

Honors: AIA Honor Award, 1956.

See: *Architectural Forum* 102 (January 1955): 130–33. *Arts + Architecture* 72 (February 1955): 14–16. *Domus,* no. 329 (April 1957): 3–6.

■ **502**

Ghirardelli Square; San Francisco, CA; 1965.
Quaint old red brick buildings, once occupied by a chocolate-manufacturing firm, have been converted here into an enticing restaurant/shopping complex. New buildings designed to blend in with the old and an underground garage for 300 cars have been added.
Structural engineer: Gilbert-Forsberg-Diekmann-Schmidt. Landscape architect: Lawrence Halprin & Associates. General contractor: Swinerton & Walberg Co.

Honors: AIA Merit Award, 1966; AIA Bicentennial List, three nominations.

See: *AIA Journal* 46 (July 1966): 46–47. *Interiors* 125 (October 1965): 98–109. *Process: Architecture,* no. 4 (February 1978): 103–18.

■ **503**

Ice Houses I and II; San Francisco, CA; 1968.
An improbable but highly successful example of adaptive reuse: two staunchly handsome brick warehouses, originally built in 1914 for cold storage, turned into wholesale showrooms for interior furnishings. The architects made the most of original interior brick walls, high ceilings, and wooden columns; they connected the two buildings at all upper levels with a boldly contrasting steel and glass "concourse tower" and added a plaza.
Engineers: G. F. D. S. Engineers (structural); G. L. Gendler & Associates (mechanical/electrical). Landscape architect: Lawrence Halprin & Associates. General contractor: Dillingham Construction Co.

Honors: AISC Architectural Award of Excellence, 1969 (for concourse tower connecting the two renovated icehouses); AIA Honor Award, 1972.

See: *AIA Journal* 57 (May 1972): 40. *Interiors* 129 (July 1970): 73, 84–85. *Interior Design* 40 (September 1969): 160–63.

WURSTER, BERNARDI & EMMONS; SKIDMORE, OWINGS & MERRILL

■ **504**

Bank of America World Headquarters; San Francisco, CA; 1969.
A 52-story office tower, faced with red granite and set on an appealing plaza, whose intriguing facade derives from San Francisco's traditional bay windows. Above its plaza/lobby level, the building rises as a zigzag series of sawtooth bays unbroken except for contrasting detailing at the fifteenth and thirty-seventh floors and a series of irregular setbacks near the top.
Consulting architect: Pietro Belluschi. Engineers: H. J. Brunnier & Associates (structural); Skidmore, Owings & Merrill (mechanical/electrical). Landscape architect: Lawrence Halprin & Associates. Contractor: Dinwiddie-Fuller-Cahill (joint venture).

Honors: AISC Architectural Award of Excellence, 1970.

See: *AIA Journal* 69 (August 1980): 48–55 and cover. *Architectural Forum* 131 (October 1969): 70–71. *Architectural Record* 148 (July 1970): 126–32. *Baumeister* 68 (March 1971): 262–65.

Minoru YAMASAKI

■ 505

The ANR Building (formerly Michigan Consolidated Gas Company Headquarters); Detroit, MI; 1963 (see Illus. 240).

This precast concrete, 28-story office tower has surprisingly fanciful detailing in its 25-foot-high lobby and in its soaring facade set with distinctive hexagonal windows. It is topped by an unusual "crown" designed to be illuminated at night.

Associated architects and engineers: Smith, Hinchman & Grylls. General contractor: Bryant Detweiler Company.

Honors: AISC Architectural Award of Excellence, 1964.

See: Architectural Forum 118 (May 1963): 98–113. *Architectural Record* 128 (August 1960): 141–46; 133 (May 1963): 143–50.

■ 506

Reynolds Metals Sales Headquarters Building, Great Lakes Region; Detroit, MI; 1959, later modified for use as a health club (see Illus. 241).

There was a light and airy feeling to this unusual suburban office building, constructed around a skylighted central well and almost completely surrounded by a reflecting pool. Two stories of offices supported on slim black columns hovered

240 The ANR Building (formerly Michigan Consolidated Gas Company Headquarters), Detroit, MI; 1963. *See* Entry 505. (Courtesy Minoru Yamasaki Associates; Troy, MI. Photographer: Balthazar Korab.)

240

241 Reynolds Metals Sales Headquarters Building; Great Lakes Region; Detroit, MI; 1959. *See* Entry 506. (Courtesy Minoru Yamasaki Associates; Troy, MI. Photographer: Balthazar Korab.)

241

above a recessed, glass-enclosed entry floor and looked out through a lacy sunscreen of gold-anodized aluminum. Design associates: Harold Tsuchiya and Gunnar Birkerts. Engineers: Ammann & Whitney (structural); Cass S. Wadowski (mechanical). Landscape architect: W. B. Ford Design Associates. General contractor: Darin & Armstrong.

Honors: AIA Honor Award, 1961.

See: Architectural Record 126 (November 1959): 161–68; 136 (September 1964): 169–84. *Interiors* 119 (November 1959): 102–9.

■ 507

Temple and School Buildings, North Shore Congregation Israel; Glencoe, IL; 1964 (see Illus. 242).
Graceful aspiring lines that resemble plant forms characterize this religious complex built of reinforced and precast concrete. Light flows into the sanctuary through delicately wrought skylights and petal-shaped windows; harmonious expansion space for the sanctuary is provided innovatively by means of low platforms on either side of the main seating and an adjacent lobby/memorial hall.
Resident architects: Friedman, Alschuler & Sincere. Project director: Henry J. Guthard. Engineers: Worthington, Skilling, Helle & Jackson (structural); Peter Turner (mechanical). Landscape architect: Lawrence Halprin. Contractor: Bolt, Beranek & Newman.

See: Architectural Record 136 (September 1964): 176–77, 191–96; 171 (June 1983): 104–13. *Architecture International* 1 (1965): 96–103.

242

242 North Shore Congregation Israel Temple Building; Glencoe, IL; 1964. *See* Entry 507. (Courtesy Minoru Yamasaki Associates; Troy, MI. Photographer: Hedrich-Blessing; Chicago, IL.)

■ 508

Woodrow Wilson School of Public and International Affairs, Princeton University; Princeton, NJ; 1965 (see Illus. 243).
A colonnade of gracefully sculptured columns surrounds this oblong, high-ceilinged, 2-story building of "classic monumentality." It is set on a formal podium, within which is concealed a third level containing conference and lecture halls; alongside lies a reflecting pool.
Structural engineers: Worthington, Skilling, Helle & Jackson. Contractor: William L. Crow Construction Co.

See: Architectural Record 134 (December 1963): 103–10; 138 (October 1965): 140–43. *Arts + Architecture* 80 (June 1963): 14–15, 30.

Minoru YAMASAKI; Emery ROTH & SONS

■ 509

World Trade Center; New York, NY; 1 World Trade Center, 1970; 2 World Trade Center, 1972; overhaul project, 1981 (see Illus. 244).
The twin towers of this gargantuan office complex were, at 1,350 feet, briefly the tallest in the world but were superseded by the Sears Tower (see entry no. 426). This complex also comprises four lower buildings—including the Vista Hotel—set in a spacious plaza, and an extensive system of underground concourses with

243 Woodrow Wilson School of Public and International Affairs, Princeton University; Princeton, NJ; 1965. *See* Entry 508. (Courtesy Princeton University Communications/Publications; Princeton, NJ. Photographer: Clem Fiori.)

243

244

244 World Trade Center; New York, NY; 1976. *See* Entry 509. (Courtesy Minoru Yamasaki Associates; Troy, MI. Photographer: Balthazar Korab.)

numerous shops and restaurants and with connections to several subway lines. Engineers: Worthington, Skilling, Helle & Jackson (structural); Jaros, Baum & Bolles (mechanical). Main contractor: Tishman Realty & Construction Co.

Honors: AIA Bicentennial List, one nomination.

See: Architectural Forum 134 (May 1971): 7. *Architectural Record* 155 (March 1974): 140–42. *Building* 223 (September 29, 1972): 43–47.

YAMASAKI, LEINWEBER

■510

McGregor Memorial Conference Center, Wayne State University; Detroit, MI; 1958 (see Illus. 245, 245A).
On the east and west facades of this dignified campus center, two rows of marble-faced columns rise to neatly zigzagging concrete ceilings; its other two facades, blank at the sides, open at the center to a 2-story-high lobby topped with a skylight of gleaming diamond shapes and lined with columns and zigzag ceilings that echo those outside. Engineers: Ammann & Whitney. Landscape architect: Eichsted-Johnson Associates. General contractor: Darin & Armstrong, Inc.

Honors: AIA First Honor Award, 1959.

See: AIA Journal 31 (June 1959): 81.

Architectural Forum 109 (August 1958): 78–83. *L'Architecture d'Aujourd'hui,* no. 89 (April–May 1960): 60–63.

ZEIDLER PARTNERSHIP; BREGMAN & HAMANN (see also entry nos. 66–68 and 217)

In 1986, Eberhard Zeidler received the Gold Medal of the Royal Architectural Institute of Canada.

■511

Toronto Eaton Centre; Toronto, Ontario; first phase, 1977; second phase, 1981 (see Illus. 246).
The centerpiece of this complex, located on a five-block site, is The Galleria, a shopping mall with scores of small shops; 860 feet long and 90 feet high, it is topped by an immense arching skylight. Also included in the complex are a major department store (Eaton's), high-rise office space, and a parking garage. Coordinating partner: Sidney Bregman; design partner: Eberhard H. Zeidler. Engineers: C. D. Carruthers & Wallace Consultants Ltd. (structural); H. H. Angus & Associates (mechanical/electrical). Construction management: The Foundation Co. of Canada Ltd.

Honors: Governor General's Medal, 1982.

245 McGregor Memorial Conference Center, Wayne State University; Detroit, MI; 1958. *See* Entry 510. (Courtesy Minoru Yamasaki Associates; Troy, MI. Photographer: Bill Hedrich, Hedrich-Blessing.)

245

See: Architectural Record 163 (March 1978): 117–21. *Architectural Review* 163 (February 1978): 103–8. *Process: Architecture,* no. 5 (1978): 30–41. *Architettura* 29 (April 1983): 313–23. Leon Whiteson, *Modern Canadian Architecture* (Edmonton: Hurtig, 1963), 164–67.

ZEIDLER ROBERTS PARTNERSHIP

■ 512

Queen's Quay Terminal conversion; Toronto, Ontario; 1983 (see Illus. 247).

A huge (1-million-square-foot) waterfront warehouse, originally built in 1926, adapted for multipurpose use. An unsightly annex was removed. The remaining 8-story reinforced concrete building has been dressed up with contrasting bay windows and glass-enclosed exterior stairs; its interior has been transformed into distinguished quarters for shops and restaurants, parking, offices, and a theater. Four floors added on top, set back a little and finished in a contrasting color, contain seventy-two apartments and a pool.
Partner in charge of design: Eberhard H. Zeidler. Engineers: M. S. Yolles & Partners (structural); Mitchell Partnership (mechanical). General contractor: Olympia & York.

Honors: Governor General's Award, 1986.

See: Architectural Record 173 (June 1985): 134–41. *Architektur + Wettbewerbe,* no. 121 (March 1985): 38–41. *Abitare,* no. 233 (April 1985): 84–87. *Canadian Architect* 28 (October 1983): 14–21.

246 Toronto Eaton Centre; Toronto, Ontario; 1981. *See* Entry 511. (Courtesy Zeidler Roberts Partnership; Toronto, Ontario. Photographer: Balthazar Korab Ltd.)

246

247 Queen's Quay Terminal conversion; Toronto, Ontario; 1983. *See* Entry 512. (Courtesy Zeidler Roberts Partnership; Toronto, Ontario. Photographer: Fiona Spalding-Smith.)

247

BUILDING TYPE INDEX

MANUFACTURING PLANTS see INDUSTRIAL BUILDINGS

MARKETS see STORES, MARKETS, SHOPPING CENTERS, AND SHOWROOMS

MEDICAL CENTERS see HOSPITALS, SANITARIUMS, AND MEDICAL CENTERS

MEMORIALS AND MONUMENTS

MONUMENTS see MEMORIALS AND MONUMENTS

MOTELS see HOTELS AND MOTELS

MULTIUSE COMPLEXES See also: STATE CAPITOLS, CITY HALLS, AND CIVIC CENTERS; FAIRS AND EXPOSITIONS—BUILDINGS

MUNICIPAL OFFICE COMPLEXES see OFFICE BUILDINGS AND OFFICE COMPLEXES; STATE CAPITOLS, CITY HALLS, AND CIVIC CENTERS

MUSEUMS AND ART GALLERIES See also: ARTS CENTERS

**NEW TOWNS see PLANNED
COMMUNITIES**

OBSERVATORIES

**OFFICE BUILDINGS AND OFFICE
COMPLEXES See also: MULTIUSE
COMPLEXES; STATE CAPITOLS,
CITY HALLS, AND CIVIC CENTERS**

OPERA HOUSES see CONCERT HALLS AND THEATERS

ORIENTATION CENTERS See also: ENVIRONMENTAL EDUCATION CENTERS

PARKS AND FOUNTAINS See also: RECREATIONAL BUILDINGS AND COMPLEXES

PIERS AND WATERFRONT COMPLEXES

St. John's Abbey; Collegeville, MN. Marcel Breuer and Hamilton Smith. **47**

St. Matthew's Parish Church; Pacific Palisades, CA. Moore Ruble Yudell. **268**

St. Procopius Abbey Church and Monastery; Lisle, IL. Loebl, Schlossman, Bennett & Dart. **231**

Shrine; New Harmony, IN. Philip Johnson. **191**

Temple and school buildings, North Shore Congregation Israel; Glencoe, IL. Minoru Yamasaki. **507**

Thorncrown Chapel; Eureka Springs, AR. E. Fay Jones. **201**

Unitarian Meetinghouse; Hartford, CT. Victor A. Lundy. **236**

United Church House of Worship; Rowayton, CT. Joseph Salerno. **388**

Wayfarers Chapel; Palos Verdes, CA. Lloyd Wright. **500**

RENOVATION see RESTORATION, RENOVATION, AND ADAPTIVE REUSE

RESEARCH AND TECHNICAL FACILITIES See also: INDUSTRIAL BUILDINGS; UNIVERSITIES AND COLLEGES—BUILDINGS AND CAMPUSES

Alfred Newton Richards Medical Research Building, University of Pennsylvania; Philadelphia, PA. Louis I. Kahn. **203**

Bell Telephone Laboratories Research Center; Holmdel, NJ. Eero Saarinen. **371**

Bradfield and Emerson Halls, Cornell University; Ithaca, NY. Ulrich Franzen. **100**

CBS Television City; Los Angeles, CA. Pereira & Luckman. **322**

Center for Advanced Study in the Behavioral Sciences; Palo Alto, CA. Wurster, Bernardi & Emmons. **501**

Comsat Laboratories; Clarksburg, MD. Daniel, Mann, Johnson & Mendenhall. **72**

E. R. Squibb and Sons, Inc. Worldwide Headquarters; Lawrenceville, NJ. Hellmuth, Obata & Kassabaum. **160**

Engineering Science Center, University of Colorado; Boulder, CO. Architectural Associates Colorado. **20**

General Motors Technical Center; Warren, MI. Eero Saarinen; Smith, Hinchman & Grylls. **384**

Headquarters Building, Emhart Manufacturing Co.; Bloomfield, CT. Skidmore, Owings & Merrill. **409**

Health Sciences Center, State University of New York; Stony Brook, NY. Bertrand Goldberg. **115**

Health Sciences Instruction and Research Towers, Unit 1, San Francisco Medical Center, University of California; San Francisco, CA. Reid, Rockwell, Banwell & Tarics. **341**

IBM Sterling Forest Information Systems Center; Sterling Forest, NY. Gunnar Birkerts. **39**

Johnson Wax Company Research and Development Tower; Racine, WI. Frank Lloyd Wright. **492**

Kline Science Center, Yale University; New Haven, CT. Philip Johnson & Richard Foster. **192**

Lewis Thomas Laboratory, Princeton University; Princeton, NJ. Payette Associates; Venturi, Rauch and Scott Brown. **477**

Manufacturers Hanover Trust Co. Operations Building; New York, NY. Carson, Lundin & Shaw. **55**

Multicategorical Research Laboratory, Cornell University Veterinary College; Ithaca, NY. Ulrich Franzen. **102**

National Center for Atmospheric Research near Boulder, CO. I. M. Pei. **311**

PA Technology Lab and Corporate Facility; Hightstown, NJ. Richard Rogers. **356**

Research Laboratory D, Chevron Research Company; Richmond, CA. Gerald McCue. **244**

Robert R. McMath Solar Telescope; Kitt Peak, AZ. Skidmore, Owings & Merrill. **425**

Salk Institute for Biological Studies; La Jolla, CA. Louis I. Kahn. **209**

Undergraduate Science Center and Chilled Water Plant, Harvard University; Cambridge, MA. Sert, Jackson & Assoc. **394**

Vehicle Assembly Building, John F. Kennedy Space Center; Cape Canaveral, FL. Max Urbahn. **469**

W. C. Decker Engineering Building; Corning, NY. Davis, Brody. **74**

WCCO Television Headquarters; Minneapolis, MN. Hardy Holzman Pfeiffer. **143**

Wellesley College Science Center; Wellesley, MA. Perry, Dean, Stahl & Rogers. **326**

Westinghouse Molecular Electronic Laboratory; Elkridge, MD; Vincent G. Kling. **223**

Wyeth Laboratories, Inc. office and laboratory complex; Radnor, PA. Skidmore, Owings & Merrill. **432**

RESEARCH INSTITUTES see CONFERENCE CENTERS AND STUDY FACILITIES FOR

SCHOLARS; RESEARCH AND TECHNICAL FACILITIES

RESIDENTIAL DEVELOPMENTS See also: MULTIUSE COMPLEXES. For dormitories, see: UNIVERSITIES AND COLLEGES—BUILDINGS AND CAMPUSES

Amelia Island Plantation; Amelia Island, FL. Wallace, McHarg, Roberts & Todd. **478**

Asilomar Housing, Asilomar Beach State Park; near Monterey, CA. John Carl Warnecke. **479**

Atlantis on Brickell; Miami, FL. Arquitectonica. **21**

Bolton Square; Baltimore, MD. Hugh Newell Jacobsen. **179**

Bronx Developmental Center; New York, NY. Richard Meier. **246**

Carmel Valley Manor; Carmel Valley, CA. Skidmore, Owings & Merrill. **404**

Cedar Square West; Minneapolis, MN. Ralph Rapson. **338**

Chatham Towers; New York, NY. Kelly & Gruzen. **215**

The Cloisters; Cincinnati, OH. Hardy Holzman Pfeiffer. **139**

Dunehouse; Atlantic Beach, FL. William Morgan. **27**

Eastwood, Roosevelt Island; New York, NY. Sert, Jackson. **392**

860–880 Lake Shore Drive; Chicago, IL. Ludwig Mies van der Rohe. **254**

1199 (Eleven Ninety-nine) Plaza Cooperative Housing; New York, NY. Hodne/Stageberg. **172**

Exodus House, East Harlem; New York, NY. Smotrich & Platt. **437**

Fairways; Coquitlam, British Columbia, R. E. Hulbert. **176**

500 Park Tower; New York, NY. James Stewart Polshek. **329**

Francis Greenwood Peabody Terrace (Married Student Housing), Harvard University; Cambridge, MA. Sert, Jackson & Gourley. **395**

Grove Court; Houston, TX. Taft Architects. **455**

Guild House, Friends' Housing for the Elderly; Philadelphia, PA. Venturi & Rauch. **474**

Habitat; Montreal, Quebec. Moshe Safdie; David, Barott, Boulva. **387**

Hilliard Center; Chicago, IL. Bertrand Goldberg. **116**

Housing for the Elderly; Cidra Municipality, PR. Jorge del Rio & Eduardo Lopez. **78**

Housing Union Building, University of Alberta; Edmonton, Alberta. Diamond,

RESORT COMMUNITIES see RESIDENTIAL DEVELOPMENTS

RESTAURANTS See also: MULTIUSE COMPLEXES; OFFICE BUILDINGS AND OFFICE COMPLEXES; STORES, MARKETS, SHOPPING CENTERS, AND SHOWROOMS

RESTORATION, RENOVATION AND ADAPTIVE REUSE

RETREAT CENTERS see CONFERENCE CENTERS AND STUDY FACILITIES FOR SCHOLARS

SANITARIUMS see HOSPITALS, SANITARIUMS, AND MEDICAL CENTERS

SCHOOLS, ELEMENTARY AND SECONDARY

BUILDING NAME INDEX

GEOGRAPHICAL INDEX

MASSACHUSETTS

Boston

Additions to Campus, Boston University. Sert, Jackson, Gourley; Hoyle, Doran & Berry. **396**

Boston City Hall. Kallman, McKinnell & Knowles. **210**

Boston Government Service Center. Paul Rudolph. **360**

Boston Public Library Addition. Philip Johnson/John Burgee. **195**

Children's Hospital Medical Center. The Architects Collaborative. **16**

Christian Science Church Center. I. M. Pei; Cossuta & Ponte. **315**

Faneuil Hall Marketplace and Quincy Market Restoration. Benjamin Thompson & Assoc. **464**

Federal Reserve Bank of Boston. Hugh Stubbins. **450**

Francis A. Countway Library of Medicine, Harvard University Medical School. Hugh Stubbins & Assoc. **451**

John Hancock Tower. I. M. Pei. **309**

John Fitzgerald Kennedy Library, Columbia Point. I. M. Pei. **308**

Lewis Wharf Rehabilitation. Carl Koch & Assoc. **224**

Prudential Center. Charles Luckman Associates. **233**

Cambridge

American Academy of Arts and Sciences. Kallman McKinnell & Wood. **211**

Arthur M. Sackler Museum, Harvard University. James Stirling. **443**

Baker House, Massachusetts Institute of Technology. Alvar Aalto. **1**

Carpenter Center for the Visual Arts, Harvard University. Le Corbusier (Charles-Edouard Jeanneret-Gris). **229**

Design Research Building. Benjamin Thompson & Assoc. **461**

Francis Greenwood Peabody Terrace (Married Student Housing), Harvard University. Sert, Jackson, Gourley & Assoc. **395**

George Gund Hall, Harvard University. John Andrews. **10**

Harvard University Graduate Center. The Architects Collaborative. **17**

Holyoke Center, Harvard University. Sert, Jackson & Assoc. **393**

Kresge Auditorium, M.I.T. Eero Saarinen & Assoc. **378**

Kresge Chapel, M.I.T. Eero Saarinen & Assoc. **379**

Loeb Drama Center, Harvard University. Hugh Stubbins & Assoc. **452**

Undergraduate Science Center and Chilled Water Plant, Harvard University. Sert, Jackson & Associates. **394**

Deerfield

C. Thurston Chase Learning Center, Eaglebrook School. The Architects Collaborative. **14**

Framingham

Point West Place. Robert A. M. Stern. **439**

North Dartmouth

Southeastern Massachusetts University. (Formerly Southeastern M.I.T.) Paul Rudolph; Desmond & Lord. **368**

Roxbury

Warren Gardens. Hugh Stubbins; Ashley, Myer. **453**

Stockbridge

Opera Shed, Berkshire Music Center. Saarinen, Swanson & Saarinen. **386**

Waltham

Interfaith Center, Brandeis University. Harrison & Abramovitz. **151**

Social Science Center and Academic Quadrangle, Brandeis University. The Architects Collaborative. **19**

Wellesley

Mary Cooper Jewett Arts Center. Paul Rudolph. **363**

Science Center. Perry, Dean, Stahl & Rogers. **326**

Worcester

Robert Hutchings Goddard Library, Clark University. John M. Johansen. **182**

MICHIGAN

Ann Arbor

Legal Research Building Addition. Gunnar Birkerts. **40**

Birmingham

Greenfield Elementary School. Eberle M. Smith Assoc. **434**

Dearborn

Central Staff Office Building, Ford Motor Company. Skidmore, Owings & Merrill. **406**

Detroit

Center for Creative Studies, College of Art and Design. William Kessler & Assoc. **216**

Cobo Hall. Giffels & Rossetti. **114**

First Federal Building. Smith, Hinchman & Grylls Assoc. **436**

Fisher Administrative Center, University of Detroit. Gunnar Birkerts. **38**

Lafayette Park. Ludwig Mies van der Rohe. **257**

McGregor Memorial Conference Center, Wayne State University. Yamasaki, Leinweber & Assoc. **510**

Medical complex: Wayne State University Health Center; the Detroit Receiving Hospital; Detroit Medical Center Concourse. William Kessler; Zeidler Partnership; Giffels Associates. **217**

Michigan Consolidated Gas Company Headquarters. Minoru Yamasaki. **505**

Renaissance Center. John Portman & Assoc. **334**

Reynolds Metals Sales Headquarters Building. Great Lakes Region. Minoru Yamasaki. **506**

near Detroit

Northland Regional Shopping Center, Southfield Township. Victor Gruen Assoc. **127**

Muskegon

St. Francis de Sales Church. Marcel Breuer and Herbert Beckhard. **46**

Warren

General Motors Technical Center. Eero Saarinen; Smith, Hinchman & Grylls. **384**

MINNESOTA

Collegeville

St. John's Abbey. Marcel Breuer & Hamilton Smith. **47**

Minneapolis

Butler Square. Miller Hanson Westerbeck Bell Architects Inc. **259**

Cedar Square West. Ralph Rapson. **338**

Christ Church. Saarinen, Saarinen & Assoc. **385**

East Bank Bookstore/Admissions and Records Facility, University of Minnesota. Myers & Bennett. **290**

Federal Reserve Bank of Minneapolis. Gunnar Birkerts & Associates. **37**

Hennepin County Government Center. John Carl Warnecke & Associates. **480**

IDS Center. Philip Johnson/John Burgee. **197**

Sunar Showroom. Michael Graves. **126**

Tyrone Guthrie Theater. Ralph Rapson. **339**

Walker Art Center. Edward Larrabee Barnes. **25**

WCCO Television Headquarters. Hardy Holzman Pfeiffer. **143**

St. Paul

Mount Zion Temple and Center. Erich Mendelsohn. **253**

MISSISSIPPI

Tougaloo

Library and two dormitories, Tougaloo College. Gunnar Birkerts & Assoc. **41**

INDEX OF DESIGN, ENGINEERING, AND CONSTRUCTION PROFESSIONALS AND FIRMS